D0912484

Larry A. Henderson

The Sweet Breathing
of Plants

Edited by Linda Hogan and Brenda Peterson

LINDA HOGAN has published three award-winning novels and collections of poetry and essays, including *Woman Who Watches Over the World: A Native Memoir*. BRENDA PETERSON is the author of three novels and five works of nonfiction, including *Build Me an Ark: A Life with Animals*. They are co-editors of *Intimate Nature: The Bond Between Women and Animals*. They live, respectively, in Colorado and Seattle.

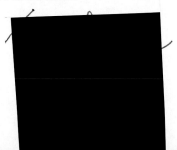

Also by Linda Hogan

Also by Brenda Peterson

Edited by Linda Hogan, Deena Metzger,
and Brenda Peterson

Also by Linda Hogan and Br

The Sweet Breathing of Plants

The Sweet Breathing of Plants

Women Writing on the Green World

Edited by Linda Hogan and
Brenda Peterson

North Point Press
A division of Farrar, Straus and Giroux
New York

North Point Press
A division of Farrar, Straus and Giroux
19 Union Square West, New York 10003

Distributed in Canada by Douglas & McIntyre Ltd.
Printed in the United States of America
Published in 2001 by North Point Press
First paperback edition, 2002

Library of Congress Cataloging-in-Publication Data
    The sweet breathing of plants : women writing on the green world /
edited by Linda Hogan and Brenda Peterson.—1st ed.
        p. cm.
    ISBN 0-86547-625-X (pbk.)
    1. Gardening.   2. Plants, Cultivated.   3. Gardening—Literary
collections.   4. Plants, Cultivated—Literary collections.   I. Hogan,
Linda.   II. Peterson, Brenda, 1950–

SB455.3 .S95 2001
635.9—dc21   00-057862

The following selections are included by arrangement with the authors:
Anita Endrezze, "Corn Mother," copyright © 2001 by Anita Endrezze;
Laura Bowers Foreman, "For the Maples," copyright © 2001 by Laura
Bowers Foreman; Linda Hasselstrom, "Mulch," copyright © 2001 by
Linda Hasselstrom; Linda Hogan, "Bamboo," copyright © 2001 by Linda
Hogan; Donna Kelleher, "Living Medicine for Animals," copyright
© 2001 by Donna Kelleher; Claudia Lewis, "Ode to Mold," copyright
© 2001 by Claudia Lewis; Trish Maharam, "Plantswomen," copy-
right © 2001 by Trish Maharam; Teresa tsimmu Martino, "Alder," copy-
right © 2001 by Teresa tsimmu Martino; Lesa Quale, "Radioactive
Tumbleweeds," copyright © 2001 by Lesa Quale; Linda Jean Shepherd,
"My Life with Weed," copyright © 2001 by Linda Jean Shepherd;
Annick Smith, "Huckleberries," copyright © 2001 by Annick Smith;
Mary Troychak, "Miriam Rothschild: Through the Eyes of a Butterfly,"
copyright © 2001 by Mary Troychak; Louise Wisechild, "La Limpia,"
copyright © 2001 by Louise Wisechild; Linda Yamane, "My World Is Out
There," copyright © 2001 by Linda Yamane.

Additional permission credits can be found on pages 287–288, which
constitute an extension of this copyright page.

Illustrations by Karen M. Koehler
Designed by Cassandra J. Pappas

www.fsgbooks.com

10   9   8   7   6   5   4   3   2   1

For the wisdom of the green world
and the women who keep it well

". . . the voice of the Great Spirit is heard in the twittering of birds, the rippling of mighty waters, and the sweet breathing of flowers . . ."

—GERTRUDE SIMMONS BONNIN [Zitkala-Sa]
(1876–1938), Dakota Sioux

Contents

xx great!

Flora for Fauna

Preface

The green world has long been the province of women. To our gathering ancestors, a knowledge of plants—their healing powers, sacred purposes, and green intelligence—was synonymous with feminine wisdom. And this green wisdom was acknowledged as power, too. In the Western tradition, the goddess Demeter, who in ancient Greek mythology controlled the growth of crops, had the power to withhold plant nourishment until the return of her daughter Persephone, who had been kidnapped and taken to the underworld. It was not until the Inquisition, which declared herbalists, midwives, and healers—most of them women—to be witches, that the long symbiosis between women and plants was severed. It was never utterly eradicated, however, and nurtured by lay practitioners who passed down their know-how mother to daughter, plantswoman to plantswoman, it slowly grew back.

Meanwhile, in other places, native peoples carried on a vibrant relationship with the plant world. In the New World the two strands met in a powerful hybrid. Until the early decades of the twentieth century, many rural American women not only farmed but knew and used herbs and herbal potions for everything from cramps to abortion to childbirth. There was always the local yarb doctor, root worker, healer, or midwife to call on along with—and often instead of—the family physician. And women began to codify their knowledge so that it might be formally disseminated, as did Almira Hart Lincoln Phelps in her *Familiar Lectures on Botany* (1800), a bestseller. So the literature as well as the practice of feminine plant wisdom has long roots.

As women have planted, gathered, preserved, and used herbs and plants, they have also reflected upon the emotional, philosophical, and spiritual aspects of the relationship between humans and the plants who give us food, breath, and medicine. Our connection to the green world is practical, but also, and originally, primal and sensual. The passion we feel for plants extends not only to lovely flowers, but also to mold, mulch, and compost, as a number of writers reveal in the section "A Passion for Plants." Plants are fundamental to who we are, as Isabel Allende knew when she brought with her into exile from her native Chile "a little bag containing dirt from my garden, intending to plant forget-me-nots in that unknown country where I was to begin a new destiny." Out of this vital, primal connection with plants, women have created rituals of homecoming, harvest, and holiness, such as the wedding-day preparations Zora Neale Hurston describes.

In developing countries, the practical knowledge of plant use among laypeople faded with the growth of mass agriculture, and more and more, those who have cultivated a relationship with the green world have done so primarily out of passion. But elsewhere in the world, native peoples continue to know and use plants not only as food but as medicine. Some of them were using white-willow bark as a painkiller and fever reducer long before the advent of aspirin. Many contemporary medicines, in fact, have exploited that wisdom, or imitated it in the production of synthetic drugs. Steroids are produced from yams; penicillin is a creation of mold. After a long period of inattention, contemporary Western medicine is awakening to a greater awareness of traditional plant knowledge. Pharmaceutical companies are even trying to purchase plant wisdom from the native peoples of South and Central America. The section "Keepers of the Plants" pays tribute to this indigenous knowledge.

Yet for all the practical importance plants have for native peoples, traditional knowledge systems and stories give equal attention to expressions of love and praise for plants: "Our earth is turning over and turning green," sang the Shoshone woman Emily Hill. She is echoed here by basket-weaver Linda Yamane of the Rumsien Ohlone native people of Monterey, California, who leaves a song of thanksgiving after she gathers sedges for her baskets: "It is good to hear the language of my ancestors as it drifts across the land."

The green world is fundamental to our identity. Knowing it intimately has been a way of knowing who we are, and passing on that knowledge has been a way of ensuring not only our own survival but the survival of our species. Thus Marjory Stoneman Douglas's ability to capture the unique ecology of the Florida Everglades makes her selection read more like a character sketch than a scientific treatise; the intimacy with which she conveyed what she saw was instrumental in changing people's views on the preservation of wetlands. Yet women's intense spiritual as well as practical connection with the plant world has often aroused suspicion and hostility, as Jeanne Achterberg documents in her powerful survey of the persecution of witches.

Today we are grateful for these women who collected themselves and conserved the green world. With prescient figures like Rachel Carson, whose seminal *Silent Spring* helped encourage the banning of the poisonous insecticide DDT and inspired the modern environmental movement, they paved the way for a more wide-ranging approach to science and ecology, which is reflected here in the section "The Science of Green." As Nobel Prize–winning geneticist Barbara McClintock said, in the style that distinguished her work and life, "All around you, there is much pleasure, if you think about it." McClintock, conceiving of plants as sentient beings, learned their secrets by knowing them intimately, by developing a "feeling for the organism," as Sharon Bertsch McGrayne shows in her portrait of the scientist.

The same embracing experience inspires the writers collected in "The Forest for the Trees," who speak out on behalf of the Amazon rain forest and old-growth "elders," and against the practice of clear-cutting. Sometimes these voices are elegiac and dreamy, sometimes matter-of-fact, sometimes outraged; outrage begins in love, scientific "neutrality" in passionate engagement. In the end, all discussion of nature is really a dialogue *with* nature, as exemplified by Carolyn Kizer's majestic "Index, a Mountain," which chronicles the birth of the Cascades, the history of lumbermen, and the tragic fate of the mountain of the title, with its "scarred flanks" and "raw summit." *"Serve as God's tombstone,"* she urges it. *"Have no green mercy on us."*

Humans are not the first or only animals to enjoy an intricate relationship with the green world, as the selections in "Flora for Fauna" remind us. Indeed, many of our ancestors learned which plants were safe to eat by watching animals, and horses and chimpanzees are among those animals known to medicate themselves with plants as well. Ultimately we must see the green world "through the eyes of a butterfly," as gardener and lepidopterist Miriam Rothschild tells us, if we are to see what is necessary to preserve it, and ourselves.

These days, plant knowledge seems to be flowering anew. Gardening is on the upswing, with women not only participating in it but taking a lead in directing it, through seed businesses, research, and plant development. Women—and men—are rediscovering how to use plants for health as well. A look at any health-food store's bookshelf reveals a multitude of guides to herbal and natural plant remedies. A recent government study showed that 80 percent of American medical patients, looking for ways to supplement or replace conventional medical treatment, were consulting practitioners of alternative medicine. In the United States, organic farming, herbal medicines, and natural foods are gaining the widespread popularity that they have enjoyed in Europe for generations. And a widespread resurgence of environmentalism has inspired a new generation of Rachel Carsons. Whether by initiating communal gardens or participating in reforestation and native-plant salvage projects, women are exercising their citizenship in the green world as never before, restoring and fortifying an ancient bond.

LINDA HOGAN
BRENDA PETERSON

A Passion for
Plants

Susan Orlean

Orchid Fever

 he Orchidaceae are a large, ancient family of perennial plants with one fertile stamen and a three-
petaled flower. One petal is unlike the other two.
In most orchid species this petal is enlarged into a
pouch or lip and is the most conspicuous part of
the flower. There are close to forty thousand known orchid species,
and there may be thousands more that haven't yet been discovered
and maybe thousands that once lived on earth and are now extinct.
Humans have created another hundred thousand hybrids by cross-
fertilizing one species with another or by crossing different hybrids
to one another in plant-breeding labs.

Orchids are considered the most highly evolved flowering
plants on earth. They are unusual in form, uncommonly beautiful in
color, often powerfully fragrant, intricate in structure, and different
from any other family of plants. The reason for their unusualness
has always been puzzled over. One guess is that orchids might have
evolved in soil that was naturally irradiated by a meteor or mineral

deposit, and that the radiation is what mutated them into thousands of amazing forms. Orchids have diverse and unflowerlike looks. One species looks just like a German shepherd dog with its tongue sticking out. One species looks like an onion. One looks like an octopus. One looks like a human nose. One looks like the kind of fancy shoes that a king might wear. One looks like Mickey Mouse. One looks like a monkey. One looks dead. One was described in the 1845 Botanical Registry as looking like "an old-fashioned head-dress peeping over one of those starched high collars such as ladies wore in the days of Queen Elizabeth; or through a horse-collar decorated with gaudy ribbons." There are species that look like butterflies, bats, ladies' handbags, bees, swarms of bees, female wasps, clamshells, roots, camel hoofs, squirrels, nuns dressed in their wimples, and drunken old men. The genus *Dracula* is blackish-red and looks like a vampire bat. *Polyrrhiza lindenii*, the Fakahatchee's ghost orchid, looks like a ghost but has also been described as looking like a bandy-legged dancer, a white frog, and a fairy. Many wild orchids in Florida have common names based on their looks: crooked-spur, brown, rigid, twisted, shiny-leafed, cow horn, lipped, snake, leafless beaked, rat tail, mule-ear, shadow witch, water spider, false water spider, ladies' tresses, and false ladies' tresses. In 1678, the botanist Jakob Breyne wrote: "The manifold shape of these flowers arouses our highest admiration. They take on the form of little birds, of lizards, of insects. They look like a man, like a woman, sometimes like an austere, sinister fighter, sometimes like a clown who excites our laughter. They represent the image of a lazy tortoise, a melancholy toad, an agile, ever-chattering monkey." Orchids have always been thought of as beautiful but strange. A wildflower guide published in 1917 called them "our queer freaks."

The smallest orchids are microscopic, and the biggest ones have masses of flowers as large as footballs. Botanists reported seeing a cow-horn orchid in the Fakahatchee with normal-sized flowers and thirty-four pseudo-bulbs, which are the bulging tuber-shaped growths at the base of the plant where its energy is stored, each one over ten inches long. Some orchid flowers have petals as soft as powder, and other species have flowers as rigid and rubbery as inner tubes. Raymond Chandler wrote that orchids have the texture of human flesh. Orchids' colors are extravagant. They can be freckled or mottled or veiny or solid, from the nearly neon to spotless white. Most species are more than one color—they'll have ivory petals and a hot pink lip, maybe, or green petals with burgundy stripes, or yellow petals with olive speckles and a purple lip with a smear of red underneath. Some orchids have color combinations you wouldn't be caught dead wearing. Some look like the results of an accident involving paint. There are white orchids, but there is no such thing as a black orchid, even though people have been wanting a black orchid forever. It was black-orchid extract that Basil St. John, the comic-book character who was the boyfriend of comic-book character Brenda Starr, needed in order to control his rare and mysterious blood disease. I once asked Bob Fuchs, the owner of R.F. Orchids in Homestead, Florida, if he thought a black orchid would ever be discovered or be produced by hybridizing. "No. Never in real life," he said. "*Only* in *Brenda Starr.*"

Many plants pollinate themselves, which guarantees that they will reproduce and keep their species alive. The disadvantage of self-pollination is that it recycles the same genetic material over and over, so self-pollinating species endure but don't evolve or improve themselves. Self-pollinated plants remain simple and common—weeds. Complex plants rely on cross-fertilization. Their pollen has to be spread from one plant to another, either by the wind or by birds or moths or bees. Cross-pollinating plants are usually complex in form. They have to be shaped so that their pollen is stored someplace where it can be lifted by a passing breeze, or they have to be found attractive by lots of pollinating insects, or they must be so well suited and so appealing to one particular insect that they will be the only plant on which that insect ever feeds. Charles Darwin believed that living things produced by cross-fertilization always prevail over self-pollinated ones in the contest for existence because their offspring have new genetic mixtures and will then have the evolutionary chance to adapt as the world around them changes. Most orchids never pollinate themselves, even when a plant's pollen is applied artificially to its fertile stigma. Some orchid species are actually poisoned to death if their pollen touches their stigma. There are other plants that don't pollinate themselves either, but no flower is more guarded against self-pollination than orchids.

The orchid family could have died out like dinosaurs if insects had chosen to feed on simpler plants and not on orchids. The orchids wouldn't have been pollinated, and without pollination they would never have grown seeds, while self-pollinating simple plants growing nearby would have seeded themselves constantly and spread like mad and taken up more and more space and light and water, and eventually orchids would have been pushed to the margins of evolution and disappeared. Instead, orchids have multiplied and diversified and become the biggest flowering-plant family on earth, because each orchid species has made itself irresistible. Many species look so much like their favorite insects that the insect mistakes them for kin, and when it lands on the flower to visit, pollen sticks to its body. When the insect repeats the mistake on another orchid, the pollen from the first flower gets deposited on the stigma of the second—in other words, the orchid gets fertilized because it is smarter than the bug. Another orchid species imitates the shape of something that a pollinating insect likes to kill. Botanists call this pseudo-antagonism. The insect sees its enemy and attacks it—that is, it attacks the orchid—and in the process of this pointless fight the insect gets dusted with orchid pollen and spreads the pollen when it repeats the mistake. Other species look like the mate of their pollinator, so the bug tries to mate with one orchid and then another—pseudo-copulation—and spreads pollen from flower to flower each hopeless time. Lady's-slipper orchids have a special hinged lip that traps bees and forces them to pass through sticky threads of pollen as they struggle to escape through the back of the plant. Another orchid secretes nectar that attracts small insects. As the insects lick the nectar they are slowly lured into a narrowed tube inside the orchid, until their heads are directly beneath the crest of the flower's rostellum. When the insects raise their heads the crest shoots out little darts of pollen that are instantly and firmly cemented to the insects' eyeballs but then fall off the moment the insects put their heads inside another orchid plant. Some orchids have straight-ahead good looks but deceptive and seductive odors. There are orchids that smell like rotting meat, which insects happen to like. Another orchid smells like chocolate. Another smells like an angel-food cake. Several mimic the scent of other flowers that are more popular with insects than they are. Some release perfume only at night, to attract nocturnal moths.

No one knows whether orchids evolved to complement insects or whether the orchids evolved first, or whether somehow these two life forms evolved simultaneously, which might explain how two totally different living things came to depend on each other. The harmony between an orchid and its pollinator is so perfect that it is kind of eerie. Darwin loved studying orchids. In his writings he often described them as "my beloved Orchids," and was so certain that they were the pinnacle of evolutionary transformation that he once wrote that it would be "incredibly monstrous to look at an Orchid as having been created as we now see it." In 1877, he published a book called *The Various Contrivances by Which Orchids Are Fertilised by Insects*. In one chapter he described a strange orchid he had found in Madagascar—an *Angraecum sesquipedale*, with waxy white star-shaped flowers and "a green whip-like nectary of astonishing length." The nectary was almost twelve inches long, and all of the nectar was in the bottom inch. Darwin hypothesized that there had to be an insect that could eat the unreachable nectar and at the same time fertilize the plant—otherwise the species couldn't exist. Such an insect would have to have a complementarily strange shape. He wrote: "In Madagascar there must be moths with prosboces capable of extension to a length of between ten and twelve inches! This belief of mine has been ridiculed by some entomologists, but we now know from Fritz Muller that there is a sphinx-moth in South Brazil which has a proboscis of nearly sufficient length, for when dried it was between ten and eleven inches long. When not protruded the proboscis is coiled up into a spiral of at least twenty windings. . . . Some huge moth with a wonderfully long proboscis could drain the last drop of nectar. If such great moths were to become extinct in Madagascar, assuredly the *Angraecum* would become extinct." Darwin was very interested in how orchids released pollen. He experimented by poking them with needles, camel-hair brushes, bristles, pencils, and fingers. He discovered that parts were so sensitive that they released pollen upon the slightest touch, but that "moderate degrees of violence" on the less sensitive parts had no effect, which he concluded meant that the orchid wouldn't release pollen haphazardly—it was smart enough to save it for only the most favorable encounters with bugs. He wrote: "Orchids appeared to have been modelled in the wildest caprice, but this is no doubt due to our ignorance of their requirements and conditions of life. Why do Orchids have so many perfect contrivances for their fertilisation? I am sure that many other plants offer analogous adaptations of high perfection; but it seems that they are really more numerous and perfect with the Orchideae than with most other plants."

The schemes orchids use to attract a pollinator are elegant but low-percentage. Botanists recently studied one thousand wild orchids for fifteen years, and during that time only twenty-three plants were pollinated. The odds are bad, but orchids compensate. If they are ever fertilized, they will grow a seedpod that is supercharged. Most other species of flowers produce only twenty or so seeds at a time, whereas orchid pods may be filled with millions and millions of tiny, dust-sized seeds. One pod has enough seeds to supply the world's prom corsages for the rest of eternity.

Some species of orchids grow in the ground, and others don't live in soil at all. The ones that don't grow in soil are called epiphytes, and they live their lives attached to a tree branch or a rock. Epiphytic orchid seeds settle in a comfortable spot, sprout, grow, dangle their roots in the air, and live a lazy life absorbing rainwater and decayed leaves and light. They aren't parasites—they give nothing to the tree and get nothing from it except a good place to sit. Most epiphytes evolved in tropical jungles, where there are so many living things competing for room on the jungle floor that most species lose the fight and die out. Orchids thrived in the jungle because they developed the ability to live on air rather than soil and positioned themselves where they were sure to get light and water—high above the rest of the plants on the branches of trees. They thrived because they took themselves out of competition. If all of this makes orchids seem smart—well, they *do* seem smart. There is something clever and unplantlike about their determination to survive and their knack for useful deception and their genius for seducing human beings for hundreds and hundreds of years.

Orchids grow slowly. They languish. They will produce a flower and a seedpod, maybe, and then rest for months at a time. A pollinated orchid seed will mature into a flowering plant in about seven years. Over time, an orchid will wither away in back but it will keep growing from the front. It has no natural enemies except bad weather and the odd virus. Orchids are one of the few things in the world that can live forever. Cultivated orchids that aren't killed by their owners can outlive their owners and even generations of owners. Many people who collect orchids designate an orchid heir in their wills, because they know the plants will outlast them. Bob Fuchs of R.F. Orchids has some plants in his nursery that were discovered by his late grandfather in South America at the turn of the century. Thomas Fennell III, of Fennell Orchids, has plants that his grandfather collected when he was a young man orchid-hunting in Venezuela. Some orchids at the New York Botanical Garden have been living in greenhouses there since 1898.

Orchids first evolved in the tropics, but they now grow all over the world. Most of them spread from the tropics as seeds that were lifted and carried on air currents. A hurricane can carry billions of seeds thousands of miles. Orchid seeds blown from South America to Florida will drop in swimming pools and barbecue pits and on shuffleboard courts and gas stations, on roofs of office buildings and on the driveways of fast-food restaurants, and in hot sand on a beach and in your hair on a windy day, and those will be swept away or stepped on or drowned without being felt or seen. But a few might drop somewhere tranquil and wet and warm, and some of those seeds might happen to lodge in a comfortable tree crotch or in a crack on a stone. If one of those seeds encounters a fungus that it can use for food, it will germinate and grow. Each time a hurricane hits Florida, botanists wonder what new orchids might have come in with it. At the moment, they are waiting to see what was blown in by Hurricane Andrew. They will know the answer around the seventh anniversary of the storm, when the seeds that landed will have sprouted and grown.

———

Nothing in science can account for the way people feel about orchids. Orchids seem to drive people crazy. Those who love them love them madly. Orchids arouse passion more than romance. They are the sexiest flowers on earth. The name "orchid" derives from the Latin *orchis*, which means "testicle." This refers not only to the testicle-shaped tubers of the plant but to the fact that it was long believed that orchids sprang from the spilled semen of mating animals. The British Herbal Guide of 1653 advised that orchids be used with discretion. "They are hot and moist in operation, under the dominion of Venus, and provoke lust exceedingly." In Victorian England the orchid hobby grew so consuming that it was sometimes called "orchidelirium"; under its influence many seemingly normal people, once smitten with orchids, became less like normal people and more like passionate orchid collector and breeder John Laroche. Even now there is something delirious in orchid-collecting. Every orchid-lover I met told me the same story—how one plant in the kitchen had led to a dozen, and then to a backyard greenhouse, and then, in some cases, to multiple greenhouses and collecting trips to Asia and Africa and an ever-expanding orchid budget and a desire for oddities so stingy in their rewards that only a serious collector could appreciate them—orchids like the *Stanhopea*, which blooms only once a year for at most one day. "The bug hits you," a collector from Guatemala explained to me. "You can join A.A. to quit drinking, but once you get into orchids you can't do anything to kick the habit." I didn't own any orchids before I went down to Florida, but Laroche always teased me and said that I'd never get through a year around orchid people without getting hooked. I didn't want to get hooked—I didn't have the room or the patience to keep plants in my apartment, and I suppose I also didn't want Laroche to feel too smug about his predictive power. In fact, nearly every orchid-grower I talked to insisted on giving me a plant, and I was so leery of getting attached that I immediately gave them all away.

Currently, the international trade in orchids is more than ten billion dollars a year, and some individual rare plants have sold for more than twenty-five thousand dollars. Thailand is the world's largest exporter of cut orchids, sending thirty million dollars' worth of corsages and bouquets around the world. Orchids can be expensive to buy and expensive to maintain. There are orchid baby-sitters and orchid doctors and orchid boardinghouses—nurseries that will kennel your plants when they're not in bloom and then notify you when they've developed a bud and are ready to take home to show off. One magazine recently reported that a customer of one orchid kennel in San Francisco had so many plants that he was paying two thousand dollars in monthly rent. There are dozens of orchid sites on the Internet. For a while I checked in on "Dr. Tanaka's Homepage"; Dr. Tanaka described himself as "a comrade who love Paph!" and also as "so bad-looking, I can not show you my photo." Instead, his homepage had stories about new "splendid and/or marvelous Paphiopedilums in the Recent Orchid Show in JAPAN" and photographs of his greenhouse and his family, including one of his daughter, Paphiopedilum. "Junior high school, 1st year," he wrote under the picture of a smiling Miss Paphiopedilum Tanaka. "She is at a cheeky age. But I put her name to almost all selected clones of Paphs. First of all, I put 'Maki' and the next, 'Dreamy Maki,' 'Maki's Happiness,' etc." As for his wife, Kayoko, Dr. Tanaka wrote, "Her age is secret. She is worried about developing a middle aged spread as me. She never complain of my growing orchids, Paphiopedilums, and let me do as I like. . . . Before we have a daughter, I have put my wife's name to the all of selected clones of my Paphs. But after that, I have forgotten her name entirely."

I heard countless stories of powerful orchid devotion during the time I hung around with Laroche. I heard about a collector who had two greenhouses, on top of his town house in Manhattan, where he kept three thousand rare orchids; the greenhouses had automatic roof vents, gas heaters, an artificial cloud system, and breeze-simulating fans, and he, like many collectors, took vacations separately from his wife so one of them could always be home with the orchids. I heard about Michihiro Fukashima, the man who founded Japan Airlines, who said he found the business world too cruel, so he retired early, turned his assets over to his wife, severed all other ties to his family, and moved to Malaysia with his two thousand orchid plants. He had been married twice before and told a reporter that he felt "he had made his wives unhappy because of his orchid obsession." Charles Darrow, who invented the game Monopoly, retired with all his Monopoly money at the age of forty-six to devote himself to gathering and breeding wild orchids. A young Chinese collector, Hsu Shehua, recently described himself as a fanatic and said that even though he had been hauled into court four times for possessing wild orchids he considered it worthwhile.

Collecting can be a sort of lovesickness. If you collect living things, you are pursuing something imperfectible because, even if you manage to find and possess the living things you want, there is no guarantee they won't die or change. A few years ago, thirty thousand orchids belonging to a man in Palm Beach all died. He blamed methane fumes from a nearby sewage station. He sued the county and received a settlement, but began what his family called "a downhill slide." He was arrested for attacking his father, then for firing a sixteen-gauge shotgun into a neighbor's house, then for carrying a concealed knife, pistol, and shotgun. "It was the death of his orchids," his son told a reporter. "That's where it all began." Beauty can be painfully tantalizing, but orchids are not simply beautiful. Many are strange-looking or bizarre, and all of them are ugly when they aren't flowering. They are ancient, intricate living things that have adapted to every environment on earth. They have outlived dinosaurs; they might outlive human beings. They can be hybridized, mutated, crossbred, and cloned. They are at once architectural and fanciful and tough and dainty, a jewel of a flower on a haystack of a plant. The botanical complexity of orchids and their mutability makes them perhaps the most compelling and maddening of all collectible living things. There are thousands and thousands of orchid species. New orchids are being created in laboratories or being discovered every day, and others are nearly unfindable because they exist in tiny numbers in remote places. In a sense, then, the number of orchid species on the planet is uncountable, because it is constantly changing. To desire orchids is to have a desire that will never be, can never be, fully requited. A collector who wants one of every orchid species on earth will certainly die before even coming close.

Sharman Apt Russell

Smelling like a Rose

I n the aisles of every department store are products that use the brand names of rose, orchid, violet, honeysuckle, magnolia, narcissus, orange blossom, carnation, and hyacinth. We use these scents in our soaps and in our perfumes, in our bubble baths, lotions, shampoos, deodorants, even in our air fresheners and cleaning products.

We want to smell like flowers.

We are no different from most cultures, ancient or modern. The Hindus and Egyptians worshipped their gods with fragrance. The Greeks specialized in perfumery. The Bible reeks of incense. Europeans thought eaux de cologne could ward off the plague. The people of Tehuantepec washed their clothes in iris-scented water. Aztec noblemen carried fresh bouquets. In all of human history, there has been hardly a time or place that has not shared our preoccupation with smelling good.

Most perfume today has three odor groups, or notes. The top note is what we smell first. It grabs our attention and is usually a floral highlight such as lilac or lily. The middle note provides body and uses the essential oils in jasmine, lavender, or geranium. The third, or base, note often includes animal products—musk from the glands of rutting deer, or the pasty secretions from the genital areas of civet cats. These products also add the intangible qualities of body and "warmth."

The human body has its own array of scent from glands scattered on the face, scalp, breasts, under the arms, and in the genital area. Oddly, humans are desensitized to the smells of this last region. Long ago, we suppressed our ability to sniff out ovulation. One theory suggests that when we began living in complex social groups, smells of sexual readiness threatened the pair bonding needed to raise children.

Culturally, frankly, we are often disgusted by our own odor. We do not want to smell too human. But we do want to smell like *something*. And we want to attract mates.

So the top notes of perfume are from flowers that use scent to attract pollinators. The middle notes are oils and resins that resemble sex steroids. The base notes, at low concentrations, are obvious.

Still, we don't want to overstate our case. We don't want to smell too much like a deer or civet cat. We want to smell like a rose. We want to smell like orange blossoms. We want to smell like jasmine.

For their part, most flowers want to smell like food. Some flowers want to smell like a rotting corpse. Some flowers want to smell like excrement. Some flowers want to smell like fungus.

Flowers have their own agenda.

A single flower can produce as many as a hundred chemical compounds, with each part of the flower smelling different from the other parts. The smells mix in patterns that change over time, conveying a variety of signals: lay your eggs here, nectar over there, eat now.

In large quantities, the chemicals that produce scent are often toxic. To protect the plant, they are stored as volatiles (oils that convert easily from a liquid to a vapor) in special cells, usually in the flower itself. The petal tissue manufactures some of these volatiles; the reproductive organs are responsible for others.

Odor molecules are released through the process of evaporation. Once in the air, the molecules begin to move about randomly, growing farther and farther apart until they are carried away from their source by the wind. For a while, though, there is a coherent trail of molecules known as an odor plume. This plume has a destination. More often than not, it is meant to intersect with an insect's antenna, which has hundreds of cells designed to catch it. The area the antenna can sweep is the insect's nostril, in effect. In some moths this "nostril" can be as large as a small dog's.

Entering a plume, insects tend to zigzag, casting down or to the side when they lose the odor. When a zigzagging insect gets close enough to see a flower, it may suddenly "beeline" to its destination.

Flowers smell so good because insects smell so well. Some moths can detect scent a mile away. And most moths, like poodles, can smell just about everything. Other pollinators, especially bees, also distinguish and remember odor. In response, flowers seem to have evolved a complex mix of smells, trying to encourage what most botanists call flower constancy.

Flower constancy is the "loyalty" of a pollinator to a specific flower or species. First a flower species wants to smell and look different from competing species. Then a flower wants to attract a pollinator who will recognize and remember the difference. Furthermore, a flower wants that pollinator to be loyal, flying off with a load of pollen to fertilize a compatible flower.

For their own reasons, insects often oblige. Even when other flowers are blooming, a bee will continue to visit the familiar red clover or pink four-o'clock. The flower gets fertilized by a similar flower, and the bee becomes adept at handling that species. A honeybee might visit five hundred flowers in one foraging trip. Any savings in energy or time adds up quickly. We choose the same strategy when we shop at the same grocery store every day, or drive the same route to work.

Different flowers open and release their scent at different times, so an insect can have many loyalties. The blue chicory has nectar in the morning. Red clover is best after lunch. The four-o'clock opens in late afternoon. The evening primrose follows the four-o'clock.

A honeybee's memory for odor is linked to the relevant times of day. Typically, bees "trap-line" a series of flowers, moving from one to another at the appropriate hour, then heading home.

The timing of scent production contributes to a flower's reproductive success. Some flowers, like roses and clover, are scented only during the day. Some flowers are scented only at night.

There are smells you and I will never know, because we are not nocturnal. There are smells like maps to the country of loyalty.

In concealed nectaries or in open pockets, nectar is the pollinator's reward. It is mainly sugar water, sometimes containing sucrose or cane sugar, sometimes a mix of sucrose, fructose, and glucose. Most of us understand the butterfly. We also extend our mouthparts, automatically, toward a candy bar, the equivalent of nectar. In different species, nectar is secreted by different parts of the flower. Nectar-rich flowers often have a strong, sweet fragrance that does not necessarily come from the nectar. (And bird-pollinated flowers are often rich in nectar but relatively unscented, because birds do not have a good sense of smell.)

A flower's strong perfume is a lure, a dinner bell, and an advertisement. Up close, scent marks on the flower direct an insect right to the source of food. Nuances of smell may help some bees to determine if the flower is full of nectar or empty. Flower mites use nectar to recognize their host species. Mites ride from flower to flower in the nostrils of hummingbirds; when they smell the right nectar, they gallop home down the bird's beak.

In many flowers, pollen is the reward, and the odor of pollen is the primary scent. This is particularly true of plants visited by pollen-eating beetles. Bees are also good at smelling and distinguishing pollen from different flowers.

Perhaps the best image for pollen is the kind of breakfast only a farmworker should have: eggs, bacon, ham, cheese, potatoes, biscuits, and gravy. The steaming plate sends out a strong odor plume that draws the insect to the rich, messy food. Invariably, pollen grains stick to the legs or thorax, the head, the back; under the wings. Eventually, some grains dislodge onto another flower, and pollination takes place.

Pollen can also be sexy. In the sunflower moth, when virgin females are exposed to the odor of pollen, they begin signaling for males earlier and spend more time signaling. Later, more of their eggs mature.

This interplay of food, scent, and sex is a common theme. Some flowers smell like the sex pheromones of a butterfly. The male carpenter bee attracts females with a pheromone that smells like a flower good enough to eat. (A pheromone is a chemical used as a device to communicate between members of a species.) Through millennia of mimicry and exploitation, flower volatiles and insect pheromones have intertwined, with flowers imitating pheromones and pheromones imitating flowers.

We want to smell like a rose. We want to smell like a butterfly. We want to smell like an insect pheromone.

It doesn't stop there. A major ingredient in the sex pheromone of many moths is also found in the sex pheromone secreted in the urine of female Indian elephants. The urine is meant to attract the attention of a bull, the bigger the better.

In one experiment, women who sniffed musk, the sex attractant of Himalayan deer, developed a shorter menstrual cycle, ovulated more often, and conceived more easily. The smell of musk resembles the smell of steroids found in human urine. The chemical structure of steroids like testosterone resembles plant resins such as myrrh. We use these resins in our perfumes, just as we use the volatiles of flowers.

The fact that so many things smell like one another is partially explained by nature's efficiency. A compound that works here will also work there. We all came from the same primordial soup. Poets, who equate one thing with another, often echo scientists. Similes are real. Metaphors are chemical.

In the Bible's lyric poem, the Song of Solomon, odor is the language of love: "My beloved is unto me as a bag of myrrh that lieth between my breasts. My beloved is unto me as a cluster of henna flowers in the vineyard of Engedi."

The flowers of henna, lime, and chestnut smell like semen. The smell of myrrh has been compared to the oils secreted by glands in the human scalp.

W e want to smell like a rose. We want to smell like a henna flower. But we don't want to smell like the largest inflorescence in the world, the nine-foot-tall titan arum, mythically pollinated by elephants, which gives off a stench so revolting it has made men faint.

We don't want to smell like the dead-horse arum, a flower that evolved near gull colonies and came to resemble the rotting carcass of a bird. The arum is round and plate-sized, grayish-purple, blotched with pink, and covered with coarse dark-red hairs, or trichomes. Its smell of decay draws blowflies, which come to feed and lay their eggs. The flies crawl into what appears to be an empty eye socket or an inviting anus, deep into the flower, where they are trapped, the exit closed by bristly hairs.

Fed by nectar, the flies lay eggs that will later hatch and die for lack of food. Then the flower releases its pollen, which covers the blowflies. The bristly hairs wilt. The flies crawl out again.

Other flowers pollinated by flies and beetles smell variously like dead animals, rotting fish, or dung. Shades of red, purple, and brown add to the effect. Dark spots or warty areas look like clusters of insects already feeding. The common names of many plants tell the story: skunk cabbage, corpse flower, stinking goosefoot.

We don't want to smell like a dead-horse arum.

But we do want to smell like jasmine, which also has a distinct fecal odor beneath the top notes of cloying sweetness. At very low levels, at levels that reach deep into childhood and evoke the unconscious mind—that define our kinship with the rest of the world—urinary and fecal smells are commonly added to our best perfumes.

———

Most flowers smell like a restaurant. They use scent to signal an insect that they have food, or to deceive an insect into believing that they have food.

Some flowers smell like home, a good place to raise a family. A fungus gnat wants to lay its eggs where the eggs can hatch and eat fungus. Fungus mimics grow low in the forest, with dark-purple or brown flowers. Fleshy parts of the flower seem to be what the fungus gnat wants. One orchid has a creamy gill-like area that resembles, precisely, the underside of a mushroom.

A few flowers are drag queens who advertise for sex and use scent as part of their costume. A Mediterranean orchid has a convex oval lip that glistens metallic violet-blue. Its narrow yellow border is fringed with reddish hairs. Dark-red threadlike upper petals move in the wind like an insect's antenna. The orchid looks and smells like a female wasp. When the male wasp lights and tries to copulate, pollen is transferred onto its head.

Pseudo-copulation is rare, but not unique. All over the world, certain bees, wasps, and other insects try to mate with flowers that appear to be what they are not. (The bee fooled only by a flower may be lucky. The larvae of blister beetles clump together to look, and perhaps smell, like a female bee. The larvae attach themselves to a male bee and then try to find their way into a bee nursery, where they feed on pollen.)

Occasionally, a cigar is just a cigar. The boldest and most bizarre use of scent may be that of "perfume flowers," whose smell tells a male euglossine bee that this flower has . . . scent. Like someone at a department store stocking up for a big date, the bee mops up the perfumed liquid with feathery brushes on its front feet and stores it in a pouch on its back leg, where it can be combined with other odors to create a uniquely irresistible pheromone.

Smell is a come-hither. It can also be a go-away. Some fertilized flowers change their scent to signal pollinators to pollinate elsewhere. Many flowers stop producing scent, the most definitive no.

Pollinators also use scent. Bees secrete a pheromone to mark recently visited flowers. The odor is a memo to itself: this flower is out of nectar. Other bees get the message, too. No one wants to crawl up an empty corolla tube.

The most expensive perfume in the world, Joy, mixes a little jasmine with lots of rose. The rose has always generated passion. The Romans created a holiday, Rosalia, which they celebrated to excess. When the prophet Muhammad rose to heaven, drops of sweat fell to earth and turned into roses. The Christian rosary was originally made from 165 dried and rolled-up rose petals.

The smell of a rose is first absorbed by the mucus membranes in our nasal cavity. Next, receptor cells fire a message to the limbic system, an ancient part of our brain, the seat of emotion.

Memories associated with the sense of smell decay more slowly than visual memories.

We want to smell like a rose. Of course we do. Everything else is smelling like something. Molecules everywhere are drifting into the wind, jostling against one another, grabbed by a sensory cell, by the antenna of a moth, by a dog's nose, by a lover's inhalation. We want to be part of that movement. We want to move. We want to be moved.

Isabel Allende

The Language of Flowers

here does taste end and smell begin? They are inseparable. The temptation of coffee is not born of the taste, which leaves smoky dregs in memory, but in that intense and mysterious fragrance of remote forests. With our eyes closed and nostrils pinched shut, we can't distinguish between a raw potato and an apple, between lard and chocolate. The nose is capable of detecting more than ten thousand odors, and the brain of distinguishing among them, yet that same brain cannot distinguish between lust and love. The olfactory sense is, from the viewpoint of evolution, our oldest sense. It is precise, swift, and powerful, and it bores into our memory with persistent tenacity, hence the efficacy of perfumes. The secret is always to wear the same scent, until it becomes a personal, untransferable trademark, something that identifies us.

Cleopatra knew this and, as with everything else she did, carried it to an extreme. In ports along the Nile, the breeze announced the impending arrival of her gilded barge hours in advance because it bore the fragrance of the roses of Damascus in which that spellbinding queen drenched her sails. During her celebrated visit to Rome, where she traveled with Caesarion, her son by Julius Caesar, the center of a formidable social and political scandal that she ignored with the natural arrogance of the pharaohs, essence of rose became the fashion, and every woman of style, except Calpurnia, the humiliated wife of Julius Caesar, used it. Sometimes that perfume lingered in the streets like an Egyptian mockery, reminding the citizens of Rome that their invincible empire could be lost in the bedsheets of a foreign woman. At the banquets of powerful Romans, slaves counted among their tasks perfuming the rooms by blowing sweet attars through ingenious silver tubes and tossing a rain of flower petals from the ceiling. The aroma of roses, as costly as liquid myrrh but much more erotic, was sprinkled upon the guests—roses everywhere: from his followers, flattery for his Egyptian queen; from his enemies, ironic obeisance for his Egyptian whore. Several centuries later, in medieval castles, the floor was covered with flower petals and aromatic herbs to mask the stench of garbage and excrement. Those were times when nobles and lackeys relieved themselves behind the draperies: the toilet is a much later invention. There were French monarchs who lavished liters of floral essences on themselves to conceal the fact that they never bathed.

In the past, flowers, among their many enchantments, had the task of transmitting subtle amorous messages, but in all the haste of the twentieth century this art has become a dead language. I don't see any advantage to reviving it. It's like Sanskrit: there's no one to speak it with. But just in case the reader of these pages is given to moments of madness, I'm going to devote a few paragraphs to the language of flowers. My experience is that in the Western world it doesn't pay to invest too much effort in details as delicate as these, because most of the time they are totally ignored. Drastic methods yield better results.

The symbolism of flowers reached its apogee in the midnineteenth century during the reign of Queen Victoria in England, although it wasn't there the language originated but in Turkey, where it was used to send coded love notes within the harem. Lady

Mary Wortley Montagu, who as the wife of a British ambassador lived in that country from 1716 to 1718, introduced the language of flowers into England. It evolved through several decades until it became a romantic epidemic so sophisticated that by using different combinations in a bouquet it was possible to maintain a long correspondence without a single written word.

Ladies placed great care in the selection of the paper for their notes, because even printed flowers could convey messages. A handkerchief embroidered with pansies was an indication that the lady would never forget her sweetheart; with roses, a promise of love. If the needle masterfully re-created the quince flower, the recipient could consider himself fortunate, because quince indicated lifelong fidelity. Things reached the point where the placement of the ribbon on a bouquet determined whether the sentiments expressed referred to the giver or to the receiver, and the hand with which flowers were presented or accepted affected their meaning, as did the place on her body the woman chose to wear the offering: the nearer the heart, the more accessible she was to love. Thence the tradition of giving a corsage before a dance; the lady selects the place she wants to pin it, whether at hip, waist, hair, or bosom. Any way you look at it, it's an abominable custom; no dress ever looked good with all that rubbish attached to it.

If flowers were handed or accepted with the blossoms pointing downward and the stems up, their meaning was completely reversed. So, if a swain came to call carrying a bouquet of tulips with a bow on the left, which was tantamount to a declaration of love, and the lady handed them back with the heads upside down, that meant there was no shred of hope for the suitor; his rejection was final. The interpretation was not that dramatic in every case; it depended on the variety of the flowers. Anemones, for example, represented forgetfulness, but a bouquet presented with the flowers pointing down did not translate as nostalgia, and a hyacinth, which from the time of Greek mythology spoke of sorrow, or a calendula, which also embodies suffering, did not turn into an expression of joy.

No one has time for such complexities nowadays, and we have to imagine that, if you've progressed to the stage of cooking aphrodisiac dishes for your date, it won't matter with what hand he gives you the red rose or where you decide to pin the camellia. A few basics are more than enough: the color red proclaims passion; white, purity; pink, tenderness; yellow, forgetfulness; purple, modesty (although now feminists claim that color). To a Victorian it would have been maladroit to give yellow flowers to someone you wanted to win, but today flowers are so expensive that we appreciate the gesture without dwelling on such details. I still remember with pleasure the last time someone brought me a flower: a thirsty, newspaper-wrapped sunflower in the hands of my five-year-old grandson.

Wild daisies, from which we plucked the leaves when I was young to find out whether the redhead on the corner loved us, symbolize innocence. Once it was believed that a libation brewed from these humble flowers and drunk with regularity could assuage the pain of madness and reintegrate dispersed spirits. The narcissus is, logically, the flower of vanity and egotism. Its name derives from the Greek legend of Narcissus, a shepherd in love with his own reflection in a pool, who died trying to kiss that image. Besides conceited, not too bright. The poppy—opium flower—expresses surcease from sorrow, temporal pleasure, and relief from shortness of breath, but for the English, because of its color, it also symbolizes the blood of soldiers fallen in war. Geraniums, which rarely are included in a bouquet because of their sharp odor, are by their color a representation of sadness, disillusion, consolation, and other rather useless sentiments.

The heliotrope, whose name in Greek means "with the head turned toward the sun," indicates sincerity and devotion in love; it is given as a promise or allegation of fidelity should one have been detected in a compromising situation. Lilies predict a message. This is an interesting flower; in some cultures of the Middle East and Mediterranean it is associated, because of its shape, with the female genitals, as is true of the orchid as well, but the lily is also the flower of purity, the Virgin Mary's flower, and, not least, the emblem of France, the fleur-de-lis. The flower of the lavender signifies distrust. The perfumes of violets and jasmines have such high aphrodisiac qualities—especially at night—that they can turn the most virtuous of maidens into an insatiable nymphomaniac, yet in the language of flowers violets symbolize modesty and jasmine represents elegance, discretion, and grace. The scent of the tuberose is also irresistible to women, although nauseating to most men. Lilacs connote humility, but ever since the Renaissance these flowers have been credited with the ability to excite men. I had them in my garden for years and never knew that because of them the postman harbored lustful intentions. To the Victorians, incapable of confessing thoughts of passion in the presence of a lady, lilacs also stood for the first move toward professing their love; they were a way of testing the water before making a more explicit declaration, which might consist of a bouquet of white roses—purity—followed immediately by another of red roses—love. Never together, because that would mean separation and death, as in the fate of Tristan and Isolde or Romeo and Juliet. Finally, after formalizing the betrothal, if the suitor was very bold he might offer his fiancée branches of the flowering almond to express his sublime passion without beating about the bush—almond or any other.

According to the classic language of flowers, the forget-me-not meant true love and remembrance. An Austrian legend tells the story of two lovers who were walking along the Danube when the girl, who always had her way, saw a small blue flower floating in the water, and nothing would do but that her young man get it for her. He leaped into the river at her bidding but was caught in the current and pulled under. With his last burst of strength, he reached the flower and tossed it to his sweetheart, calling, "Forget me not." For me, nevertheless, this small blue blossom will always be the symbol of exile. When it became my fate to leave my country following the military coup of 1973, I was able to take very few things with me. My grandfather, my mother-in-law—whom I loved with rare devotion—my friends, my family, and the incomparable landscape of my homeland were all left behind in Chile. As for Lot's wife when she was fleeing Sodom, the rule was not to look back, but who can leave the house where her children were born without one last look? I didn't as yet know that I was cutting off my roots with a brutal slash, that little by little I would dry up like a mutilated tree, and that only the unrelenting exercise of memory would keep me, again like Lot's wife, from turning into a pillar of salt. In the bottom of my suitcase I carried a little bag containing dirt from my garden,

Claudia Lewis

Ode to Mold

I grow fungi—the only flora able to survive my well-intentioned but fickle care. And these fungi more than survive; they thrive. I specialize in two types. One is wild, the other tame.

Scrutiny of the shy, tenacious, wild fungi that grow at my house regardless of place or season reveals subtle colors, variety, and unrelenting optimism. Exquisitely soft, dove-gray pads of mold float like velvet lilies on a calm pond of yogurt in the back of my refrigerator, silently expanding across the thick liquid. On a lower shelf puffs of cottony growth dot a can of forgotten refried beans. Yesterday there was a single white patch on the inside of the can. Today there are six. Soon, I know from experience, the surface will be shrouded under a delicate quilt. *Penicillium* expands in a circle of green dust on an orange at the bottom of the fruit bowl. *Aspergillus niger* sprouts on the last bagel in the breadbox. Tiny black specks wag hopefully from the ends of tiny stalks. Propagules—the fungal equivalent of seeds—cluster at the ends of knobby threads, ready to burst into the air to be carried aloft by a draft from an open window, by a tailwind of someone racing past, by a sneeze.

"Surprise me!" I think to myself as I retrieve a plastic carton that has been lurking behind successive gallons of milk. Someone must have put it back half finished. I can't resist peeking to see what Dr. Seuss–like forms flourish inside.

Once, while searching my car for misplaced airline tickets, I discovered that an apple had been left in the lidded compartment of an armrest. Its perfect apple shape was still recognizable even though it had tripled in size and had been transformed into an extravagant, gauzy bloom of finespun filaments the color of exotic jade. The mold's matrix was so fragile it barely supported the delicate drops of amber liquid that glistened at the surface. Such avid decay was strangely appealing and yet disturbing. The cobwebbed growth looked as gentle as sleep, as sinister as suffocation. I was reluctant to disturb this phenomenon of opportunism, afraid airborne spores might desire to colonize my skin, my lungs, or a sluggish corner of my heart. Though I appreciate mold as a metaphor for change, I am not yet ready to surrender to its spores. I put on rubber gloves, held my breath, and carefully scooped up the spoilage along with its host.

Wary of these wild mold intruders that arrive uninvited to bloom without encouragement, I nevertheless cherish their tame cousin, a sourdough yeast culture that is the second type of fungus I grow. And though I am a reluctant gardener in the macroscopic world of flowers and fruits, I am devoted to this yeast of the class Ascomycetes that I have had with me for most of my life.

Forty years ago my mother was given a cup of sourdough starter that originated in the Coeur d'Alene mining district of Idaho and dated back to 1888. She taught me how to make sourdough pancakes and gave me a cup of my own starter when I went off to college. I would take it with me west across the Pacific Ocean to Hawaii and back.

When I married, in 1975, my husband and I left San Francisco to live in a rural town in Alabama. Every night of our cross-country drive I'd have to convince a different but consistently doubtful motel proprietor to let me store my Mason jar of starter, which was clearly neither medicine nor baby formula, in his or her refrigerator.

It was all the dowry I had. Every morning I'd fill a chest with ice to keep the starter cool for the long hours we were on the road.

This steady, eager, budding yeast is as dear to me as the roses, lilacs, and rhubarb plants I've known friends to dig up and take with them when they move from one house to another. Just like my friends and their flowers, I lovingly cultivate my starter, this "bonsai of the food world," and pass it on to relatives and interested friends.

Sourdough yeast lives in a companionable symbiosis with lactobacillus bacteria. The association between these two dissimilar organisms—the yeast more plant than animal, the bacteria more animal than plant—is mutually beneficial. As long as that relationship is stable, the starter is stable and will remain unchanged indefinitely as each new generation replicates the qualities of the original species.

I marvel at the way the DNA of its original yeast compels my starter to grow and expand with consistent enthusiasm, just as it used to do for some grizzled miner, just as my own DNA compels me to get up every morning and brew tea. And sometimes I wonder about the original character of my own cells. Like those of my starter, my cells are constantly being replaced, more or less, as I age. And yet, like my starter, some distinct essence of me remains the same. At fifty-two I wonder what there is of me now as a middle-aged woman that was also present when I was a baby, a teen, a new mother. The older I get, the more I appreciate the paradox of continuity and change, that life is wholly connected, a sustained, enduring expression of meaning, however mysteriously it is transformed.

Luckily, my starter's patient torpor is perfectly suited to my unreliable attention. Starters can lie fallow in the refrigerator for months, or in the freezer for years, ready to spring to life whenever the steps are taken that, like rain after drought, bring growth. We have created our own stable symbiosis, my starter and I: it secures me to my memories while I give it a future.

During the dark and erratic winters of refrigeration, my starter and its bacteria convert carbohydrates derived from flour and milk into sugar, producing a clear grain alcohol that collects at the top of the jar. The tangy fragrance of this hooch jolts me every time I open the lid. Like many women, I have a particularly acute sense of smell. It is my most reliable pathway to memory. When I take my usual stiff whiff of starter, the way some people sniff roses, it is as if a jumble of emotions and memories have come tumbling out of the jar as well, like eager genies, to take me back to my adolescence. My mother stands at the stove while my sister and I sprawl on the cool tile floor of the last house we lived in as a family. I am reading the funnies. My father makes fresh orange juice. I recall how I would relax in these oases of tradition and camaraderie. The pancakes are as sharply sour as the syrup we poured on top was sweet, a marvelous balance of opposites, a yin and yang of flavor, the taste of our destinies.

In my family we moved a lot. And it's only lately, by willing myself to stay put, that I've been able to resist the haul-ass blues and nomadic life-style I learned from my parents. It seems to me that the desire to garden is the emotional opposite of the desire to move. People who garden commit themselves to place. They also risk being caught by entropy. My sourdough starter is like an herbal remedy for the restlessness I constantly try to suppress. Like a miniature, portable bog, my starter goes where I go, even as it connects me to my past.

My mother, who at eighty has finally lost her desire to move, now lives alone in a cozy house with a big backyard. She has become a gardener. She grows irises. Her flowerbeds are full of splashy, ruffled blooms in gorgeous shades of maroon, copper, and purple; some exotic few sport beards. "I love my irises so much I kiss them!" she confessed the other day. Fully *compos mentis*, my mother has found a way to express her gratitude for her flowers' faithful company. And when the seasons wheel past, gathering momentum, she greets each fearlessly, ready to dig and replant rhizomes in the fall, to await their resurrection in the spring. But does she sense that, like her irises, she will also lie in this earth, absorbed into its cycles?

Sometimes I find myself racing forward, as if what I dread is behind me, not ahead. If only the beautiful wild molds and my steady starter were proof that death is not a terminus but part of a continuous cycle, proof that the grave is neither ominous nor lonely, proof that neither lovelessness nor disappointment will overtake me just because I lingered too long in one place. If only I were convinced that the paradox of continuity and change is benign.

Hungry for reassurance, taking comfort in family customs, I complete the steps in my sourdough-pancake recipe. It takes two days. Batter rises in a big yellow bowl on my kitchen counter. My three kids sprawl on the floor, watching cartoons they have long outgrown. I look for my husband in the garden he loves. His ambition is to grow an heirloom tomato so big a single, luscious slice will fill a whole plate. He smiles through a sweaty smudge of dirt when I bring him a glass of orange juice. After twenty-three years of marriage, our Sunday-brunch routine is as familiar to him as it is to me. "Come on in; pancakes are ready," I say, pausing for a moment in the sunshine and fresh air. Out here I can escape my preoccupation with the molds that transform matter of one kind into something else, escape even my dear yeast that connects me with an irretrievable past. Standing under this sweet sun with my husband, I feel safe and far away from the softly silent decay that transpires in all the dark corners of our house and across the entire world. In this moment of perfect equipoise, the earth firm beneath my feet, I feel the warm and gentle sun dissuade for now the spores of change that have arrived too soon on this living skin.

Linda Hasselstrom

Mulch

A mulch is a layer of organic matter
used to control weeds,
preserve moisture,
and improve the fertility of the soil.
You will not find naked soil
in the wilderness.

I started cautiously: newspapers,
hay, a few magazines;
Robert Redford stared up
between the rhubarb and the lettuce.

Then one day, cleaning shelves,
I found some old love letters.
I've always burned them, for the symbolism.
But the ashes, gray and dusty as old passions,
would blow about the yard for days

stinging my eyes,
bitter on my tongue.

So I mulched them:
gave undying love to the tomatoes,
the memory of your gentle hands to the squash.
It seemed to do them good,
and it taught me a whole new style
of gardening.

Now my garden is the best in the wilderness,
and I mulch everything:
bills; check stubs;
dead kittens and baby chicks.
I seldom answer letters; I mulch them
with the plans I made for children of my own,
photographs of places I've been
and a husband I had once;
as well as old bouquets
and an occasional unsatisfactory lover.

Nothing is wasted.

Strange plants push up among the corn,
leaves heavy with dark water,
but there are
no weeds.

Zora Neale Hurston

Wedding Day

hese specialists are always women. They are old women who have lived with a great deal of subtlety themselves. Having passed through the active period and become widows, or otherwise removed from active service, they are reinducted in an advisory capacity.

The young girl who is to be married shortly or about to become the mistress of an influential man is turned over to the old woman for preparation. The wish is to bring complete innocence and complete competence together in the same girl. She is being educated for her life work under experts.

For a few days the old woman does not touch her. She is taking her pupil through the lecture stages of instruction. Among other things she is told that the consummation of love cannot properly take place in bed. Soft beds are not for love. They are comforts for the old and lackadaisical. Also she is told that her very position must be an invitation. When her lord and master enters the chamber she must be on the floor with only her shoulders and the soles of her feet touching the floor. It is *so* that he must find her. Not lying sluggishly in bed like an old cow, and hiding under the covers like a thief who has snatched a bit of beef from the market stall. The exact posture is demonstrated over and over again. The girl must keep on trying until she can assume it easily. In addition she is instructed at length on muscular control inside her body and out, and this also is rehearsed again and again, until it is certain that the young candidate has grasped all that is meant.

The last day has arrived. This is the day of the wedding. The old woman gives her first a "balm bath," that is, a hot herb bath. Only these old women know the secret of which herbs to use to steep a virgin for marriage. It is intended, this bath is, to remove everything mental, spiritual, and physical that might work against a happy mating. No soap is used at this point. It is a medicinal sweating tub to open the pores and stimulate the candidate generally. Immediately that the virgin leaves the bath she is covered and sweated for a long time. Then she is bathed again in soapy water.

Now the subtleties begin. Jamaica has a grass called khus khus. The sweet scent from its roots is the very odor of seduction. Days before, the old woman has prepared an extract from these roots in oil and it is at hand in a bowl. She begins and massages the girl from head to foot with this fragrant unction. The toes, the fingers, the thighs, and there is a special motional treatment for every part of the body. It seems to me that the breasts alone are ignored. But when the body massage is over, she returns to the breasts. These are bathed several times in warm water in which something special had been steeped. After that they are massaged ever so lightly with the very tips of the fingers dipped in khus khus. This fingertip motion is circular and moves ever toward the nipple. Arriving there, it begins over and over again. Finally the breasts are cupped and the nipples flicked with a warm feather back and forth, back and forth, until there is a reaction to stimulation. The breasts stiffen and pout, while the rest of the body relaxes.

But the old woman is not through. She carries this same light-fingered manipulation down the body and the girl swoons. She is revived by a mere sip of rum in which a single leaf of ganga has been steeped. Ganga is that "wisdom weed" which has been brought from the banks of the sacred Ganges to Jamaica. The girl revives and the massage continues. She swoons again and is revived. But she is not aware of the workaday world. She is in a twilight state of awareness, cushioned on a cloud of love thoughts.

Now the old woman talks to her again. It is a brief summation of all that has been said and done for the past week.

"You feel that you are sick now but that is because the reason for which you were made has not been fulfilled. You cannot be happy or complete until that has happened. But the success of everything is with you. You have the happiest duty of any creature on earth and you must perform it well. The whole duty of a woman is love and comfort. You were never intended for anything else. You are made for love and comfort. Think of yourself in that way and no other. If you do as I teach you, heaven is with you and the man who is taking you to his house to love and comfort him. He is taking you there for that reason and for no other. That is all that men ever want women for, love and softness and peace, and you must not fail him."

The old instructor ran over physical points briefly again. She stressed the point that there must be no fear. If the girl experienced any pain, then she had failed to learn what she had been taught with so much comfort and repetition. *There was nothing to fear.* Love killed no one. Rather, it made them beautiful and happy. She said this over and over again.

Still stressing relaxed muscles, the old woman took a broad white band of cloth and wound it tightly about the loins of the girl well below the navel. She circled the body with the band perhaps four times and then secured it with safety pins. It was wound very tightly and seemed useless at first. All the time that this was being done the girl was crying to be taken to her future husband. The old woman seemingly ignored her and massaged her here and there briefly.

They began to put her wedding clothes upon the girl. The old woman was almost whispering to her that she was the most important part of all creation, and that she must accept her role gladly. She must not make war on her destiny and creation. The impatient girl was finally robed for her wedding and she was led out of the room to face the public and her man. But here went no frightened, shaking figure under a veil. No nerve-racked female behaving as if she approached her doom. This young, young thing went forth with the assurance of infinity. And she had such eagerness in her as she went!

Annick Smith

Huckleberries

igarettes, ice cream, sex with strangers—maybe, for kicks, a roaring old-fashioned drunk. Now, there's a fistful of guilty pleasures best given up these death-fearing days of the millennium. "Nails in your coffin," says my companion, Bill, as he inhales his mentholated True. I miss the sweetness of what I've given up. The smoke. The danger. "Who cares?" I reply. I'm lying. The grandmother years are on me, and I plan to enjoy them. But huckleberries? Where is the sin in huckleberries?

In my part of the northern Rockies, women (and quite a few men) have been picking the pungent wild blueberry for, say, ten thousand years—as long as the two species have existed in proximity. The Salish and Kootenai Indians who live in the Flathead Valley, on the west side of the Mission Range, just a couple of drainages from my Blackfoot Valley home, have gleaned their wild-berry gardens for generations, reaping an important source of sugar and carbohydrates.

Gathering is the traditional work of women, and it includes the cultivation of a sustainable crop by selective picking and pruning. Old burns are a favorite place, for huckleberries, like prairies and old-growth forests, have a positive relationship with fire. The bushes need openings in the forest canopy in order to flower and bear fruit. Also, the nutrients returned to the soil after a burn fertilize the berries. If a patch isn't burned within seventy years, even the biggest bushes become sterile. In turn, the spreading rhizomes stabilize soil and hold off erosion.

Women of the berry-picking tribes know such things. They guard their patches the way men guard fishing holes, and pass their knowledge to daughters and granddaughters—a practice not limited to Native Americans. My ninety-three-year-old Hungarian Jewish mother still takes her grandchildren and great-grandchildren out into the blueberry patches that thrive in the loamy soil of the Michigan dunes, near the summer home we have frequented for over half a century. She talks as she picks. "I remember, when I was a girl . . ." Mother might say, pulling her white, wide-brimmed hat down so sun will not freckle her soft skin. "There was a sour-cherry tree in our orchard. . . ." She tells stories of Transylvania, where she grew up. She remembers what is lost: her mother and her brother, and a more gentle, slower, closer-to-earth way of life.

Grandmothers are the leaders of the cultures of gathering, and we have stories to tell. Some of them are love stories, for berry-picking was an approved courtship ritual in many tribes. I like to imagine a young man and young woman (a version of me, with long black braids) wandering away from companions in summer twilight, a half-moon rising, the undersides of clouds lit silver and apricot. There is a creek singing nearby where whitetails drink. The lovers hear a crashing in the underbrush. They freeze. It's a bear roused on the other side of the thicket. They drop their baskets, hold on to each other. Luckily, the bear stalks off in the opposite direction. But it's too late. The young couple have descended as one into the lush, sweet-scented, and sheltering brush. Their lips are blue-rimmed and taste like berries.

Like sex, eating has remained pretty much the same over eons, and the consumption of berries is a cross-cultural ceremony. In the old days, as now, women stored their huckleberries in baskets or boxes. Women of the Northwest Coast mixed theirs with whale oil as we mix ours with whipped cream. Plains-tribe ladies might have served them up with bison fat. Some batches were dried whole, or cooked to pulp and pressed into cakes, which were then dried for later use. Dried berries flavored stews, were mixed with bitterroot as a sweetener, or could be crushed into smoked meat to make pemmican—road food for travelers and warriors, or for automobile nomads like me.

I'd love to snack on pemmican as I drive toward Glacier Park with my second son, Steve. We will take the tour boat up Waterton Lakes, hike the three miles from Goat Haunt to the Kootenay Lakes. When we camped beneath the towering cirque wall a few years ago, a moose family, knee-deep in the marshy lake, kept us up a good part of the night with their slurping. Next morning, up toward the pass, we found a bounteous huckleberry patch where we filled our plastic bags in half an hour. Walking out, we heard a noise in a great hemlock. Looking down at us was a fox-faced little mammal with dark fur, a rare and voracious fisher—the only one we have ever seen.

Huckleberrying can bring such unexpected gifts, because, while we are out in the woods looking for pea-sized fruit, alert to the presence of bears, our senses are jacked up. In the cities and towns where most people live, ten thousand daily cacophonies would drive us nuts if we practiced such alertness. One reason we go into the wild is to escape to a place where elements are basic and it is necessary to notice them. Old habits return, and, like the animals we are, we tune in to actual weather. The terrain where we walk hides predators. We are cautious as prey.

People like me retreat to secret places in the mountains whenever we can, but life can be so busy that berrying gives us a good excuse. We load our old cars, our 4x4s and pickups with camping gear, kids, relatives, dogs, and head up into the hills, the trout streams, and the back-country forests—what's left of them. We find a clearing in which to make camp amid ponderosa pines and clumps of white-flowering bear grass, and then, pails clanking, trail off into thickets and avalanche chutes, along streams, or up to the edges of clear-cuts and burns where we know the berries will be.

Family gatherings like these take place from Alaska to California, and from Oregon to Michigan—in the huge cool territories where more than a dozen species of wild blueberry grow. The most familiar in my experience are the thinleaf variety in the damp cedar-and-fir-covered Cascade range of western Oregon and Washington; and the globular variety, which likes the drier, more acidic soils of ponderosa pine and larch groves in the northern Rockies. With greater moisture, Northwest berries grow larger than their Montana cousins, but the tough little Montana guys have a stronger, more concentrated flavor.

Several types of wild blueberry often grow in the same neighborhood. In Glacier National Park, for instance, six varieties intermingle: blue huckleberry, tall huckleberry, dwarf huckleberry, velvet-leaved huckleberry, dwarf billberry, and grouse whortleberry. Only the blue and the tall are sought by grizzlies. And, a woman researcher has discovered, the hucks become sweeter, more packed with nutrition, as altitude rises, which is a good thing for bears, who follow ripening crops from river valleys to high mountain ridges when autumn approaches.

Huckleberries ripen in late July or early August at their lowest elevations (about thirty-two hundred feet in western Montana) and keep on ripening into mid-September at elevations of up to seven thousand feet. Bears must accumulate enough fat to survive in winter dens, and to birth and suckle their young through the snowy spring emergence. In my part of the northern Rockies, most of their fat-producing calories come from huckleberries. The search for hucks usually keeps grizzlies and black bears safely in the back country, where they roam higher as winter calls, until the last berries are stripped.

Berrying is a favorite pastime in the mountain West, but now some alarmists are telling us to stop the picking, hold off on that pie, nix the huckleberry ice cream. We must boycott the commercially sold jams and the berry-filled chocolates in their Made-in-Montana wooden boxes. Why? Because huckleberries are getting scarce in this region, and bears who depend on them are starving, and the ecosystem is skewed (or screwed), and we're partway to blame.

The scarcity was palpable during the summer of 1998 in western Montana: huckleberry bushes were barren, their bright-green ovate, minutely toothed leaves spotted yellow or turning a premature red. The few berries I found in my home patches were shriveled, dead white, inedible. This was true all over Montana's huckleberry country, from the forested foothills of the Flathead and the Swan to the berry heavens of Glacier National Park.

The failure could have been caused by weather: premature budding brought on by February thaws; late freezes that nipped the tiny bell-like flowers; a record thirty-two days over ninety degrees from July through September in 1998—climate changes that may themselves be caused by boundless human appetites for energy and more energy.

Charles Jonkel, a rosy-cheeked, white-bearded expert on bear behavior, believes that bumblebee pollinators flew in too late in 1998 to service the surviving early blooms, causing mass infertility. The same sexual miscues were likely to blame for the fruitlessness of serviceberry and chokeberry bushes, which abound in our valleys and hills, and usually serve as backup food for bears and other foragers.

"It's a five-hundred-year event," said Jonkel. He was sanguine about future crops. He pointed at Mount Sentinel, which rises behind the University of Montana. "Looks like we'll have a helluva season. See, the mountain's white with serviceberries in blossom." But a few days later, we had a twenty-degree night and woke to a two-inch crust of snow lying deadly white on Mount Sentinel's blossoms.

By harvest time, feeling the threat of starvation and with almost no backup food sources, a passel of bear mothers discarded their usual caution and came plundering into human territory. Instructing their hungry cubs, they raided orchards and gardens and garbage. Many sows were shot. Wildlife rehabilitation centers in Kalispell, Helena, and the Bitterroot Valley took in nearly seventy orphans.

I saw for myself how desperate the situation had become when, in midsummer, I went up into the larch and ponderosa and Douglas-fir stands above my meadow to scout the berry patches where we gather each year, and was astonished to find no berries, no bears. Not even bear scat. Climbing higher, into Plumb Creek's logged "industrial" forests, through clear-cuts and burns where the brush is thick, I still found no huckleberries worth taking. Poor bears, I thought.

They did not come down until late August. It was about three in the afternoon, sun shining on the sere grass. I'd been hanging sheets to dry (I love the ozone scent of sun-dried sheets) when I looked up to see a honey-and-amber panda-striped black bear sow and her two chocolate cubs walk out of the woods and across the meadow in plain view. They went directly to the thorn-apple bush on the stone pile and commenced the work of eating. I called Andrew, one of the twins, who was back home from Brooklyn. We whispered by the deck, binoculars in hand, our old German shepherd, Betty—nearly blind, and oblivious to any intruders except coyotes and meter-readers—at our feet.

The mama bear lifted her nose to the wind, seemed to look at us an instant, then returned to browsing. Her two cubs rose on their hind legs and pulled down branches with their paws, raking in the fruit through open jaws. We could barely believe what we were seeing. In the thirty years my family has lived on this meadow, we have spotted a number of bears in berry brush or raiding wild apple trees at dawn or dusk (our creek is, after all, named Bear Creek), but never at midday, out in the open. And during the last few years, none of us has sighted any bears in the meadow—only their telltale piles of berry-rich scat.

The retreat of the bears has worried me. In the past, I attributed it to hunting, for Montana has a black-bear season in the spring. One ranger told me that too many mature bears have been taken, leaving untutored teenagers, not enough newborns. Add scarce food and disappearing habitat to hunting, and the sum is a major threat to survival. I wish I could protect all the bears, but I can promise safety only on my quarter-section of land, which is a mere mini-mart snack stop within the huge wild habitat they need in order to survive.

Through the rest of the summer, our bear trio came again and again for their snacks, always in daylight, until the thorn apples were gone. I was glad to see they were still shy enough to keep away from the wild apple tree, with its rosy fruit, growing a few yards from my house. I hope they found great thorn-apple feasts down the brushy slopes above Bear Creek, where grouse and wild turkeys hang out. I hope they made it through the winter. I hope to see them again this summer, but not starving at midday.

Whatever the cause of the recent berry failures, we know that pickers have an impact on the huckleberry crop—especially in popular harvest areas where berries are accessible and lush. Some of the most prolific huckleberry gardens are no longer family secrets. Patches that nurtured rural, self-sufficient, earth-connected ways of life are being depleted by commercial pickers. The middlemen who hire them, and the businesses and markets that sell huckleberry products, are reaping profits from a resource that belongs to all Americans.

The gleaners scour brushy habitat near back-country trails and roads in national parks and forests, often setting up camp. Many use homemade rakes or combs to strip berries from limbs, or beaters to shake them onto ground cloths, and some people break off loaded branches, hauling them to camp to be picked after dark.

Although the picker may claim she is merely pruning, or wreaking no more havoc than an average bear, such methods wound or destroy the growth points at the tips of branches, leaving only the weakest shrubs to bear fruit the following year.

In addition to kids wanting to earn summer bucks, and the usual itinerants, recent immigrants such as the Hmong people from Laos are becoming huckleberry entrepreneurs. After the Vietnam War, some Hmong tribes that had aided the CIA and American troops were transported to the U.S. for safety. One group chose to settle in Montana's Bitterroot Valley. There, they've become meticulous and successful truck farmers, but like many old-time ranchers and farmers in the West, they seem to feel no need for stewardship in the wild. Unlike most other Westerners, however, the Hmong are willing to pursue back-aching hand labor from dawn to dusk, bushwhacking into the back country to pick huckleberries for much-needed dollars. Because they are conscientious workers, leaving no bush unpicked, they may become serious competitors of the black bears and grizzlies, grouse and songbirds who depend on the same huckleberry crops for sustenance.

Not until the early 1990s was the commercial picking of huckleberries even partially regulated on public lands. The wild crop seemed endless as the spawning salmon that ran up every clear, gravelly stream. Now salmon are mostly gone from the waters of Oregon, Washington, Idaho, and Montana, but huckleberries are still here and ripe for protection. These days, if you want to pick hucks for profit in our national forests, you must get a permit from the ranger of the district you wish to enter. Day-use permits are four dollars (twenty dollars minimum), or eighty dollars per season, which is not prohibitive when pint bags are selling for five dollars or more in the Missoula Public Market. Wilderness and research areas, campgrounds, and developed recreational sites are off limits, and off-road vehicles and mechanisms that damage plants are prohibited, as is the severing of branches. But the consequence for disobeying such rules is only a ticket, carrying no standard fine or punishment.

Even if there were stiff fines, what agency can police the hundreds of thousands of acres of back country available to pickers. Huckleberries are one natural resource that remains largely unstudied and unguarded—free for the taking from nature's lunch pail. Few opportunists can resist a free lunch, especially in an economy as poor as Montana's, where tourism is a growth industry offering a market for the million-dollar huckleberry business, which is value-added and regional—just what the economic doctors ordered.

The have-your-cake-and-eat-it answer would be to grow huckleberries as a crop on private ground. Unfortunately, it is difficult, if not impossible, to successfully plant *Vaccinium membranaceum* (thin-leaf huckleberry) or *V. ovalifolium,* the oval-leaved species that grows alongside it in Northwestern forests, or *V. globulare* (blue or globe huckleberry), the most common species east of the Cascades. As long as the berries' habits of growth and production remain whimsical, unpredictable, and largely mysterious, domestication does not seem imminent. And a domesticated berry would not be as valuable. We might think of them as common, like supermarket blueberries. We would believe they had lost the taste of wildness so much to be desired.

W alk into the berry woods some bright early August afternoon, with children or sisters or lovers or neighbors, and you will realize that we belong in this habitat. We are as natural browsing in the underbrush as rabbits and grouse and bedding does. Women especially seem at home here, humming as we stoop to pick the ripe huckleberries, tasting every so often because we can't resist the stomach's call.

Every summer for thirty years I have climbed into the rocky pine woods in the foothills above my meadow to go berrying. My neighbor took me the first time—an act of generosity, this sharing of territory, but my boys and I were no competition for her deft-fingered girls, who filled pail after pail while I scrambled after the wandering, eat-all-you-can-on-the-spot four-year-old twins.

Though I sometimes go alone, berrying is better done communally. Once, long ago, when friends from Seattle were visiting, Bill, my true companion for nearly a quarter of a century, came along. We had been drinking red wine, and he'd imbibed more than the rest of us. Bill is a burly man with a big head of thick, wavy hair, and when we found him under a prize bush, swiping berries into his open mouth, all of us burst into laughter, for if any person ever looked like a happy bear it would be him.

Picking berries is not work for us, but celebration. Even in a good year, my family does not harvest many hucks, just three or four cottage-cheese cartons full, enough for a pie or two, some for cereal or pancakes or to sprinkle over ice cream, maybe a few jars of preserves. We might freeze a couple of pints for treats next Thanksgiving or Christmas—the scent of huckleberries in winter bringing the promise of summer to come.

For generations, there has been plenty of berry-rich country to make both bears and people fat. Loggers' wives in Libby, or ranch-women in Drummond, or professors in Missoula made syrups and preserves from recipes passed down, perhaps, by pioneer great-grandmothers. Cooks in Florence or Arlee or Yaak baked all the huckleberry pies and made all the berry-dotted pancakes they wanted, and hikers stuffed their pockets and rucksacks with impunity. In good years, such small-scale picking still offers little threat to the berry supply and the bears who depend on it. The only solution in bad years is to leave *all* the hucks to the bears.

But the commercialization of huckleberries and demands from a growing market pose real dangers to a diminishing resource. Not long ago, we experienced mushroom wars in the national forests—shootings and gangs protecting their special patch of morels or chanterelles (only it was *our* patch, *our* forest). Soon, I'm afraid, we'll be having berry wars, too, with competing gangs blasting away at each other on the public lands that are our nation's wild commons.

Boycotting commercial huckleberry products and the plastic bags of fresh berries sold in markets is one way to send the message that we care about our wild gardens. Abstinence is another. And we could adopt stricter, better-enforced rules governing the gathering of wild plants, similar to the rules that govern hunting. No one argues that commercial hunters should be free to shoot all the elk they can find on public lands, then market them for profit. The world changes, and we must adjust.

These days, Bill's hair is gray and mine is white, and the boys are grown up, and we don't drink quite so much red wine. Still, when we all get together this summer, we'll likely go berrying. There may be girlfriends, wives, a granddaughter, a great-grandmother. The dogs will be at our heels, and we will be singing or talking loud to alert the bears, for if huckleberries are ripe and abundant, bears will surely be nearby.

The air in early August will be dry and intoxicating: sun on pine needles, dust rising, earth musty under the low-spreading branches. Soon our fingers and mouths will be stained purple with the tart juice—mottled like the tongue of Little Red Dog, my runaway part-chow mongrel, whose spirit haunts these woods. There will be animal scent in the air, perhaps a whiff of elk or skunk, or the musk of a mother bear carried downwind. Old Betty will snap berries right off the branches. We'll shoo her away, but gently, this Huckleberry Hound who is like a maiden aunt.

Gathering wild food makes many of us inordinately happy because, I believe, it connects us to our deep past. To pick the wild blueberry is to take one's place in a fast-diminishing ecology populated by plants and creatures that we did not create or domesticate—a connection impossible to experience in Safeway. Food is a gift, no matter how it grows, but when we partake of wild food we feel the giving of it intensely. The berries fall ripe into our open palms.

You may think your own preservation has nothing to do with the preservation of huckleberries—or of black bears and grizzlies, grouse and wild turkeys and songbirds, or the small berry-eating mammals who forage in huckleberry habitat from the Pacific Coast to the Midwest. You may think you have nothing in common with Salish grandmothers and Libby housewives, or with me and my family on our meadow above Bear Creek.

Think again. If you are reading this, you are imagining something. Maybe you are remembering an old story your grandmother told. Or inventing a new story for your children. About bears. About picking berries. About hope that what is imagined and remembered may continue to exist, so that, if we travel to where the wild things grow, they will be there for our gathering hands.

Elaine Scarry

Columbine

he first garden I lived in was very steep. The ground rose so steadily that, if you were to enter from the front street and climb up the sequence of garden staircases to the dirt road at the top, you would have ascended to the height of a fourteen-story building.

The house in the garden was itself four stories high. But even to reach its front door you had first to climb up through a steep bank of lavender and blue phlox and then go up a second, briefer staircase that passed through a privet hedge and lifted you to the level of the morning glories by the front door. This second stairway was made of concrete and was walled in on either side to hold back the ground you were climbing through. At its bottom step, your head was below ground level; then, as you climbed, your eyes came level with the roots of the privet (which you were obliged to inspect for copperheads); then, in another step or two, you were safer, since it was no longer your face but only your shoulders, waist, legs that took their turn rising out of the ground.

From here the garden kept rising, sometimes in a sharp incline, sometimes by a wall where the ground level suddenly jumped, and running beside it were the walkways and staircases that lifted you up past pansies, lilies, columbine, hydrangea and iris, dahlias and zinnias, until the top, steepest staircase, which rose up beside the stalks of sunflowers, whose faces were exactly even with the ground of the upper road. From the road, you could watch the garden dropping back down into its deep well of color.

This steepness—this sense of life tilted on its side—belongs to all perennials, but above all to columbine. My garden is level now, but everywhere the columbine rises and flies, floats and falls, its blossoms turning up by my face, my feet, my waist, my thighs. I am steeped in them and can measure them against every part of me.

Their fluty colors—light pinks, light blues—mix with air and disappear into the sky like something that has flown too high to be identified. Uncertain bird: aquilegea-columbine. The tallest in the garden has blossoms that are three yellow shades: the petals are cornsilk, the spray of stamens the color of buttercups, and tawny spurs kick out behind. Each blossom looks like a shooting star itself shooting stamen-stars out in front and carrying four comets behind. Taller than I, its array of blossoms point up, point down, lift, dive, and dart away, their spurs curving under or arching out until the whole plant seems about to pitch and roll and wheel away. What keeps it trim, balanced, are the tiers of leaves stacked neatly below, like layers of mica or lace, or like the plumes of a dove when she ruffs her feathers and breaks the smooth surface into looping rows.

Steep flowers confound up and down, air and ground, as though there is no difference between being above and below. First perennial out of the earth, the columbine comes into the world fully formed. Not a shaft or a stem but a delicate curled ball of already lobed leaves, each layer perfect, lying inside the next, folded up like a nested staircase. It is as though no adjustment has been required. It is as though it had already leafed out underground, then packed up, arriving in the light like laughter (or a soft drumroll), ready to ruffle out in all directions.

This continuity between the below- and above-ground layers was in my first garden. The gardener was a coal miner and spent the first six hours of each day underground; then, after bathing, eating, and resting, he spent the afternoon working the earth from above. In summers, I would wake in mid-morning, climb up the garden stairways at noon, and walk along the top road watching for him; I stood at the hinge of his day. We would travel back to the garden together, dropping down all the garden staircases to the kitchen door, never cutting through the upper rooms of the house.

The gardener's boy had died when he was nine, and every four or five days we carried a basket of tall flowers to his grave. The cemetery (like everything in the town) was on the same steep incline as the garden, though it started one street lower on the mountainside, the graves proceeding downward like a grassy stairway counted off by the stone markers. The boy's grave was at the very bottom, but he was part of the high world, mixed in our minds with the tall flowers and only pressing on our attention in the late half of the day.

This confounding of up and down happened even when you were just walking inside the house. The doorsill on the bottom floor was at ground level; but as soon as you walked deeper into the room, the ground was already rising, so that soon you could see flower stems through the window, and at the backmost room there was no window at all, since you were now deep underground. There was no horizontal plane: just moving about already pitched you onto the vertical. The same was true on the second floor and the third: their front rooms hung suspended out into the air; their backmost rooms met the steep ground, so that you were always traveling either down or up, depending on whether you were moving toward the back or toward the front. The attic had side windows, equidistant from the ground; the front and back had closed-in eaves, which held the fragile objects the gardener had carried in the war.

The very steepness that ought to have made upper and lower distinct instead made the two interchangeable. In the steady roll of the earth, up and down somersault over and take one another's place. My first winter in the level garden, the plants all died. It was as though my hands, my eyes, my mouth had all been struck, bruised, and emptied. I had lost not just the things that had been sensed but the act of sensing itself. I cut up bright picture books, putting their colors everywhere on the walls, and tried to fill the windows with colored glass.

When the columbine came up, it was as though I were the first person on earth to see this happen. Only common sense restrained me from carrying the news all over town ("My garden, which died, has come back"). The airy cartwheel that carried it down out of view in November now carried it up in March. Trim soldier, at ease in its yearly spin, Columbine.

Naomi Shihab Nye

Mint Snowball

y great-grandfather on my mother's side ran a drugstore in a small town in central Illinois. He sold pills and rubbing alcohol from behind the big cash register and creamy ice cream from the soda fountain. My mother remembers the counter's long polished sweep, its shining face. She twirled on the stools. Dreamy fans. Wide summer afternoons. Clink of nickels in anybody's hand. He sold milkshakes, cherry Cokes, old-fashioned sandwiches. What did an old-fashioned sandwich look like? Dark wooden shelves. Silver spigots on chocolate dispensers.

My great-grandfather had one specialty: a Mint Snowball, which he invented. Some people drove all the way in from Decatur just to taste it. First he stirred fresh mint leaves with sugar and secret ingredients in a small pot on the stove for a very long time. He concocted a flamboyant elixir of mint. Its scent clung to his fingers even after he washed his hands. Then he shaved ice into tiny particles and served it mounded in a glass dish. Permeated with mint syrup. Scoops of rich vanilla ice cream to each side. My mother took a bite of minty ice and ice cream mixed together. The Mint Snowball tasted like winter. She closed her eyes to see the Swiss village my great-grandfather's parents came from. Snow frosting the roofs. Glistening, dangling spokes of ice.

Before my great-grandfather died, he sold the recipe for the mint syrup to someone in town for one hundred dollars. This hurt my grandfather's feelings. My grandfather thought he should have inherited it to carry on the tradition. As far as the family knew, the person who bought the recipe never used it. At least not in public. My mother had watched my great-grandfather make the syrup so often she thought she could replicate it. But what did he have in those little unmarked bottles? She experimented. Once she came close. She wrote down what she did. Now she has lost the paper.

Perhaps the clue to my entire personality connects to the lost Mint Snowball. I have always felt out of step with my environment, disjointed in the modern world. The crisp flush of cities makes me weep. Strip malls, poodle grooming and take-out Thai. I am angry over lost department stores, wistful for something I have never tasted or seen.

Although I know how to do everything one needs to know— change airplanes, find my exit off the interstate, charge gas, send a fax—there is something missing. Perhaps the stoop of my great-grandfather over the pan, the slow patient swish of his spoon. The spin of my mother on the high stool with her whole life in front of her, something fine and fragrant still to happen. When I breathe a handful of mint, even pathetic sprigs from my sunbaked Texas earth, I close my eyes. Little chips of ice on the tongue, their cool slide down. Can we follow the long river of the word "refreshment" back to its spring? Is there another land for me? Can I find any lasting solace in the color green?

Keepers of the Plants: Native Women

Linda Hogan

Bamboo

First woman was made of slender bones
like these that stand upright together
in the rich, green world of daylight.

At night, they are a darkened forest
of sisters who grow quickly
in moving water
and talk in the clattering breeze
as if each is an open throat, rising
to speak.

I tell a man about this beautiful,
creaking world, how it flowers all
at once. He has been to war. He says
with bamboo they do terrible things
to men and women.

I look at this bamboo.
It did not give permission to soldiers.
It is imprisoned in its own skin.
The stalks are restless about this.
They have lived too long in the world of men.
They are hollow inside.

Lord, are you listening to this?
Plants are climbing to heaven
to talk to you.

Linda Yamane

My World Is Out There

he morning is clean and quietly still as I open my
front door to greet the first day of the last year of
the millennium. Sparrows and jays flit and glide
about their business, and even the crows seem to
be observing a vow of silence, though I know it is
only temporary. The day is warm, even for a California winter, and
because it is a day of symbolic beginnings, I ponder what to do that
is worthy of this auspicious occasion. After some thought, I decide
to follow my heart outdoors. I will begin the year gathering roots for
baskets beneath a canopy of ancient oaks, surrounded by the peace
and beauty of the world as it was meant to be.

While I am driving the short distance from my home, my
thoughts travel back to last night, the eve of the new year, when I
did something I have never done before. I went to a party at a
nearby hotel where Taj Mahal and his band were performing. I have
never felt comfortable in such settings, but I love Taj and I love the
blues, and with my fiftieth birthday approaching, it seemed time to

indulge in a bit of fun. And so it happened that I found myself sandwiched among hundreds of other bouncing fans, stomping and clapping. When Taj sang, I sang along, or screamed in pure excitement. At times, I could have sworn it was Coyote's voice coming from my mouth.

All too soon the concert ended. My partner and I wandered about the hotel atrium, sampling the food and watching the many people who had come in their party finery to celebrate. Balloons overhead shifted ever so delicately, waiting to be released at the stroke of midnight. It wasn't long before both hands of the clock were about to point upward, signaling the first minute of the new year. That's when I realized this was not where I belonged.

I belonged outside the hotel door, just beyond the parking lot, alongside the little lake where I often walk and gather willow sticks for my baskets. There, the crows bed down in the willow thicket each evening, their hundreds of voices squawking as they attempt to calm themselves for the night ahead. There, the Canada geese congregate with their young, claiming the lakeside for themselves except when they take to the water or rise into the air, arranging themselves in neat formation and honking as they move through the sky.

I asked my friend, "Would you mind if we go outside? I just realized that my world is out there, not in here." I felt small as the great glass doors opened to let us out into the cold night air, and I pulled my fleece scarf snug around my neck. We crossed the parking lot to stand at the water's edge. In the darkness were the pointed profiles of tules I sometimes shape into little boats and houses, miniature versions of those my ancestors made. Nearby, the willows stood quietly. It is their resting time of year. But soon, in early spring, they will begin to swell with budding leaflets, and it will be time to gather the straight, healthy shoots that will later curve, one after another, forming the foundation of many future baskets.

Today, as I drive, I am in no hurry. A few short miles from home I turn off the main road, entering the back country of a former army base. The chaparral appears desolate, but as I pass through acres and acres of manzanita, I can almost see myself and my friends, in the long days of summer, reaching into the brittle bushes, knocking the dry orangish berries into baskets and bowls. The lure of another cluster draws us from one shrub to another. As our bowls and baskets fill, we empty them into larger containers for the ride home. Back home, I put them in my openwork cleaning basket, shaking it to let the berries roll to one end, a few at a time, leaving behind the leaves and stems we gathered along with the berries. Now they are ready to be made into the delicately tart manzanita cider traditional to California Indian people.

When I wrap my hands around a stone pestle to pound the berries into a dry meal, I imagine the many hands that have held this tool before me. I lift and drop, lift and drop, until the little berries break down into a coarse, rosy powder. I transfer the meal to a basket or a cloth-lined colander and bathe it with cool water. As the water drips through the crushed berries, it is infused with their flavor, very subtly at first. But as the same bath is poured repeatedly through the manzanita mash, it lifts more and more of the flavor and goodness from the berries, and the resulting drink is as refreshing and healthful as any I have ever tasted.

These are the things I think of as I drive along the quiet, ribbon-like road that has now taken me into land graced by sprawling coastal live oaks. At a remote and little-used intersection stands an enormous elderberry tree whose branches are bare of leaves and clusters of distinctive purple berries at this time of year. A friend and I were traveling this same road on our way to gather roots when I noticed this tree for the first time. Instinctively, I put my foot on the brake and rolled to a stop at the side of the road. The tree was clearly in need of help. It had not been cut back for a long, long time, if ever, and many of its branches were dead or dying. I opened the trunk of my car and pulled out my pruning shears, and we picked our way through the dry grasses to investigate. We began clipping and clearing, relieving the tree of lifeless limbs, until we arrived at the center, where we found a few straight, healthy branches pointing skyward. Some were just the right diameter for making the clapper sticks we use to beat a rhythm to our songs. And so we exchanged one gift for another: our pruning would stimulate new growth and vitality, while the branches we gathered would add voice to our songs for a long time to come.

A little farther along I arrive at a seasonal lake teeming with life. Here I must turn to pass through a locked gate. Although these are now public lands, roads are still off-limits to most private vehicles. I have a special permit that allows me access in order to harvest the plants needed for our traditional baskets. I also have a key, which I slip into the padlock and jiggle ever so slightly to get the lock to open.

On this very spot perhaps two years past, I noticed two turkey vultures in a tree just across the water. I was surprised to see them there, as if they must perpetually be soaring in the distance, with their slow toggling motion. I remembered the binoculars I keep in my car but rarely use. Just as I took them from their case and brought them to my eyes, the birds lifted from the branches and took flight. I tried to locate them in that narrow field of vision, but my sight was more impeded than enhanced by the little lenses, and after a few moments I lowered the binoculars. When I looked up, I discovered that one of the vultures was flying just feet above my head. I could see its face clearly, could see the details of its body, the dark feathers, and the way it glanced down at me as it passed. I watched the enormous wings rise and fall; the only sound breaking the silence was a rhythmic *whh, whh, whh, whh*, as the wings pushed a path through the air. Then it was gone, almost as quickly as I realized it was there.

From here, the narrow road begins to climb, winding past places marked by memories of many plant friends. To my left, I can see the slope as it appears in spring, when the *brodeias*, the Indian potatoes, dot the hillside with delicate splashes of lavender and yellow. Their bulbs are both delicious and nutritious, and in times past were baked slowly in the earth, becoming succulent and even caramelizing. There, on the right, is the place where the bracken ferns abound, where I have sweated while digging their thick, gnarly rhizomes from the ground. It is even harder work to extract and clean the dark woody bands within, which become patterns in my weaving, adorning the baskets not only with their color, but with the spirit and memories of the land.

I follow the road as it winds and turns, dropping to the place where my path once crossed with Coyote's. Then the road climbs, a long, steep grade, until the Salinas Valley stretches below, against a hazy backdrop of mountain ranges to the east. Soon the road tires of turning, bringing me to lower land. On either side, the earth rises in gently undulating hills that are freshly greened from early winter rains. The live oaks reach out on this land of my ancestors, their great lichen-draped arms never tiring. In summer they shelter the earth, keeping it damp and cool. In fall they drop their leaves, building layers of healthy soil upon these ancient sand dunes. When coastal fogs creep silently into the hills, the oaks capture their moisture and give it drop by drop to the land below.

Here, beneath these oaks, our baskets begin. Here I spend many hours each year, digging the rich, soft earth. It is quiet and peaceful as I make my way toward the dense green bed of sedges, where the long, slender blades rise from the ground in clumps, swaying gently with the breeze. Carefully, I push aside a thick layer of leaves and other plant material until I reach the soil, remembering the salamanders I sometimes encounter here.

I begin digging, searching for the long rhizomes that connect one sedge plant with another. My garden claw begins the job, but soon my hands take over, probing for the roots I have come to know so well. Years of practice have taught my fingers that sedge runners are more yielding than the roots of oak, poison oak or blackberry, their frequent companions. Before long, I recognize the familiar feel and pull away the dirt, little by little, until the full length of the rhizome is exposed. It is long and straight, not too old, and I know that beneath its bearded, reddish-brown bark lies the flexible, woody material I need.

I continue digging, gathering one runner after another. The shorter ones will be used by new weavers to practice the techniques of splitting and trimming. A novice can quickly reduce a forty-inch length of sedge into a pile of unusable scraps; these roots are too precious, and the gathering is too labor-intensive, for such waste. I will save the longest for my twined baskets, which begin with a framework of willow sticks. I weave them together with long strands of moistened sedge, and as the basket grows, a row at a time, I add more willow sticks to create the shape.

The sedges I gather today will also be used for my coiled baskets, which are constructed in a very different way. I begin by wrapping a single strand of sedge around a small bundle of sedge, until it is completely encased. With this I form a tight coil that becomes the bottom of the basket. I continue wrapping, and coiling, securing each layer of wrapped sedges to the coil by poking a small hole with a sharp awl, pushing the strand of sedge through, and pulling the stitch tight. In this way, and very slowly, the basket grows. When the diameter is large enough to be negotiated by flexible willow rods, they are inserted in place of the sedge bundle as the foundation, and the process continues. I wrap and stitch, wrap and stitch, shaping the basket in the same manner as coiled pottery.

As I dig, I see the baskets of the past and those I will make in the future. Soon I'll begin a *pechump tiperin*, a name that translates as "stuck-on basket." It has no bottom, but sits over a shallow stone mortar, to which it is sometimes attached with pitch or asphaltum, a naturally occurring asphalt. When acorns are pounded in the mortar, the stray pieces that jump about hit the basket wall and fall back down for further pounding. There is a shallow mortar, found near my ancestral village, that still bears the broad ring of asphaltum that once held such a basket in place. It is waiting to hold a "stuck-on basket" again, and I will not disappoint it.

Some of these sedges may become a tall burden basket, of the sort that was once commonly used by my people for carrying large or heavy loads. The basket was pointed at the bottom, and a broad strap was looped around it, then placed across the forehead or chest to support the basket and its load. A bundle of long willow sticks waits at home, resting against my wall, until the day it will become just such a basket. None of our burden baskets has survived into the present, and so I must make one. I imagine how I will weave and pattern it, and remember a story told by my Monterey Ohlone people. Once there was a witch woman named Shelp who cooked her acorn soup in the bottom of her burden basket. She was at a dance, and when the people got hungry she invited them to eat of the acorn soup. There were many people at the dance and just a small amount of acorn soup at the bottom of her basket, but no matter how much the people ate, that little bit of soup never ran out— because it was her witchcraft that was making it!

To my surprise, morning has become afternoon, and my bucket has slowly filled. It is not easy work, and my arms, hands, back, and legs are aching from the posture and effort. I think of the several hours of work that remain to be done after I return home. Each root must be split in half lengthwise, and the bark removed. With this in mind, I begin to close the ground, replacing the leaves and other debris I have pushed aside. Out of respect for the land and for others who may come this way, I am careful to repair the evidence of my intrusion. When I have finished, it is my time to say thank you. Today, I will leave a quiet song of long ago: *Ono kah weh-weh nah, ono kah weh-weh nah* . . . It is good to hear the language of my ancestors as it drifts across the land. At other times, I may leave glittering bits of abalone shell or, if the weather is warm and the earth is dry, I will sprinkle water over the places I have disturbed.

Although I am dirty and tired, I am happy. I look out at this beautiful place and feel lucky that it is here, so little changed from the past. Modern times have left their mark, but the oaks and sedges, the grasses and wildflowers are still here. Red-tailed hawks still soar overhead, and red-shafted flickers still flash their color from brush to branch. As I work, coyotes sometimes howl their soulful song, reminding me I am not alone. Deer bed down in the sedges at night; bobcats travel about swiftly and silently, appearing briefly, then disappearing into the cover of plants and the darkness.

I retrace my route home, dreaming of baskets that want to be made; there's a mush bowl and little drinking cup, a water jug with a narrow neck, and a ceremonial basket covered with little olivella-shell beads and the red feathers of the acorn woodpecker. There is much work to be done, little sedges, so rest assured that I will return.

Anita Endrezze

Corn Mother

Beneath Mexico City, there is a lake
sealed tightly below concrete boulevards
and buildings of blind glass
windows where the pigeons batter their wings
and the cleaning women press damp cloths,
dreaming of the lake beneath the city where skulls
have been crushed into mud and the long paths
out of the palaces, markets where the ripe fruit rotted,
tables where chocolate pots tipped over,
unattended, bone ladles clinking to the floor.

Where are we? stories above
the lake and the dead Aztecs
who were kinsmen of the Yaquis,
in some northern desert way,
and I won't pause because history didn't,
if you know your history: you know
that Cortés killed thousands of people,

by sword, hunger, sickness
and all their bones fell into the lake,
the water of floating gardens.

So drill into the sediment
and this is what you'll find:
jade flute music, bamboo combs,
a woman's shy whisper,
small clay statues,
a woman giving birth
in a warm bath,
a hunchbacked old man
touching earth with the palms
of his hands
in his oath to the earth,
royal seals with jaguars,
and jugglers.

Drill deeper into the core:
these are the grasses,
teosinte, *Gramineae, Zea mays,*
maize, corn;
20,000 years ago the seeds
inherited the hands of women.
They cultivated the shaggy heads,
the sacred ears, so that humans
became the same flesh.

6500 B.C.
They sifted soil over Mexica
and gave corn a family:
maize,
beans,
squash.

Maize journeyed to Ontario, Canada,
before 1200 A.D.

blue corn
yellow corn
white corn
black corn

Table #1
Corn: endosperm, germ, pericarp, tip cap
16% moisture (rain, sweat, prayers)
72% starch (sun, moon, finger prints)
10% protein (Indian flesh, Corn Mother, the Virgin of Guadalupe)

zinc: good for your immune system
iron: improves your blood, whether full-blood, mestizo, or Other
aluminum, phosphorus, potassium, boron: chant these minerals
like a prayer, with both hands folded over the earth

Blue corn: tortillas, piki (paper bread
you can write on with the hieroglyphics of your teeth),
chaqueque (cornmeal mush),
atole (cornmeal drink),
corn flakes, syrup,
chips for salsa,
muffins, popcorn,
pancakes,
polenta.

Table #2:
Set plates the color of polished sun
for the three sisters

One loves to eat corn on the cob slathered with butter,
sprinkled with salt.
She props her elbows on the table, leans over the plate,
and grins, corn sticking between her teeth.

One loves to eat spoonfuls of yellow squash.
Later, she takes the dried gourd and carves out a door

like the mouth of a woman surprised in a dark window
as a lover plays a jade flute.
She hangs the gourd up in a willow,
so that small brown birds nest
and sleep
warm in the belly of a sister.

And one loves to cook beans
as she sings away the day's complaints:
red, black, white, pinto, kidney, green,
lima, butter, navy, pole, frijole,
spotted, striped:
all snap like Nahuatl vowels.

Set the table for the Corn Mother and her family: Alamo,
Utton, Curry, Santa Ana, Taos,
Rose, Best, Average, Yellow, White,
Kinsman.

To prepare corn: Boil it in lime
(it dissolves flesh and bone)
and water ancient as language.
Steep
overnight
while the moon is
an Aztec calendar
dividing centuries
into the green silk body
of the Virgin of Guadalupe,
her chocoatl sex,
her serpent-skirted hips,
her yellow teosinte heart.
In the morning,
take two dark reeds,
pounded into paper,
and using ink from beans,
write poems about maize,

then throw out
the liquid.

Rinse, discard
the splattered
blood of innocent
cracked kernels.

Drain, wash, drain.
Grind with stone
in a skull bowl.
Grind for 500 years
until the flour is fine
as Indian bones,
and shape into hands,
brown faces, virgins,
and mothers,
small icons of corn women
carrying bags of groceries
in Los Angeles, Guaymas,
Spokane, Portland, Seattle.

Mary Crow Dog

Peyote

he Aztec word for the sacred herb was *peyotl,*
meaning "caterpillar," because this cactus is fuzzy
like the hairs on a caterpillar. Our Sioux word for
medicine is *pejuta.* Peyote, *pejuta*—that sounds
very close. Maybe it is just a coincidence. It is certain that peyote came to us out of Mexico. In the 1870s, the Kiowas
and Comanches prayed with this medicine and established what
they called the Native American Church. By now the peyote religion is common among most tribes all the way up to Alaska. Since
peyote does not grow farther north than the Rio Grande, we must
get our medicine from the border region. It is in the Southwest that
we have our "peyote garden."

Peyote came to the Plains Indians just when they needed it
most, at a time when the last of the buffalo were being killed and
the tribes driven into fenced-in reservations, literally starving and
dying of the white man's diseases, deprived of everything that had
given meaning to their lives. The Native American Church became
the religion of the poorest of the poor, the conquered, the despoiled.

Peyote made them understand what was happening and made them endure. It was the only thing that gave them strength in those, our darkest days. Our only fear is that the whites will take this from us, too, as they have taken everything else. I am sure there are some people at this moment saying, "This is too good for those dumb Indians. Let us take it away from them and get high." Sometimes whites come to Leonard to "see the medicine man," like somebody at a country fair comes to see the calf with two heads, and often the first words they say are "Hey, got any peyote, chief?" Already I have seen white people misusing peyote, using it just like another drug to get stoned on. Already our sacred medicine is getting scarce.

It is perfectly legal for Indians to buy and use peyote as a sacrament in a religious ceremony—to buy it at a price, that is. As peyote is being fenced in, like us Indians, and as it is getting harder to come by, all along the Texas border dealers are selling it at exorbitant prices to the Native American Church people. For the sellers it is something like a gold rush. Peyote has been hit by inflation. It has been subjected to the rule of supply and demand, and selling it has become a business—can you imagine, an herb that grows wild in abundance, which nature has put on this earth for the use of the native peoples since the beginning of time.

Peyote makes me understand myself and the world around me. It lets me see the royalness of my people, the royalness of peyote, how good it can be. It is so good, and yet it can be dangerous if a person misuses it. You have to be in the right mind, approach it in the right way. If people have the wrong thoughts about it, it could hurt them. But peyote has never hurt me, it has always treated me well. It helped me when nothing else could. Grandfather Peyote knows you; you can't hide from him. He makes the unborn baby dance inside its mother's womb. He has that power. When you partake of this medicine in the right way, you feel strength surging through you, you "get into the power," other-world power given specially to you and no one else. This also is common to all Indians, whether or not they use peyote, this concept of power.

Peyote is a unifier; that is one of its chief blessings. This unifying force brought together in friendship tribes who had been enemies before, and it helped us in our struggle. I took the peyote road because I took the AIM road. For me they became one path. I have visited many tribes. They have different cultures and speak different languages. They may even have different rituals when partaking of this medicine. They may be jealous of each other, saying, "We are the better tribe. Our men used to fight better than yours. We do things better." But once they meet inside the peyote tipi, all differences are forgotten. Then they are no longer Navajos, or Poncas, Apaches, or Sioux, but just Indians. They learn each other's songs and find out that they are really the same. Peyote is making many tribes into just one tribe. And it is the same with the Sun Dance, which also serves to unite the different Indian nations.

The words we put into our songs are an echo of the sacred root, the voices of the little pebbles inside the gourd rattle, the voices of the magpie and scissortail feathers which make up the peyote fan, the voice from inside the water drum, the cry of the water bird. Peyote will give you a voice, a song of understanding, a prayer for good health or for your people's survival. Once I saw a star shining through the opening on top of the tipi. It shone upon the sacred altar and it gave me a song. Many songs have no words, but you can put in words if you want to. It's up to the peyote to put words into your song. Women always took part in peyote meetings but for a long time they were not supposed to sing. They were not supposed to pray with the staff, because the staff is a man and women should not try to be men. I was one of the first women to sing during meetings. I have a very high voice, and I am told that I sound like a sad little girl. Leonard's sisters are all fine singers—especially Christine, with her deep, strong voice. Now many women sing while holding the staff and shaking the gourd.

When I sit in the circle with Poncas, Otos, Winnebagos, or Cheyennes, I feel as if I am among my own people. We cannot understand each other except by talking English, but through peyote we speak one tongue, spiritually. The ceremony might change a little from tribe to tribe, but not much. Essentially it is always the same. The Navajos might use cornhusk cigarettes during their ritual, whereas we use the pipe and can-shasha, Indian willow-bark tobacco. The Navajos form their main altar in the shape of a half-moon; another tribe may shape it another way. In some places they have their meetings inside the house, in an ordinary room, cleared and purified for the purpose. Somewhere else they prefer to meet in a tipi. When Navajo people visit Leonard, he runs his ceremony Navajo-style. If we go down to Arizona, the Navajos might put up a meeting for us in the Sioux manner. The differences are minor. Always the meeting lasts from sundown to sunup, always you have the songs, the staff, the gourd, the fan, the drum, the smoking, the fire, the drink of cold water. It is only when you travel below the border that peyote is worshipped in a markedly different way. In 1975, Leonard held a Ghost Dance at his place and to our great surprise a couple of Mexican Indians showed up—Yaqui, Huichol, and Nahuatl. How they knew about the Ghost Dance and what exactly had made them travel this long distance to Crow Dog's place was something of a mystery. One, a guy from Oaxaca, came in his typical Mexican Indian outfit and told us that his Nahua name was Warm Southwind. The Sioux, with their peculiar kind of Lakota humor, immediately named him "Mild Disturbance." We found out that these Indian brothers from Aztec and Maya country also were peyote people, but from what they told us their rituals were not at all like ours, going back to the dawn of history.

The peyote staff is a man. It is alive. It is, as my husband says, a "hot line" to the Great Spirit. Thoughts travel up the staff, and messages travel down. The gourd is a brain, a skull, a spirit voice. The water drum is the water of life. It is the Indians' heartbeat. Its skin is our skin. It talks in two voices—one high and clear, the other deep and reverberating. The drum is round like the sacred hoop which has no beginning and no end. The cedar's smoke is the breath of all green, living things, and it purifies, making everything it touches holy. The fire, too, is alive and eternal. It is the flame passed from one generation to the next. The feather fan is a war bonnet. It catches songs out of the air. Crow Dog's father, Henry, had a fan of magpie feathers, and the magpie taught him a song. Magpie feathers are for doctoring. Water-bird feathers are the road man's companions. The water bird is the chief symbol of the peyote religion. A fan made from its feathers is used by the road man to bless the water. Hawk feathers are for good understanding. A scissortail fan represents the Indian mothers, Indian maidens with black hair wearing white buckskin dresses. Everybody would like to own a macaw-feather fan, but these are hard to come by. The macaw speaks all tongues and unifies the tribes. You can see good things in a macaw-parrot fan. The strange thing is that, in prehistoric Indian ruins going back a thousand years, in New Mexico, Arizona, and Colorado, the feathers and remains of macaws have been found. I have also seen many centuries-old rock paintings depicting parrots. The feathers, mummies, and paintings of these macaws are found some fifteen hundred to two thousand miles north of the nearest place where these huge parrots occur in the wild. It proves that the North American Pueblos were in communication with the Aztecs and Toltecs. I often wonder whether the prehistoric Anasazi were peyote people and imported their macaws to use the feathers during their rituals. Maybe someday I will find out.

After Wounded Knee, when I became Crow Dog's wife, I started to go down south with him to what he called his "peyote gardens." This always involved a round trip of some three thousand miles and staying with various tribes along the way. I have to admit that in the beginning I had the typical Sioux prejudice against some of the southern tribes. To me they seemed at first to be too peaceful and self-contented, not "committed to the struggle," the Pueblos especially. They did not have the Plains tribes' aversion to farming and were growing their corn and squash on fields they had tended for hundreds of years before the first white man set foot on this continent. In time I recognized that they had an inner strength that we Plains people lacked, strength without macho, without bragging about what great warriors they were, or had been. I had to admire the way they kept the government at arm's length, kept tourists and photographers out, and managed to hold on to their old ways without theatrics or confrontations. They worked and kept themselves busy. They had, on the whole, fewer problems with alcoholism than we did. Of course, they had been farmers since the dawn of history, and great potters, and nowadays were also jewelry makers. Through their farming and craftwork they had been able to adapt to the system without being overrun by it.

Having our certificates and other documents proving that we are acting on behalf of all the Native American Church people in the

Dakotas, and that Leonard is an official as well as priest of that church, we may now legally go down into Texas and Mexico to harvest our medicine. Leonard only has to show his papers to get all the peyote he wants—if he has the money to pay for it. It took some tough court battles to bring this about. One of the funniest court cases he won arose from an incident on the Navajo reservation. Leonard had been invited to a peyote meeting by some Navajo friends. It was run by a Navajo, but they gave Leonard the job of fire chief. At the beginning an Indian woman came in with a white man. She explained, "He is my husband. That makes it all right for him to partake." This white guy was dressed like a hippie. He had long hair and beads all over him. He was dressed like an Indian. He took some medicine and seemed to be affected by it. He acted drunk. Halfway through the meeting he suddenly got up to take a leak outside. As he stumbled back into the tipi, he did not bend down low enough to clear the entrance hole. His long hair got caught and came off. It was a wig. Underneath he had a crew cut. At once he said, "I am the sheriff of Holbrook, and I arrest the whole bunch of you." All the Indians burst into laughter, it was so grotesque.

When the trial came up, one of the charges was that the Indians had let a white man participate. Of course, Leonard had only been a guest. It had not been up to him to let or not let the white man participate. When it was Leonard's turn to speak, he said: "Judge, if it is illegal for a white man to take this medicine, then the sheriff has broken his own law. We did not break it, because we have been allowed to use this herb as a sacrament for a long, long time. But I think the sheriff has not broken any law, because this was a religious meeting and even a white man has the right to participate—if we let him—as long as it is a strictly conducted ceremony. Freedom of religion doesn't stop at the door of a peyote tipi. Also, the sheriff had no jurisdiction on Indian land in the first place. Inside the reservation he was just a tourist. Only the tribal police would have had the right to make an arrest. This is all I have to say." We won that case and it was a landmark decision in favor of the peyote church.

When we go down to the peyote gardens, we usually travel in four or five cars or trucks. It takes a good number of people to do the harvesting. They have "distributors" on the border, peyote dealers.

The last time we had to pay over a hundred dollars for a thousand buttons. Five years ago it was twenty-five dollars. That's inflation for you. But on the last few trips we did not go to a dealer; we did the harvesting on our own. It is not only cheaper, but a lot more fitting to get the medicine in the right, sacred way, than just to buy it like aspirin or cough drops.

We found a place where we saw the desert sprinkled with peyote. It is a kind of cactus plant. We got up at sunrise and Leonard performed a prayer ceremony that he said would make us find plenty of medicine—would help us go to the right spots. We all spread out and looked around. The whole area was covered with cactus, Joshua trees, chaparral, and creosote bushes. Some of the cactuses were gigantic, up to twenty feet high. The peyote was sitting there between all those thorns, prickles, and spikes. It was really hard to get at. I felt it was good that we had to work for it and got scratched up. It gave the harvest a special meaning for me.

Some people take the whole peyote plant, but we decided to take only the tops and leave the roots so that the peyote could grow again. It took us a little more than two weeks to harvest about thirty-five thousand peyotes, enough for the whole tribe and for a whole year. While we were gathering our medicine, the rancher who owned the land came up and asked what we were doing on his property. When we explained, he smiled and said we were welcome anytime. If we had been forced to pay for them all at the price the dealers were charging just then, it would have meant no shoes for the kids. We would have had to save on food and everything else for the rest of the year. Thirty-five thousand buttons! Maybe all that medicine on his land had influenced the man's thinking—"sensitized" him, as the AIM guys would say. The first harvesting was a new experience for me. It made me want to go back and do a little better each time, do the gathering in an ever more sacred way, more knowingly.

Once we went harvesting in Old Mexico. As we drove back to the States, we had little peyotes lying all over the car, all those little buttons on the dashboard. Somebody said, "Jesus! It's illegal to bring it across the border. They'll arrest us and take our medicine away." I did not want to throw our medicine out the window. So I and another girl decided to eat it. It seemed more respectful. When we got back to our motel in Texas, we were all peyoted up. My head was spinning. When you take medicine in a ceremonial context, it does not affect you that way. There I was, sitting on the carpet in our room, and I sure was in the power. Later, we found out that the customs inspectors had known all about us, had seen Crow Dog's certificate, and had waved the other cars ahead of us through with a smile—buttons and all. And there I had struggled getting a record amount of our medicine down into my stomach in record time; for nothing. But later, in the motel, it felt so nice!

Paula Gunn Allen

The Woman I Love Is a Planet; the Planet I Love Is a Tree

ur physicality—which always and everywhere includes our spirituality, mentality, emotionality, social institutions and processes—is a microform of all physicality. Each of us reflects, in our attitude toward our body and the bodies of other planetary creatures and plants, our inner attitude toward the planet. And as we believe, so we act. A society that believes that the body is somehow diseased, painful, sinful, or wrong, a people that spends its time trying to deny the body's needs, aims, goals, and processes—whether these be called health or disease—is going to misunderstand the nature of its existence and of the planet's and is going to create social institutions out of those body-denying attitudes that wreak destruction not only on human, plant, and other creaturely bodies but on the body of the earth herself.

The planet, our mother, Grandmother Earth, is *physical* and therefore a spiritual, mental, and emotional being. Planets are alive,

as are all their by-products or expressions, such as animals, vegetables, minerals, climatic and meteorological phenomena.

Believing that our mother, the beloved earth, is inert matter is
destructive to yourself. (There's little you can do to her, believe it or
not.) Such beliefs point to a dangerously diseased physicality.

Being good, holy, and/or politically responsible means being
able to accept whatever life brings—and that includes just about
everything you usually think of as unacceptable, like disease, death,
and violence. Walking in balance, in harmony, and in a sacred manner requires staying in your body, accepting its discomforts, decay-
ings, witherings, and blossomings and respecting them. Your body is
also a planet, replete with creatures that live in and on it. Walking in
balance requires knowing that living and dying are twin beings, gifts
of our mother, the earth, and honoring her ways does not mean
cheating her of your flesh, your pain, your joy, your sensuality, your
desires, your frustrations, your unmet and met needs, your emotions, your life. In the end you can't cheat her successfully, but in
the attempt to do so you can do great harm to the delicate and subtle
balance of the vital processes of planetary being.

A society based on body hate destroys itself and causes harm to
all of Grandmother's grandchildren.

In the United States, where milk and honey cost little enough,
where private serenity is prized above all things by the wealthy,
privileged, and well-washed, where tension, intensity, passion, and
the concomitant loss of self-possession are detested, the idea that
your attitudes and behaviors vis-à-vis your body are your politics
and your spirituality may seem strange. Moreover, when I suggest
that passion—whether it be emotional, muscular, sexual, or intellectual—*is* spirituality, the idea might seem even stranger. In the
United States of the privileged, going to ashrams and centers to
meditate on how to be in one's immediate experience, on how to be
successful at serenity when the entire planet is overwrought, tense,
far indeed from serene, the idea that connected spirituality consists
in accepting overwroughtness, tension, yes, and violence, may seem
not only strange but downright dangerous. The patriarchs have long
taught the Western peoples that violence is sin, that tension is the
opposite of spiritual life, that the overwrought are denied enlighten-

ment. But we must remember that those who preached and taught serenity and peacefulness were teaching the oppressed how to act— docile slaves who deeply accept their place and do not recognize that in their anguish lies also their redemption, their liberation, are not likely to disturb the tranquillity of the ruling class. Members of the ruling class are, of course, utterly tranquil. Why not? As long as those upon whose labor and pain their serenity rests don't upset the apple cart, as long as they can make the rules for human behavior— in its inner as well as its outer dimensions—they can be tranquil indeed and can focus their attention on reaching nirvanic bliss, transcendence, or divine peace and love.

And yet the time for tranquillity, if there ever was time for it, is not now. Now we have only to look, to listen, to our beloved planet to see that "tranquillity" is not the best word to describe her condition. Her volcanic passions, her hurricane storms of temper, her tremblings and shakings, her thrashings and lashings indicate that something other than serenity is going on. And after careful consideration, it must occur to the sensitive observer that congruence with self, which must be congruence with spirit, which must therefore be congruence with the planet, requires something more active than serenity, tranquillity, or inner peace.

Our planet, my beloved, is in crisis; this, of course, we all know. We, many of us, think that her crisis is caused by men, or white people, or capitalism, or industrialism, or loss of spiritual vision, or social turmoil, or war, or psychic disease. For the most part, we do not recognize that the reason for her state is that she is entering upon a great initiation—she is becoming someone else. Our planet, my darling, is gone coyote, *heyoka*, and it is our great honor to attend her passage rites. She is giving birth to her new consciousness of herself and her relationship to the other vast intelligences, other holy beings in her universe. Her travail is not easy, and it occasions her intensity, her conflict, her turmoil—the turmoil, conflict, and intensity that human and other creaturely life mirror. And as she moves—learning and growing ever closer to the sacred moment of her realization—her turmoil, intensity, agony, and conflict increase.

We are each and all a part of her, an expression of her essential being. We are each a small fragment that is not the whole but that, perforce, reflects in our inner self, our outer behavior, our expressions and relationships and institutions, her self, her behaviors, her expressions and relationships, her forms and structures. We humans and our relatives the other creatures are integral expressions of her thought and being. We are not her, but we take our being from her, and in her being we have being, as in her life we have life. As she is, so are we.

In this time of her emergence as one of the sacred planets in the Grandmother galaxy, we necessarily experience, each of us in our own specific way, our share or form of her experience, her form. As the initiation nears completion, we are caught in the throes of her wailings and contractions, her muscular, circulatory, and neurologic destabilization. We should recognize that her longing for the culmination of the initiatory process is at present nearly as intense as her longing to remain as she was before the initiation ceremony began, and our longing for a new world that the completion of the great ceremony will bring, almost as great as our longing to remain in the systems familiar to us for a very long time, correspond. Her longing for completion is great, as is ours; our longing to remain as we have been, our fear that we will not survive the transition, that we will fail to enter the new age, our terror at ourselves becoming transformed, mutated, unrecognizable to ourselves and all we have known, correspond to her longing to remain as she has been, her fear that she will fail the tests as they arise for her, her terror at becoming new, unrecognizable to herself and to all she has known.

What can we do in times such as these? We can rejoice that she will soon be counted among the blessed. That we, her feathers, talons, beak, eyes, have come crying and singing, lamenting and laughing, to this vast climacteric.

I am speaking of all womankind, of all mankind. And of more. I am speaking of all our relatives, the four-leggeds, the wingeds, the crawlers; of the plants and seasons, the winds, thunders, and rains, the rivers, lakes, and streams, the pebbles, rocks, and mountains, the spirits, the holy people, and the gods and goddesses—of all the intelligences, all the beings. I am speaking even of the tiniest, those no one can see; and of the vastest, the planets and stars. Together you and I and they and she are moving with increasing rapidity and under ever-increasing pressure toward transformation.

Now, now is the time when mother becomes grandmother, when daughter becomes mother, when the living dead are released from entombment, when the dead live again and walk once again in her ways. Together we all can rejoice, take up the tasks of attending, take up the joy of giving birth and of being born, of transforming in recognition of the awfulness of what is entailed, in recognition of what it is we together can and must and will do. I have said that this is the time of her initiation, of her new birth. I could also say it is the time of mutation, for transformation means to change form; I could also say it is the climacteric, when the beloved planet goes through menopause and takes her place among the wise-women planets that dance among the stars.

At a time such as this, what indeed can we do? We can sing *Heya-hey* in honoring all that has come to pass, all that is passing. Sing, honoring, *Heya-hey* to all the beings gathering on all the planes to witness this great event. From every quadrant of the universe they are coming. They are standing gathered around, waiting for the emergence, the piercing moment when she is counted among those who are counted among the wise. We can sing *Heya-hey* to the familiar and the estranged, to the recognized and the disowned, to each shrub and tree, to each flower and vine, to each pebble and stone, to each mountain and hill. We can sing *Heya-hey* honoring the stars and the clouds, the winds and the rains, the seasons and the temperature. We can think with our hearts, as the old ones do, and put our brains and muscles in the service of the heart, our Mother and Grandmother Earth, who is coming into being in another way. We can sing *Heya-hey*, honoring.

What can we do, rejoicing and honoring, to show our respect? We can heal. We can cherish our bodies and honor them, sing *Heya-hey* to our flesh. We can cherish our being—our petulances and rages, our anguishes and griefs, our disabilities and strengths, our desires and passions, our pleasures and delights. We can, willingly and recognizing the fullness of her abundance, which includes scarcity and muchness, enter inside ourselves to seek and find her, who is our own dear body, our own dear flesh. For the body is not the dwelling place of the spirit—it is the spirit. It is not a tomb, it is life itself. And even as it withers and dies, it is born; even as it is renewed and reborn, it dies.

Think: How many times each day do you habitually deny and deprive her in your flesh, in your physicality? How often do you willfully prevent her from moving or resting, from eating or drinking what she requests, from eliminating wastes or taking breath? How many times do you order your body to produce enzymes and hormones to further your social image, your "identity," your emotional comfort, regardless of your actual situation and hers? How many of her gifts do you spurn, how much of her abundance do you deny? How often do you interpret disease as wrong, suffering as abnormal, physical imperatives as troublesome, cravings as failures, deprivation and denial of appetite as the right thing to do? In how many ways do you refuse to experience your vulnerability, your frailty, your mortality? How often do you refuse these expressions of the life force of the Mother in your lovers, your friends, your society? How often do you find yourself interpreting sickness, weakness, aging, fatness, physical differences as pitiful, contemptible, avoidable, a violation of social norm and spiritual accomplishment? How much of your life is devoted to avoiding any and/or all of these? How much of her life is devoted to avoiding any and all of these?

The mortal body is a tree; it is holy in whatever condition; it is truth and myth because it has so many potential conditions; because of its possibilities, it is sacred and profane; most of all, it is your most precious talisman, your own connection to her. Healing the self means honoring and recognizing the body, accepting rather than denying all the turmoil its existence brings, welcoming the woes and anguish flesh is subject to, cherishing its multitudinous forms and seasons, its unfailing ability to know and be, to grow and wither, to live and die, to mutate, to change. Healing the self means committing ourselves to a wholehearted willingness to be what and how we are—beings frail and fragile, strong and passionate, neurotic and balanced, diseased and whole, partial and complete, stingy and generous, safe and dangerous, twisted and straight, storm-tossed and quiescent, bound and free.

What can we do to be politically useful, spiritually mature attendants in this great transformation we are privileged to participate in? Find out by asking as many trees as you meet how to be a tree. Our Mother, in her form known as Sophia, was long ago said to be a tree, the great tree of life. Listen to what they wrote down from the song she gave them:

> I have grown tall as a cedar on Lebanon,
> as a cypress on Mount Hermon;
> I have grown tall as a palm in Engedi,
> as the rose bushes of Jericho;
> as a fine olive on the plain,
> as a plane tree I have grown tall.
> I have exhaled perfume like cinnamon and acacia;
> I have breathed out a scent like choice myrrh,
> like galbanum, onzcha and stacte,
> like the smoke of incense in the tabernacle.
> I have spread my branches like a terebinth,
> and my branches are glorious and graceful.
> I am like a vine putting out graceful shoots,
> my blossoms bear the fruit of glory and wealth.
> Approach me, you who desire me,
> and take your fill of my fruits.

Rigoberta Menchú

Maize

he times we spend up in our village are happy times because we're there to harvest the maize, and before we harvest the maize, we have a fiesta. The fiesta really starts months before, when we asked the earth's permission to cultivate her. In that ceremony we burn incense, the elected leaders say prayers, and then the whole community prays. We burn candles in our own houses and other candles for the whole community. Then we bring out the seeds we will be sowing. With maize, for instance, the seeds for the coming year are picked out as soon as the cobs start to grow. We choose them and put a mark on them. The cob is peeled or left in its leaves, but those grains are taken off, and the big ones are wrapped in the leaves and made into a little ball. The small ones are cooked straightaway and made into a tortilla the next day and eaten, so we don't waste even the smallest part of these cobs. The big seeds, wrapped in the leaves in little balls, are left in the branches of a tree to wait, to be dried as carefully as possible. It has to be a place where none of the women pass over them, or jump on them or anything, nor where the hens and chickens or any other animal can walk on them—where dogs, for example, can't get them. In front of our house there is a big tree where we put everything like that. A child stands watch to see that nothing gets at them.

Before the seeds are sown in the ground, we perform a ceremony. We choose two or three of the biggest seeds and place them in a ring, candles representing earth, water, animals, and the universe (that is, man). In our culture, the universe is man. The seed is honored because it will be buried in something sacred—the earth— and because it will multiply and bear fruit the next year. We do it mainly because the seed is something pure, something sacred. For us the word "seed" is very significant. The candles are lit in every house. We put in some *ayote* too, because that will be sown together with the maize. And we do the same with beans. It is like an offering to the one God. This will be our food for the coming year. During the fiesta, prayers are given up to the earth, the moon, the sun, the animals, and the water, all of which join with the seed to provide our food. Each member of the family makes a vow and promises not to waste the food.

The next day we all call to each other to go and start sowing. The whole community rejoices when we begin to sow our maize. When we reach the fields, the men sow the maize and the beans. The seeds go in the same hole. The women follow, planting the *ayotes* in between the furrows to make the most of every bit of land. Others, children usually, follow, sowing gourds, *chilacayotes*, or potatoes. Children like sowing potatoes. We plant everything at the same time. Then we have to look after the maize, because there are many kinds of animals in the mountains and, at sowing time, they come and dig up the seeds. So we take it in turns to keep watch in the fields, taking a turn around the fields now and again during the night. Raccoons, squirrels, *taltuzas*, and other rodents are the ones that come at night. During the day, it's the birds. We're happy to take turns keeping watch, because we fall asleep by the tree trunks. We like setting traps everywhere we think an animal is likely to come. We set traps, but when the poor animals cry out, we go and see. Since they are animals and our parents have forbidden us to kill them, we let them go after we've given them a telling off so that they won't come back. If the dogs kill them we eat them, but, generally, we don't kill animals. We only kill them accidentally. When the leaves start sprouting, they stop digging up the seeds.

When the maize starts growing, we all go back down to the *fincas* on the coast to work. When we come back, the maize has grown and needs attention. It needs weeding out. When that's done, we go back to the *finca*. When the maize is high, it needs attending to again. These are the two most difficult parts of growing maize; after that it can be left to itself. We have to put little pieces of earth round the roots so that the stalks don't get knocked over by the wind. While it is growing, the women often don't go to the *fincas* but stay and look after the beans, putting in little sticks for them to wind round so they don't interfere with the maize. They look after the *ayotes* too, and all the varieties of gourds.

Maize is the center of everything for us. It is our culture. The *milpa* is the maize field. *Maíz* is the grain. The *mazorca* is the body of the maize, the cob. The *tuza* is the leaf that envelops the cob, especially when it's dry. The *xilote* is the core. That's why we call it *xilotear* when the fruit begins to grow. Maize is used for food and for drink, and we also use the *xilote* for bottle stoppers and food for the dogs and pigs.

The animals start coming into the maize fields again when the cobs appear. The birds eat them and the animals come from the mountains for them. So we have to keep guard again. It's usually the children who look after the fields, shouting and throwing earth all day to keep the birds away. All the neighbors are in their fields shouting. When the cob starts to grow, we have other customs. One custom is when we start using the leaves of the maize plant to make tamales. We don't cut them or use them straightaway, but have a special ceremony before we cut the first leaf. All our village sows their maize in the same way, but it doesn't always grow the same. Some turn out small, some big, and some even bigger. So the neighbors with the most maize must share their big leaves with the others. For us, using a maize leaf for our tamales makes them very tasty, and we want to give some meaning to it, so that's why we celebrate the first leaves. Then comes the fiesta. After we've used the first leaves, when we've eaten the tamales inside, we don't throw the leaves away but make a pile of them. We roll them up and hang them in a corner of the house in remembrance of the first harvest the earth gave up. Then comes the ripe maize cob. Sometimes we eat it when it's still very young, but only if we really need to, because it's bigger when the cob has matured. But it's mountainous there and the cobs fall off with the winds. We have to pick up the maize that falls and eat that too.

At harvest time, we also celebrate the first day we pick the maize cobs, and the rest of what our small plots of land yield. The women pick the beans and the men pick the maize; we all harvest the fruits of our labor together. But before we pick them, we have a ceremony in which the whole community thanks the earth and the God who feeds us. Everyone is very happy because we don't have to go down to the *finca* and work now that we have food. The ceremony to celebrate the harvest is nearly the same as the one where we ask the earth's permission to cultivate her. We thank her for the harvest she's given us. Our people show their happiness, their gratitude for this food, this maize, which took so long to grow. It's a victory for the whole community when they harvest their crops and they all get together for a feast. So we have a celebration at the beginning of the *tapizca*, and at the end of the *tapizca* we have another.

Every village has a community house which is used for meetings, for prayers, for fiestas, or anything else. It's a big house that can hold a lot of people. It has a kitchen, and a *tapanco* to store the communal maize. The whole community assembles there to celebrate our faith, to pray. If we don't do it every Friday, then it's every Monday. So the whole village gets together, even when there are no special ceremonies or fiestas to celebrate. We get together to pray or just to talk to each other. We tell each other our experiences. We don't need an agenda, it's a dialogue between us. We also play with the children for a while. This happens once a week, either on a Friday or a Monday.

At the beginning everybody works communally, clearing the bush in the mountains. How many years would that take one family? We work together: the women pulling out the small plants below and the men cutting down trees on the mountainside. When sowing time comes, the community meets to discuss how to share out the land—whether each one will have his own plot or if they will work collectively. Everyone joins in the discussion. In my village, for example, we said it was up to all of us if we wanted our own plot or not. But we also decided to keep a common piece of land, shared by the whole community, so that anyone who was ill or injured would have food to eat. We worked in that way: each family with their own plot, and a large piece of common land for emergencies in the community or in the family. It was mostly to help widows. Each day of the week, someone would go and work that common land.

Teresa tsimmu Martino

Alder

By the circle of trees
are many tall leafless people.
It is winter.
They stand near the pond.
The wolves and I
ran by one day
and those people called to me.
I stopped and listened to them.
They sang together.
Then sometimes one among them would speak.
"We're frightened, but we do not run.
We have great fear, but we face it with peace.
We turn and stand,
our hands gripping our grandmother's flesh,
our hands holding our grandfather's body.
"What will happen, tsimmu?
Eh? What do you think?"
I said, "I don't know."

"We wait, we'll stand here and wait."
"I will wait too," I said.

"Tell the others what we think,
what we think, what we say,
we the Alder People,
that's what they call us."

In any Mexican market, there are stalls that offer natural remedies: sheets of bark, enormous dried flowers, slivers of wood, curly
surrealistic roots overflowing burlap bags. *"Compuesto para diabetes,"*
one is labeled; another, *"Cancerina para inflamación del estómago."*
Nearby, bunches of fresh herbs are heaped chest-high on tables.
Entire stalks of chrysanthemum, basil, pirul, rosemary—even *hierba
del diablo,* the herb of the devil, with its trumpeting lavender flower,
good for hemorrhoids and inflammation. The vendor will usually
display eggs—white, speckled, and brown—in a small basket. These
are not for eating but for the ceremonies of healing.

Traditional medicine in Mexico involves herbs, water, eggs, and
household tools in rites enacted by a healer, variously called a *curandera, bruja,* or *chamaya.* Healing is an occupation that is usually
passed down within families, one generation to the next, and is
open to both men and women. It is assumed that the healer is
involved in the world of the spirit as well as the body. Though there
are many different indigenous groups in Mexico, with diverse
beliefs, nearly all of them have some form of *limpia,* cleansing.

Underlying the *limpia* is a belief in duality and balance that is
fundamental to indigenous cosmologies. The *limpia* is for the healing of fright, *susto,* believed to be the cause of diabetes, wasting diseases, gastrointestinal problems, insomnia, and excessive sleepiness
as well as other infirmities. It is thought that when a person is frightened the spirit leaves the body and then, sometimes many years
later, she or he becomes physically ill. *Limpias* restore personal balance by cleaning away the fear, the cause of the imbalance, using
ancient remedies of plant and egg as well as more recent additions.

The *curandera,* Margarite, wore a gleaming white T-shirt over a
printed skirt, protected by a blue gingham apron with deep embroidered pockets, and sturdy black shoes. Her long black hair was
pulled back from a moon face of rare sweetness. At thirty-eight, she
seemed sturdy and calm. Married, she had two sons and many relatives in this pueblo of weavers tucked into the hills. Here she grew
up, married, raised a family, participated in community fiestas, and
worked. In the pueblo, reputation, prestige, and moral status are valued equally with wealth; a *curandera* is an important person there.

Harriet and I were led through the family compound, past two threaded looms. At one end of a room with a long table and a painting of a *campesino* holding a lamb in his lap, an altar with lit candles held fat bunches of herbs and flowers, an egg, and the other tools of the *limpia*. Carmen, Margarite's silver-haired mother-in-law, had bought the herbs and flowers earlier at the market, and also purchased the candles from the church. Margarite spoke to her in Zapotec, an ancient tongue in which words are formed far back in the throat, in contrast to Spanish, which is formed at the front of the mouth.

A low chair for Harriet was placed facing the altar. Margarite took stalks of young green bamboo and branches of purple and white chrysanthemums and knelt on the ground, making a cross or a tree of life on the floor with the plants. She stood and motioned Harriet to stand, then she took a mouthful of water from the glass on the altar, pursed her lips, and sprayed a fine ring of mist all the way around Harriet. Harriet's eyes were closed, and her hands relaxed as she stood. I imagined the fine spray felt pleasant in the close air of the afternoon.

Margarite filled her mouth with water once again but held it, gargling softly as she moved her face along Harriet's body, lips almost touching Harriet's T-shirt and jeans, her pale arms and hands, her face. I thought of a statue I had seen of Tlazoltéotl, the Mesoamerican goddess of love who is also the eater of filth—her head forward, her mouth open. The smoke of copal, the blond resin of the copal tree, rose from the altar, in a prayer older than Jesus.

In *Medicine Women, Curanderas, and Women Doctors*, H. Henrietta Stockel writes: "In most Native American and Hispanic American societies, it is the authority of tradition that confers lasting credibility on medicine women and *curanderas*, healers who gain legitimacy within their communities through skill, spirituality, religion, and reputation." In a pueblo with evidence of thousands of years of tradition, where medicines are ground on a *metate* and sold in the *mercado*, it seems as if it should have been easy for Margarite to become a healer. Observing the ease with which she used her body to make a connection with Harriet in this opening water dance, I would not have guessed that she had doubted her right to practice this ancient ceremony. But earlier she told me she had been ashamed of being a healer and had worked steadily at it only for the past four years. Although as a child she had watched her grandmother work as a *curandera*, Margarite had not at first considered becoming one herself. When she was growing up, Mexico was becoming "modern," pushing to homogenize its population, to melt everyone into "a Mexican." Indigenous ways were regarded as backward, and the need for money dictated new choices. Like many indigenous people in the state of Oaxaca, Margarite migrated to Mexico City when she was a teenager. There she had worked for a mestizo family, cleaning the house, washing clothes, buying food at the *mercado* for her employers.

Margarite reached for the white-shelled egg which had been placed on the altar. Cupping the egg in her palms, she began rubbing it vigorously around Harriet's temples, pressing the cool shell against her closed eyes. She moved the egg across Harriet's heart and stomach, down her back and legs. Harriet's jaw loosened as Margarite worked. She sat with more ease, breathing evenly as Margarite anointed her with the egg. Margarite continued to steer the egg over Harriet's body with her fingertips. When she finished she returned the egg to the altar. Later, it would be buried, and with it the toxins that had been taken from Harriet's body.

Margarite had performed her first *limpia* for her employers in Mexico City when she was nineteen. The family's new baby cried night and day, so much so that she stopped eating. The family took the baby to doctors in Mexico City, who couldn't diagnose the problem and advised the family to consult with specialists in the United States.

"I had the thought to do a *limpia* on the child," Margarite told me. "I said, 'Let me have the child.' They put her in my arms." Margarite cradled her arm as if she were holding the baby. "I took the egg and the herbs and I started to cleanse her," she said, motioning with her other arm, enacting the gestures of the *limpia*. "I finished and handed her to her mother and she took the breast again. Then she slept. She slept to midnight. Then she ate again—and kept on sleeping until the next day!" Margarite smiled. "She didn't cry again."

Soon Margarite's employers and their friends wanted *limpias*. "But I didn't want to do them," Margarite said. After healing the baby, she did not do *limpias* for fifteen years, saying she was afraid what people would think. "I told my sister she should try to do the *limpia*. But it made her sick. I do not take the sickness into my body, but she did."

Margarite reached for a large bundle of basil from the altar and began to circle Harriet, slapping her lightly and briskly from head to foot. Harriet sat relaxed and breathing evenly in the low-backed chair. Margarite took a second bunch of herbs with tougher-looking leaves, *casahuate*, from the altar and slapped them against Harriet's body, too, as if Harriet were a carpet being gently but efficiently whacked to remove debris.

Margarite had good reason to deny her ancient profession. The Spanish, since the Conquest, had waged relentless war against traditional wisdom. Between 1558 and 1575, a monk, Fray Bernardino de Sahagún, created an invaluable encyclopedia of indigenous herbal knowledge. He recorded each of the three hundred native species of medicinal plants in the *Codice Florentino*, with detailed watercolors of flowers and roots and descriptions of their use. The *Codice* was sent to the Vatican, where it remained until the pope returned it to Mexico in 1992. But Sahagún went on to establish a distinction between a good "curer" and a bad one. The good curer incorporated techniques of Spanish medicine in the mid-sixteenth century— bleeding, purging, and setting bones as well as giving herbal medicines. Prayer was allowed if it involved Catholic saints. The bad curer invoked non-Christian deities and used "sucking" and other indigenous techniques in addition to prescribing herbs. Native practices using herbs and prayers were condemned as "magic" and punished as the relentless wave of the Inquisition reached the New World.

One of the effects of the Inquisition was to elevate the emerging patriarchal system of medicine over more organic methods of healing. Tests and machines replaced people as the instruments of healing. Pills and tablets replaced herbs. Some, like the birth-control pill, are synthetic imitations of active ingredients derived from Mexican plants and herbs, discovered by ethnobiologists who studied the use of herbs by the indigenous people.

Midway through the *limpia*, Margarite took a black clay pot from the altar and asked Harriet to say her name again. Then Margarite raised the pot to her lips, facing out from the circle. *"Arrieta, Arrieta, regressa a su casa,"* she said, blowing her voice into the body of the clay pot. *"Su familia te esperarar en su casa, viene a su casa, Arrieta"*: Harriet, come home. Your family awaits you in your house, come home. Around the circle she moved, staying about three feet away from where Harriet sat, calling for Harriet's *alma*, soul, at each of the four directions, then straight overhead, then down, the bowl like an inverted megaphone.

A friend of mine, a Mexican doctor, told me that in the oil boom of the 1970s the government had promised to meet the health-care needs of the pueblos by training more doctors. "But then they realized they couldn't afford it," he said. "There wasn't enough money to take modern medicine with all its machines and pills into the *campos*." Now the government pays him to collect information on the herbs and ceremonies of the healers. He is compiling it for further study and for the training of doctors. In acknowledgment of the power of indigenous medicine, the government encourages training in herbs and nutrition for doctors, and training in the basics of Western medicine for indigenous healers. In fact, the building that once housed the Holy Office of the Inquisition in New Spain now houses an herbal archive that is part of the collection of the University of Mexico's medical school.

To my surprise, Margarite took a large butcher knife from the altar, its wooden handle dark from use. She began stroking the air in front of Harriet with it, working longest in front of her eyes. In her hands the knife was like a feather, her movements of cutting and brushing easy and graceful. "Much enters through the eyes," she told me later. "Someone looks at you with anger, or when you see something that frightens you—that can make you sick, too."

Margarite told us that the content of all of her *limpias* is the same and that they are always for the healing of fright. For some, the fright occurred twenty or thirty years ago and was untreated until it became a disease. Such people sometimes come for ten or twelve *limpias* before there is a cure. I thought of the clients I had seen in my own practice as a bodyworker, how their continual unease caused deep muscular contraction and pain. I thought of my own fears, which have at times left me paralyzed and listless. Americans don't talk about fear. We are, after all, "the land of the brave." Fearfulness is considered weakness. Instead we have "stress," the manic cover for our accumulations of fright. But here, in a civilization much older than ours, fear is recognized as an imbalance, worthy of treatment.

Margarite said it was important for the clients to remember what had frightened them. She works with them to help them remember, or they see another type of healer—one who works with cards or hands, reading the joints, in order to identify the incident that has frightened them. In my own inner work and in working with clients, I had come to the same conclusion. People are often unable to transcend trauma without going through the act of remembering it. Memory is key, central in indigenous culture, allowing continuation of sacred ways of living. Memory is partly genetic, like the code for growth in plants, arising out of vast time spent living on the same land. But memory also requires the deliberate passing on of knowledge, the planting of seeds.

Margarite put down the knife and took up a pair of silver-colored scissors, snipping the air around Harriet as if she were trimming bangs, then working in the space above her head. Finally, she took a pocket mirror and ran its face over Harriet's body, reflecting her back to herself.

Margarite's turning point as a healer came when her brother-in-law, Lucio, became ill and her aunt, who had been with her in Mexico City, urged her to do a healing. Margarite was reluctant. She didn't want the people in her village to know. Her aunt said, "Here, I'll close the door and no one will know." So Margarite performed the healing. Lucio recovered. "And my sister told everyone!" Margarite said, smiling broadly. We laughed.

When I asked Margarite if she was ashamed of her work now, she said, "No, now I'm not ashamed. The others in the village say

no one can do the *limpia* like me. They think it's fine that I do it."
She paused. "Except my youngest son, Augustine, he's eight. He
says, 'If you don't stop healing, I am going to break your little black
pot so you can't go. Then you will be at home all the time, with
me.' " We all laughed. "But his older brother told him that it's good
I do this work, because the person needs me, and, besides, they pay
me so we have something for the food.

"I think that when you have a gift, you have to use it."

From the altar, Margarite took the bunch of basil she had
slapped Harriet with earlier. With both hands, she rubbed the basil
over Harriet's hair like a big leafy washcloth. Harriet made a small
sound of contentment. She looked dreamy and relaxed. The scent
of basil filled the room, refreshing even me in my corner.

Harriet was given a preparation to drink, to bring up the phlegm
that lay in her chest, another symptom of *susto*. Ordinarily, a patient
would prepare this at home, but since she didn't have a *metate*, Carmen ground it for her. The mixture included kernels of maize, the
most revered of all food and plants in Mexico. To the corn was
added cocoa beans and what Margarite called a meteorite, a small
rough rock that was found high in the mountains. Carmen knelt on
the cement porch and put the ingredients in the cradle of the *metate*
with a handful of water, then rolled the heavy stone cylinder over
them, leaning into the grinding, until she had a gritty mush that
Harriet needed two glasses of water to swallow. Harriet grimaced
slightly from the taste, but she looked noticeably lighter and freer in
her body, not clenched and bound up. Margarite told her that her
body was now clean and ready for her spirit. She gathered the
chrysanthemums and green bamboo from the floor and put them
into an earthenware jug along with water and some pieces of tortilla.

That night, Harriet put Margarite's flowers at the head of her
bed. And while she slept, her spirit returned, took sustenance from
the tortilla, then slipped back through the veil of basil at the top of
her head, returning to the clean home of her body.

Collecting Myself

Jeanne Achterberg

Fate of the Wise Women

s the Middle Ages waned, life lost its gentle shadings. Passion and violence, decadence and piety, the throes of death amid the dance characterized these times. Calamity struck Europe. The ecology was under stress; plagues and wars raged. Crop failures, coupled with filthy conditions in overcrowded towns and cities, opened the floodgates to diseases that would lay waste like no others before or since. These stresses led to the brutalization of women, severe sanctions on women healers, and murder of those who plied the healing arts around A.D. 1300 and into the seventeenth century.

In October 1347, twelve Genoese galleys, thought to have come from the Crimea, were guided by dying men into the harbor of Messina. One observer reported, "In their bones they bore so virulent a disease that anyone who only spoke to them was seized by a mortal illness and in no manner could evade death." The ships were ordered out of the harbor, but not before the men had come into contact with enough people to start the disease spreading, first through Sicily, then France and the rest of Europe.

The pandemic was known as the Black Death. Infection from the disease occurred in three forms: bubonic, pneumonic, and septicemic. Most victims died within three days. From one-third to one-half of Europe's population perished. According to church records, fifteen hundred people died in three days in Avignon. The Franciscan order alone claimed 124,434 losses. Total villages were wiped out; in 1350, the population of London was only half of what it had been ten years earlier.

Women were far more likely to survive the plague than men, and in some areas their recovery rate was about seven times as high. Many people believed that women were using magic to ensure their survival, and even to cause the death of men.

Women healers had to function in the midst of overwhelming devastation and tragedy, under perpetual scrutiny by church and state. Several French women in the early fourteenth century were reported to have been excommunicated under a ban by the prior of Saint Genevieve for practicing without appropriate licensure. How many more were excommunicated and how many were overlooked and allowed to practice is uncertain. A license in France, as well as in other countries, usually required an examination by self-declared masters of surgery or medicine. Most often the licensure requirements were simply ignored by both men and women. Paris, with two hundred thousand inhabitants at the end of the fourteenth century, had only ten licensed doctors. Thirty-eight (including five women) practiced "irregularly," and were taxed heavily, indicating that their earnings must have been substantial.

Late in the century, in France and England, women were rarely allowed to sit for licensing examinations. Guy de Chauliac, the most respected surgeon of the Middle Ages, argued against their presence among the ranks of medical practitioners, calling women who gathered herbs idiots and claiming they practiced religious nonsense. (Guy's own medicine was based upon unusual concoctions such as dragon's blood and mummy dust.)

The emerging guilds determined who could do what to whom, and from the guilds grew the modern professions of medicine. Exe-

cutioners could set bones; barbers could cup, bleed, and give ene-
mas. Surgeons formed their own guild in 1435, to be joined by the
barbers in 1493—a motley, unsavory lot.

Women could practice midwifery, although it too was a profession in poor repute. The midwives were frequently fined, imprisoned, or even sentenced to death if they displeased an influential
patient or assisted at the birth of a stillborn or deformed child.

In spite of sanctions against them, some women continued
to practice. The most famous case is a woman named Jacoba (or
Jacobina) Felicie, who was fined time and again for practicing medicine in Paris without appropriate credentials. Jacoba had received
her training with a mentor. (This was not an unusual practice, especially for married men, who were not allowed to attend the universities.) Nevertheless, in 1322, she was arraigned before the Court of
Justice by the dean and masters of the Faculty of Medicine. The
charges against her read, in part:

> (1) That the said Jacoba visited many sick folk labouring under
> severe illness in Paris and the suburbs, examining their urine,
> touching, feeling and holding their pulse, body and limbs, (2) that
> after this examination she was wont to say to the said sick folk, "I
> will cure you, by God's will, if you will trust me," making a com-
> pact with them and receiving money therefrom, (3) that after the
> said compact was made between the said party and the sick folk or
> their friends that she would cure them of their internal sickness or
> of wounds upon their outward body, the aforesaid party used to
> visit them several times assiduously and continually inspecting
> their urine and feeling and touching their limbs, (4) and that after
> this she gave and gives to the aforesaid folk sirups to drink confor-
> mative, laxative and digestive, as well liquid as not liquid, and aro-
> matic and other potions, which they often drink and have drunk in
> her presence and at her order.

The prosecution called witnesses to testify against Jacoba.
They all agreed that the charges were mostly accurate, but they also
said she was a wise and practiced physician who had cured them.
Some even mentioned the names of other physicians who had failed

to offer relief or cure, much to the embarrassment of the Faculty of Medicine. According to the witnesses, Jacoba had made no financial arrangements with them, suggesting that they give her what they thought appropriate after they were cured.

Jacoba argued that she should be judged by her results. Then she went on to speak of the need for women physicians:

> It is better and more seemly that a wise woman learned in the art should visit a sick woman and inquire into the secrets of her nature and her hidden parts, than that a man should do so, for whom it is not lawful to see and seek out the aforesaid parts, nor to feel with his hands the breasts, belly and feet. . . . And a woman before now would allow herself to die rather than to reveal the secrets of her infirmity to a man, on account of the honour of the female sex and of the shame which she would feel. And for these reasons many women and also men have perished of their infirmities, not being willing to have doctors, lest these should see their secret parts.

Jacoba's testimony was ignored. The prosecution argued that, since she had not been "approved" by the faculty, she must be ignorant of the practices of medicine. They discounted her patients' cures, stating that they were "certain that a man approved in the aforesaid art could cure the sick better than a woman." Finally, they decided that since women had no status as adults in a court of law, they shouldn't be practicing medicine either.

Jacoba was reprimanded and allowed a limited practice, but she could not receive remuneration for her services. Jacoba may also have been a Jew, which is another issue. Jews were banned by the church from practicing the healing arts. However, they were reputedly so skillful that they were hired at high cost and some risk by nobles and ecclesiastics. Of the few women listed as physicians on the rolls of the major cities of Europe, a surprising number were Jewish, often members of medical families who specialized in the treatment of eye diseases. In Frankfurt, for instance, fifteen women practitioners were listed between 1389 and 1497, four of whom were

Jewish. The Jewish women were likely trained through mentorship or at Salerno, the only medical school that continued to accept women as students.

Women's skill in the healing arts was generally not discounted. But since women were not officially allowed to study medicine, it was widely accepted that their information could only have come from the devil. The position of the church was "that if a woman dare to cure without having studied, she is a witch and must die."

The women who were accused of witchcraft bore no resemblance to the witches of fairy tales. The misconception that they did has inhibited, until the past hundred years or so, serious study of Western civilization's greatest crime. Yet now, as then, the "witch" is the shadow of the darkest thoughts within the human psyche.

As Christina Larner observes in *Enemies of God,* the moral and ethical crux of the persecutions was that "witch hunting *is* woman hunting or at least it is the hunting of women who do not fulfill the male view of how women ought to conduct themselves." Most studies of the era have assiduously avoided this larger issue, concentrating instead on select details of the trials, persecutions, and sociopolitical conditions. Only recently, with the probe of serious feminist historians, anthropologists, and writers—Christina Larner, Barbara Walker, Barbara Ehrenreich and Deidre English, and Mary Daly, among others—has the impact of this tragedy come to light.

In some areas, women were burned by a ratio of ten women to one man. In Scotland, where the number of men burned was exceptionally high, the ratio was still five women to one man. In twelfth-century Russia, when the authorities were looking for witches, they simply rounded up all the women in a given area. All women healers were suspect. Any woman with exceptional talent was suspect; any woman who had acquired her knowledge through the oral tradition of woman's domestic healing was suspect; any woman who had studied independently with a master healer (even a man) was suspect. Any woman who had the bad luck to be associated, by proximity or reputation, with a physician's failure to cure his patient was suspect.

Once a woman was arrested, the brutal torture accompanying her "confessions" assured that almost no one was found innocent. Arrest, then, was tantamount to death. Transcripts of the trials have been published in a number of places, each a testimony to the insanity and sadism of the accusers.

The following scenario is adapted from a report of the first day's torture of a woman accused of witchcraft in Prossneck, Germany, in 1629. First she was put on the "ladder," alcohol was thrown over her head, and her hair was set afire. Strips of sulfur were placed under her arms and ignited. Then the torturer tied her hands behind her back and hoisted her to the ceiling, where she hung for four hours while he went to breakfast. On his return, he threw alcohol over her back and set fire to it. After placing heavy weights on her body, he jerked her up to the ceiling again. Then he squeezed her thumbs and big toes in a vise, trussed her arms with a stick, and kept her hanging until she fainted. Then he whipped her with rawhide. Once more to the vises, and he went to lunch. After his lunch, she was whipped until blood ran through her shift. The next day, it was reported, they started all over again, but without pushing things quite as far as before.

This is a relatively typical case, except that some torturers used more ingenious and cruel devices. In England, however, torture was attenuated, and women were usually hanged instead of burned. Sometimes the women were mercifully strangled before they were burned in a tar barrel. On the Continent, they were more often burned "quick" (alive). In most cases, the woman was required to pay for her confinement, the activities of the torturers, the torture equipment, and the beer, meals, and banquets of the torturers, judges, clerics, and others involved in her arrest. Complete lists of official fees were published. The accused woman's estate was confiscated. (In a few areas, such as Venice, where the citizens forbade such practices, the witch-hunts were relatively minimal.) Finally, all costs of her murder were charged to her heirs. If she should be boiled in oil—a favorite in certain parts of France—the fees were especially high.

———

The actual number of women murdered will never be known. Authoritative estimates range from two hundred thousand to nine million. In Germany alone, one hundred thousand witch-burnings have been carefully documented.

In about 1600, a contemporary observer noted that "Germany is almost entirely occupied with building fires for the witches. Switzerland has been compelled to wipe out many of her villages on their account. Travelers in Lorraine may see thousands and thousands of the stakes to which witches are bound." The Inquisition acknowledged burning 30,000 witches in 150 years. In three little German villages—Rheinback, Meckenheim, and Flerzheim—from 300 households, 125 to 150 persons were executed within five years. Another small village, Riezler, Germany, could claim between 1,000 and 2,000 burnings. Some small towns were left with one woman or no women at all.

Women healers who worked out of deep commitment to a healing vocation and with exceptional skill—even though they were called "good" or "blessing" witches and practiced what authorities considered "white magic"—were also embraced in the paranoid delusions of the persecutors. Also known as wise women *(feminae sagae)*, they were accused of the "crimes" of aiding the sick, birthing babies, and caring for the dying. In areas where the emergent male professionals had their greatest strength, many of these women were accused of witchcraft.

The Dominican Johann Herolt said that "most women belie their Catholic faith with charms and spells, after the fashion of Eve. . . . Any woman by herself knows more of such superstitions and charms than a hundred men." Superstitions, charms, and spells, of course, constituted the practical medicine of the day.

Not only were wise women accused of healing without having studied, they were also charged with the ability of "laying on cures and laying them off"—transferring ailments from one person to another, or from a person to an animal.

William Perkins, a Scottish minister and leading witch-hunter, voiced the prevalent Protestant position on the healing arts of the wise women: the "good witch was more a monster than the bad. . . . If death be due to any . . . then a thousand deaths of right belong to the good witch." He went on to say that it would be better if all witches, but especially the blessing witch, were to die. For, he said, "though the witch were in many respects profitable, and did not hurt, but procured much good, yet because he hath renounced God, his king and governor, and hath bound himself by other laws to the service of the enemies of God and his Church, death is his portion justly assigned him by God: he may not live." The opinion of Protestant minister George Gifford was that a woman healer should be condemned not because of what she does but because "she dealeth with the devil."

The English authorities were unanimous in their condemnation. At the same time, they admitted that "good" witches existed, and that they should be consulted if the physician failed to cure an illness. The public, likewise, believed that the wise women were specially skilled. However, their attitude toward prosecution may have differed, since they stood to benefit from the healing. One story has it that a jailer at Canterbury Castle in 1570 released a witch because he believed she did more good for the sick than all the priests' prayers and exorcisms.

Still, any problem that eluded cure was readily attributed by the licensed doctors to witchcraft. In some instances of failure, there might be some question by the prosecuting authorities. In cases in which the prosecuting authorities had any question, the *Malleus Mallifaricum* advised: "And if it is asked how it is possible to distinguish whether an illness is caused by witchcraft or by some natural physical defect, we answer that the first is by means of the judgement of doctors."

Many instances of wise women being accused of witchcraft are reported. For instance, Alison Peirsoun of Byrehill had established her reputation as a gifted healer. Consequently, the archbishop of Saint Andrews sent for her. Afflicted with several disorders that we might call psychosomatic, he had been treated by many practitioners without relief. Alison, by whatever means, cured him. Later, he not only refused to pay her bill, he also had her arrested. She was charged and executed for witchcraft.

A wise woman whose life created a vivid stir was Gilly Duncan. Gilly was a young servant woman in the employ of David Seaton, deputy bailiff of a small town near Edinburgh. Gilly had established a reputation as a healer and cured those who were troubled or grieved with any kind of sickness or infirmity. Seaton felt her exceptional skill was unnatural. He also claimed to have seen her going to unexplained places at night. He obtained torture devices and began to question her. He jerked her head around with a rope, applied the thumbscrews, and examined her for the devil's mark. She finally confessed to the wicked allurements and enticements of the devil. Satisfied with his work, Seaton turned her over to the authorities. They forced her, with their own means, to name her accomplices. Those accused, the so-called witches of North Berwick, were tried and hanged about 1592.

These witch activities added to the fears of King James VI (James I of England), who believed that plots and supernatural forces threatened his life. It was he who commissioned the first translation of the Bible (the King James Version) in which the word "witch" appeared, the most-quoted instance being Exodus 22:18: "Thou shalt not suffer a witch to live." As early as 1584, Reginald Scot pointed out that the word *kashaph*, which appears in several places in the Old Testament, is best translated as "poisoner," and not "witch." His protests were ignored, and use of the word "witch" in the Book of God was further justification for murdering hundreds of thousands of women.

The wise woman's use of herbs was problematic, because it was widely believed that those who used herbs for cures did so only through a pact with the devil, whether implicit or explicit. The great minds of the Middle Ages wrestled with the issue of botanics. The major problem was that the plants in and of themselves could not be credited with any potent effects. Their effects, like those of chants, spells, or prayers, therefore, had to come from either God or the devil. The strongest plants, such as the mood-altering alkaloids, were mostly the devil's doing.

In Germany women could be accused of witchcraft for owning oil, ointment, pots of vermin, or human bones. All of these, of course, were common medicaments of the time—on any pharmacist's shelf, in any woman's pharmacopoeia.

What we know of these ingredients comes from the writings of the scientists, physicians, astrologers, and philosophers who were interested in *magia licita* (natural magic). These men included Agrippa of Nettesheim, Johannes Weyer, and Francis Bacon, who attribute their information to old women, wise women, or witches. If they themselves used the potions, they do not admit it.

According to reports, the women supposedly combined concoctions of plants with a fatty substance for skin absorption. (Witches were frequently accused of using the fat of dead babies for this purpose.) They would then anoint some object—brooms, pitchforks, benches, and large kneading troughs have all been mentioned—or rub the mixture directly into their "hairy parts." Sensitive vaginal tissues absorbed the mixtures especially well. Observers say the women were convinced they were flying. They remained visible, if oblivious to shovings, beatings, and the passage of time.

Reports of the exact ingredients of the oils varied, but most of the botanics listed were highly alkaloid in content. Minimally, they would cause agitation, and in large doses could induce coma or cause death. Francis Bacon offers this speculation:

> The ointment that witches use is reported to be made of the fat of children digged out of their graves; of the juices of smallage, wolf-bane, and cinque-foil, mingled with the meal of fine wheat. But I suppose that the soporiferous medicines are likest to do it; which are hen-bane, hemlock, mandrake, moonshade tobacco, opium, saffron, poplar leaves, etc.

In 1561, Porta, in *Magiae Naturalis*, wrote that the ointment contained the juice of celery, poplar leaves, calamus, nightshade (belladonna), jimsonweed, and aconite. Rübel mentions mandrake root, henbane seed, gray barley, hemlock, nightshade berries, and badger and fox grease, mixed with the juice of poppy seeds. Weyer suggests cannabis; several others cite preparations of toad. Rock crystal, fern, and rue are listed by various sources.

The ingredients, like the medicaments of the day, were often from sources like bats, snakes, dung, parts of human cadavers, and so forth. Ritual was as important as substance.

> For such travelling, both men and women, that is, the witches, use a salve called *ungentum pharelis* or "lighthouse ointment." It is prepared from seven herbs, each one of which is picked on a certain day. Thus on Sunday they pick and dig heliotrope, on Monday crescent-shaped fern, on Tuesday verbena, on Wednesday spurge, on Thursday houseleek, and on Friday maidenhair, and all this they use to make the ointment; they also add bird's gall and the fat of various animals, which I will not describe lest someone should take offense. When they feel the urge, they rub their bench, their rake or loading fork, and off they fly.

With the exception of the last recipe, most of the concoctions described are powerful psychoactive drugs. One authority on shamanic practices believes for this reason the women were not actually practicing shamanism. The drugs preferred by shamans in most cultures allow them to maintain a sense of the ordinary state of consciousness while journeying to the spirit world. Such communion at more than one state of consciousness would be impossible if the person were comatose.

However, our information on these plants is largely based on oral ingestion. A gradual diffusion through the skin may have resulted in a state more like that of the shaman's. Women who used these plants in healing probably knew how much to use to alter consciousness for pain relief, as well as how much to use to travel through landscapes of the mind, or to poison. The ingredients for each of these purposes—especially hemlock, aconite, and belladonna—are the same.

What were the putative effects of these substances and how do they fit into a modern pharmacopoeia? Some are narcotics whose

effects are well-known. Most are alkaloids with medicinal and hallucinogenic properties. Bufotenin, a chemical isolated from the glands
of toad skin, has a synergistic effect when used with plants,
although it is debatable whether it has hallucinogenic properties
itself.

Aconite (buttercup) is usually regarded as a poison, although it
may be used in homeopathic doses for epilepsy and tremors. It is
known to cause numbness, followed by paralysis of the lower
extremities, leaving the mind clear. This particular action may have
caused the women's reported long periods of immobility with their
eyes wide open. They may not have been comatose at all, just temporarily paralyzed. In ancient times, aconite was used to kill crimi-
nals, and also for euthanasia for infirm old men. In Chinese
medicine, it is used as a narcotic.

Henbane, belladonna, and mandrake all contain scopolamine,
hyoscyamine, and atropine. Although all are toxic in large amounts,
each chemical has a host of medical uses. Henbanes have been used
in domestic medicine for toothache, as sleeping aids, and nervines.
Mandrake (mandragora) has long been used as a sleeping potion, a
nerve medicine, and an anesthetic during surgery. From the time of
Trotula, mandrake, opium, and other sedatives were soaked into a
sponge, which was placed over the patient's face. It was an uncertain anesthetic, at best. Sometimes it worked well, sometimes not at
all, and sometimes it was deadly. Mandrake also has a long and magical history as an aphrodisiac. The roots of the plant resemble a
penis; thus, the widely accepted "doctrine of signatures" would
hold that it be used for disorders of the male. The more delicate
parts of the plant were used for female-oriented problems.

Belladonna has been used for a broad range of disorders, including asthma and cardiac arrhythmia. The symptoms of overdose
include flushed skin, dilated pupils, dry mouth, and delirium.
Death can occur as a result of respiratory failure.

Henbane has been related to divination. It is also sometimes
regarded as a "truth" drug.

Scopolamine, hyoscyamine, and atropine are all important anti-
spasmodics. Scopolamine is also a popular treatment for dizziness
and motion sickness. Interestingly, after decades of arguing that

nothing of medical value could be absorbed through the skin, medical science has developed infusion patches containing scopolamine (for motion sickness) and nitroglycerine (for angina). The patches deliver medication more effectively and with greater consistency than oral administration.

Some of the ingredients have mild, or uncertain, pharmacologic effects. Cinquefoil, for instance, was used in domestic medicine as a toothache remedy, but otherwise is rarely mentioned as a specific for any other condition. The frequent mention of fern, or "fern seed," in the ointments is also questionable, since it remains unclear what this might be.

All in all, the plants the women were accused of using were known to be more potent than the physician's astrological diagnoses, bleedings, and purgings, and his pharmacy of hundreds of benign ingredients, plucked and stirred together with superstition.

T he murders of women, particularly women healers, reflect the deepest human fear of power. The women's supposed jaunts into the supernatural—where the shaman seeks power—were targeted as special threats to church and state. Women who offered remedies or who promised magic in times of stress possessed an awesome power, because healing, even the simple domestic kind, is power of a very basic nature.

The belief systems that create witchcraft, magic, and religion concern power. They supply relief of anxiety in troubled times, a sense of control over what may or may not be controlled, and scapegoats in case of failure. Christine Larner, in her contribution to the growing body of information on the sociopolitical aspects of witchcraft, notes:

> The healer is a source of hope in the community. But his power is two-edged. If he should fail, demand extortionate and uneconomic returns for his services, or become hostile, then he becomes a source of menace and focus for anxiety. The refusal of Canon Law to distinguish between black and white magic, while based on the idea that all power not sanctioned by the church is either

ineffectual or demonic, regardless of whether it is intended to heal or harm, in fact reflects a peasant reality: that the healer can be dangerous.

Larner has also observed that the healer represents power at the most local level of a continuum that ends with the most abstract and social level: God and the devil.

Given the fear of power in anxious times, the mantle of power worn by healers in all times, and the primal fear of women and their mysteries, the reasons behind the murders of women healers are comprehensible, if unforgivable. Why women not involved in the healing arts were killed requires more explanation.

An extreme explanation for the persecutions is that the entire witch craze was invented by the ruling classes to quell peasant uprisings against the nobles and clergy. The attention of the peasants was thereby focused on their neighbors and distracted from the nobility, whom they blamed for their poverty and the perpetual warfare of the times. According to this line of thought, there never were any witches or anyone who practiced anything resembling witchcraft. This thesis does little to address why most of those murdered were women and why healers were singled out. Nor is it convincing in view of the theological underpinnings of the persecutions.

Another explanation is that women were not actually practicing witchcraft, but honoring the old pagan religions, worshipping old gods who had assumed the persona of the devil in Christianity. Margaret Murray, whose ideas followed the classic path set by Frazier's *Golden Bough*, held that many of the accused women were engaged in a fertility cult, worshipping a horned god (Dianus) of an earlier religion. A similar proposal was made by Anton Meyer, who believed that the women were involved in an ancient fertility cult that worshipped the earth goddess. Jules Michelet, a medieval scholar of the nineteenth century, believed that many women chose to become "Satan's bride." Woman, out of despair, he said, sought other gods, including her "ally of old and her confidant in the Garden." He also asserted that the persecuted women may have abused their power. "Great and irresponsible power is always liable to abuse; and in this case she queened it in a very true sense for three long centuries during the interregnum between two worlds, the old dying world and the new one whose dawn was still faint on the horizon.

The ideas of Murray, Meyer, and Michelet are appealing but poorly documented. Yet the old religions empowered women to a far greater extent than Christianity. We know that women carried amulets representing the Roman goddesses long after Europe was Christianized. How widespread, and how open, the practices of the old religion were will never be known. It is unlikely, though, that the church saw the old religions as much of a threat compared with the splinter sects of heretics within its own ranks.

A balanced perspective is that women are attracted to witchcraft in both its light and dark guises. Witchcraft—the generation of super-natural power—is an outlet for the spiritually unrewarded, a means of gaining status for the culturally deprived. Women, particularly those living at the edge of society, sought it as a means of control, stature, and economic survival in a world that promised none of these.

Gradually, first in the cities, then in the countryside, women ceased to be burned. In England, the last witch was officially hanged in 1684, in America in 1692, and finally in Germany in 1775. The madness wound down only when Christianity lost its strong hold on the governments of Europe. As Larner notes, the woman-hunt "could not become rampant until personal religion had become political. It could not survive the advent of secular ideologies." When religious affairs were separated from politics, women were no longer murdered for crimes they did not commit. The witch-hunts had always been most severe in the regions ruled by Roman law and in the countries where Protestantism was most integrated into government. Through the Reformation, the Counter-Reformation, and the increasing heterogeneity of religious expression, dissent became stronger. The trials came under increasing scrutiny and mistrust. It was suggested that they too might be the work of the devil and had best be stopped.

Despite the cessation of the crimes against women, they were not given full citizenship in any country, nor was their role in the healing professions reinstated. Rather, the hunts served to lower women's status and increase the level of misogyny and distrust. The persecutions halted not because the attitude toward women changed, but because the power base of governments shifted. Nor can the dawning of the scientific age be credited with stopping the madness. Most early scientists acknowledged and feared the witches. Samuel Johnson and others believed that the decrease in the number of trials was a result of women's ceasing to practice the black arts.

During the years of the witch-hunts, women healers had been edged out by guilds, and then by the incorporations of physicians, surgeons, and apothecaries. Their work was prohibited by law in every country in Europe. The Inquisition and Christian theology had been used to exclude women from the ranks of independent practitioners. In the new worldview, science and the laws of nature would be invoked for the same purpose.

Marjory Stoneman Douglas

The Grass

he Everglades begin at Lake Okeechobee.

That is the name later Indians gave the lake, a name almost as recent as the word "Everglades." It means "Big Water." Everybody knows it.

Yet few have any idea of those pale, seemingly illimitable waters. Over the shallows, often less than a foot deep but 750 or so square miles in actual area, the winds in one gray swift moment can shatter the reflections of sky and cloud whiteness standing still in that shining, polished, shimmering expanse. A boat can push for hours in a day of white sun through the short, crisp lake waves and there will be nothing to be seen anywhere but the brightness where the color of the water and the color of the sky become one. Men out of sight of land can stand in it up to their armpits and slowly "walk in" their long nets to the waiting boats. An everglade kite and his mate, questing in great solitary circles, rising and dipping and rising again on the wind currents, can look down all day long at the water faintly green with floating water lettuce or marked by thin standing lines of reeds, utter their sharp goat cries, and be seen and heard by no one at all.

There are great shallow islands, all brown reeds or shrubby trees thick in the water. There are masses of water weeds and hyacinths and flags rooted so long they seem solid earth, yet there is nothing but lake bottom to stand on. There the egret and the white ibis and the glossy ibis and the little blue herons in their thousands nested and circled and fed.

A long northeast wind, a "norther," can lash all that still surface to dirty vicious gray and white, over which the rain mists shut down like stained rolls of wool, so that, from the eastern sand rim under dripping cypresses, or the west ridge with its live oaks, no one would guess that all that waste of empty water stretched there but for the long monotonous wash of waves on unseen marshy shores.

Saw grass reaches up both sides of that lake in great enclosing arms, so that it is correct to say that the Everglades are there also. But south, southeast, and southwest, where the lake water slopped and seeped and ran over and under the rock and soil, the greatest mass of the saw grass begins. It stretches as it always has stretched, in one thick enormous curving river of grass, to the very end. This is the Everglades.

It reaches one hundred miles from Lake Okeechobee to the Gulf of Mexico, fifty, sixty, even seventy miles wide. No one has ever fought his way along its full length. Few have ever crossed the northern wilderness of nothing but grass. Down that almost invisible slope the water moves. The grass stands. Where the grass and the water are there is the heart, the current, the meaning of the Everglades.

The grass and the water together make the river as simple as it is unique. There is no other river like it. Yet, within that simplicity, enclosed within the river and bordering and intruding on it from each side, there is subtlety and diversity, a crowd of changing forms, of thrusting, teeming life. And all that becomes the region of the Everglades.

The truth of the river is the grass. They call it saw grass. Yet in the botanical sense it is not grass at all so much as a fierce, ancient, cutting sedge. It is one of the oldest of the green growing forms in this world.

There are many places in the South where this saw grass, with its sharp central fold and edges set with fine sawteeth like points of glass, this sedge called *Cladium jamaicensis*, exists. But this is the greatest concentration of saw grass in the world. It grows fiercely in the fresh water creeping down below it. When the original saw grass thrust up its spears into the sun, the fierce sun, lord and power and first cause over the Everglades as of all the green world, then the Everglades began. They lie wherever the saw grass extends: thirty-five hundred square miles, hundreds and thousands and millions of acres of water and saw grass.

The first saw grass, exactly as it grows today, sprang up and lived in the sweet water and the pouring sunlight, and died in it, and from its own dried and decaying tissues and tough fibers bright with silica sprang up more fiercely again. Year after year it grew and was fed by its own brown rotting, taller and denser in the dark soil of its own death. Year after year after year, hundreds after hundreds of years, not so long as any geologic age but long in botanic time, far longer than anyone can be sure of, the saw grass grew. Four thousand years, they say, it must at least have grown like that, six feet, ten feet, twelve feet, even fifteen in places of deepest water. The edged and folded swords bristled around the delicate straight tube of pith that burst into brown flowering. The brown seed, tightly enclosed after the manner of sedges, ripened in dense brownness. The seed was dropped and worked down in the water and its own ropelike mat of roots. All that decay of leaves and seed covers and roots was packed deeper year after year by the elbowing upthrust of its own life. Year after year it laid down new layers of virgin muck under the living water.

There are places now where the depth of the muck is equal to the height of the saw grass. When it is uncovered and brought into the sunlight, its stringy and grainy dullness glitters with the myriad unrotted silica points, like glass dust.

At the edges of the Glades, and toward those southern- and southwesternmost reaches where the great estuary or delta of the

Glades river takes another form entirely, the saw grass is shorter and more sparse, and the springy, porous muck deposit under it is shallower and thinner. But where the saw grass grows tallest in the deepest muck, there goes the channel of the Glades.

The water winks and flashes here and there among the sawgrass roots, as the clouds are blown across the sun. To try to make one's way among these impenetrable tufts is to be cut off from all air, to be beaten down by the sun and ripped by the grassy sawtoothed edges as one sinks in mud and water over the roots. The dried yellow stuff holds no weight. There is no earthly way to get through the mud or the standing, keen-edged blades that crowd these interminable miles.

Or, in the times of high water in the old days, the flood would rise until the highest tops of that sharp grass were like a thin lawn standing out of water as blue as the sky, rippling and wrinkling, linking the pools and spreading and flowing on its true course southward.

A man standing in the center of it, if he could get there, would be as lost in saw grass, as out of sight of anything but saw grass as a man drowning in the middle of Okeechobee—or the Atlantic Ocean, for that matter—would be out of sight of land.

The water moves. The saw grass, pale green to deep-brown ripeness, stands rigid. It is moved only in sluggish rollings by the vast push of the winds across it. Over its endless acres here and there, the shadows of the dazzling clouds quicken and slide, purple-brown, plum-brown, mauve-brown, rust-brown, bronze. The bristling, blossoming tops do not bend easily like standing grain. They do not even in their own growth curve all one way, but stand in edged clumps, curving against each other, all the massed curving blades making millions of fine arching lines that at a little distance merge to a huge expanse of brown wires or bristles or, farther beyond, to deep-piled plush. At the horizon they become velvet. The line they make is an edge of velvet against the infinite blue, the blue and white, the clear fine primrose yellow, the burning brass and crimson, the molten silver, the deepening hyacinth sky.

The clear burning light of the sun pours daylong into the saw grass and is lost there, soaked up, never given back. Only the water flashes and glints. The grass yields nothing.

Nothing less than the smashing power of some hurricane can beat it down. Then one can see, from high up in a plane, where the towering weight and velocity of the hurricane was the strongest, and where along the edges of its whorl it turned less and less savagely and left the saw grass standing. Even so, the grass is not flattened in a continuous swath but only here and here and over there, as if the storm bounced or lifted and smashed down again in great hammering strokes or enormous cat-licks.

Only one force can conquer it completely and that is fire. Deep in the layers of muck there are layers of ashes, marks of old fires set by lightning or the early Indians. But in the early days the water always came back, and there were long slow years in which the saw grass grew and died, laying down again its tough resilient decay.

This is the saw grass, then, which seems to move as the water moved, in a great thick arc south and southwestward from Okeechobee to the Gulf. There, at the last imperceptible incline of the land, the saw grass goes along the headwaters of many of those wide, slow, mangrove-bordered freshwater rivers, like a delta or an estuary into which the salt tides flow and draw back and flow again.

The mangrove becomes a solid barrier there, which by its strong, arched, and labyrinthine roots collects the sweepage of the fresh water and the salt and holds back the parent sea. The supple branches, the oily green leaves, set up a barrier against the winds, although the hurricanes prevail easily against them. There the fresh water meets the incoming salt, and is lost.

It may be that the mystery of the Everglades is the saw grass, so simple, so enduring, so hostile. It was the saw grass and the water that divided east coast from west coast and made the central solitudes that held in them the secrets of time, which has moved here so long unmarked.

Trish Maharam

Plantswomen

T en years ago, when I was six months pregnant, I laid the foundation for my first garden. As I planted the first seeds on our property, it dawned on me that I was a seedpod myself.

A little more than a year later, on a rainy Seattle spring night, my husband, our new daughter, Hanae, and her grandparents dug together to plant a young Japanese snowbell tree in our garden. We piled shovelfuls of dark-brown loam in small mounds around the hollow where the young tree would be planted. I took my daughter's placenta from the freezer and settled it in the moist earth. I remembered holding it the day she was born at home, a mass of nourishment and oxygen that most women discard. When I turned the placenta inside out, it had the very defined shape of a tree. The tree of life.

Many indigenous cultures make a ritual of burying the placenta in the ground and planting a tree over it. As the child grows, so does the tree. It seemed fitting to plant Hanae's placenta under a tree so like her, graceful and gentle, with white fragrant bells that bloom in late May. We stood in the pouring rain, our heads covered in plastic rain hats, each taking a turn covering the roots, Hanae in a pack on my back. "This is your tree," I told my baby daughter; "your guardian, fed by your placenta. We will watch it grow together."

Gardening has been a tradition of the women in my family. My mother learned from her aunt Hilda Gort, who had a huge perennial garden in Lawrence, Long Island. As a child, my mother visited Hilda for a week each summer, following her through the gridded paths of pastel blossoms. Hilda wore a large hat and a billowy cotton summer dress. My mother loped behind her, carrying a woven basket, while Hilda snipped flowers with silver scissors to fill the vases that adorned each tabletop in her house.

It wasn't until my mother was in her thirties that a friend with thriving herbs and perennials invited her to learn how to make a garden. There were women in our neighborhood with whom my mother had little in common, but they became gardening friends and cultivated a language with plants that bound them, talking about the morning light on wet leaves, or bending together to admire a pink penstemon, then finding themselves a half-hour later with smudged knees and an ample pile of weeds. In this way my mother grew herself as a gardener.

Now, years later, my sister Hillary and I have our own gardens on opposite coasts. We were not born to the love of gardening. Like our mother, we learned it over time. Though I grew up with the chores of weeding and gathering berries, it wasn't until I had a home in Seattle on a large south-facing lot that I found my own relationship with plants.

I was overwhelmed by our half-acre in the city, a private dead end with a few old orchard trees, and land covered in blackberries, morning glories, and horsetails. I understood nothing of the bones of gardening, the pathways and stone walls. I'd had no formal teaching and had read few books. The only language I knew was the one my mother and I shared over the telephone about colors and simple flowers. I called her and said, "I'm not equipped to make a garden of my own."

"That's ridiculous!" she said. But then: "I remember feeling that way myself." She told me a story.

"Just the other day, I was at Home Depot. They have a huge collection of orchids. A very large woman came and stood beside me to admire them. We oohed and aahed, and then she pulled a bunch of photographs from her pocketbook. I assumed they were of her children, or grandchildren, but they were pictures of her orchid collection. There were orchids on her porch, in the house, in the garden. The same orchids I love, yet used in a completely different way. You see, we all have access to the same plants. You just have to find the ones you love, the ones that belong to you, and plant them."

Around this time, in 1987, I was offered a job as the Northwest regional editor for *Better Homes and Gardens*. It was a job my mother had learned and inherited from her dear gardening friend on the East Coast. My credentials were mostly that I was a resourceful networker with a good eye. My assignment was to find suitable houses and gardens and to arrange for them to be photographed. I didn't realize then that I would be entering people's lives through their environments.

In my second year of work I met with a Frenchman who was dying of AIDS. We walked slowly through his garden as he quietly told me about his plants. Before I left, he held in his bony hands a tiny green fava bean. "When I was a child," he said, "my mother made fava bean stew. It was my favorite dish. I have always grown them." Since meeting him I grow those long, bumpy beans, and his memory lives on in my yard.

When I was eight months pregnant with Hanae, I had an assignment to photograph a garden layered in perennials, petticoats of roses and white phlox laced in clematis and honeysuckle. For three days the homeowner brought me tea as I worked. During lunch, she invited me to lie down on her tall bed, which I reached by climbing a small ladder. When I left she gave me a fairy rose, which has grown full and abundant planted beside the gate I pass through each day going in and out of my home.

For seven years I visited and photographed the garden of a woman who looked like Audrey Hepburn. She had made her garden her lifework. There were paths of stone, each one hand-collected and carefully placed. There were birdhouses she constructed herself, and jams she made from marionberries and gooseberries, served to me on muffins fresh from the oven. We ate them seated by the small pond where the first water lilies were opening. She taught me to have a large view of the garden but to focus on one small piece at a time.

Each gardener I met gave me a list of his or her favorite gardens. That is how I found my way from one place to the next. Over the years, a number of people had mentioned a garden in Victoria, British Columbia, and finally I called to set a time for a visit.

When I opened the wooden gate, a woman in her fifties scurried toward me. She was of medium height and lean, and though she smiled, her face was hawkish.

She welcomed me into her yard, an exquisite foliage garden. A small fountain bubbled calmly in the foreground. Layered in gradations of green, symmetrical but loosely planted, the shapes and textures were carefully and thoughtfully placed. There were slender paths woven throughout. It is always a treat to come upon a garden like this one, to set up the camera in soft morning or early-evening light and compose pictures. It is the way I learn best about plants in combination. I was already looking forward to the time I would spend there.

We sat down together at a small table perched at one side of a courtyard.

"What magazine are you working for?" she asked, her lips pulled tight into her face.

I had brought her an issue. She leafed through it quickly, barely glancing at the contents. "Well, you know, I've been in *Fine Gardening* and *Horticulture* and many other serious magazines, and this looks rather superficial."

"It's new," I countered with discretion, "but I don't believe it's superficial. It offers contemplation for gardeners, and an invitation for beginners."

Turning on me, her eyes narrowed, she said, "And what about you? Do you have a garden?"

I kept my eyes level with hers. "Yes. It's ten years old now."

"And are you a *plantswoman*," she hissed, "or do you simply gather pretty flowers?"

She craned her neck, stretching her head up over me. The gesture reminded me of a bird puffing out its feathers to appear larger than it is.

"We all have to start somewhere." I kept my voice steady. "I have my whole life to learn about plants."

In the end, I had no desire to view her garden. It seemed tainted, like the woman. I closed the gate quietly and left, but her words had unsettled me.

Back in my own garden, I asked myself, What is a plantswoman? Was I really one? Often I felt inadequate in the presence of long-time gardeners, as though I wasn't serious enough or devoted enough. Over the years I had tried to study Latin names of plants, but I retained only the common names. I thought about my slow toil of digging out horsetail and blackberry, amending soil that was once so hard I'd had to jump on the shovel to pierce the ground. Now I could easily dig down two shovelfuls deep and find worms instead of rocks and clumps of clay.

I'd made many mistakes in the garden, such as planting whole beds with smatterings of perennials that made it spindly and unappealing. But over time I had learned to think in combinations, to use one kind of plant generously, so that it grew full and textured beside another—the loose roundness of the standard Hiroki Nishiro willow, for example, its variegated leaves and thin reddish limbs surrounded by the tall deep purple orbs of allium "Globemaster." I had learned how to choose from the nursery or others' gardens what belonged in my own. But perhaps that made me a mere gatherer of pretty flowers.

Over the next month, I contacted many women, gardeners and nurserywomen, in my quest to define what a "plantswoman" is.

"The garden," said Karen Jennings, a member of a family-owned South Carolina seed business, "is an extension of our living space, and I think that's one reason why it belongs to women. Plants have always been there at times when women didn't have many avenues for creativity. Whether it was food production or perennial gardens, it was their province."

Renee Shepherd, a seed gatherer and provider living in California, explained to me that gardening is an exchange of information. For her, "being a seed gatherer means having a link with every culture."

Jane Lappin, a grower and designer on eastern Long Island with a formal education in horticulture, has a voice to match her person, deep and gutsy. "When I began in the 1970s, I remember going to my first Long Island growers' meeting. I was one of only three women. I wanted to grow rare and unusual plants that I couldn't get anywhere else, and I wanted to grow the majority from seed. The men laughed at me. But I was driven, and excited about the growing."

When I asked for her definition of a plantswoman, she responded, "Being a plantswoman is a buildup of knowledge and experience." As an example, she mentioned a large sweep of ocean-front property in the Hamptons that she'd recently been asked to landscape. It had taken her fifteen years of planting by the sea to be able to know which plants were going to make it and which ones wouldn't. "Now I get to think about contrasting foliages, about what it's going to look like through the seasons beside another plant"— her speech quickened with enthusiasm—"the flowers, the textures, how it handles the wind. It's so exciting when you have the knowledge to put this whole picture together properly, to plant it, and stand back, and see it completed."

Each time I finished speaking with a plantswoman, I refined my own definition of the term. Over time I began to understand the language of plants and their nature. Some years are just about maintenance, other years are about change. One year, during a bout with pneumonia, I was unable to tend my plants. Instead, I sat in a chair and observed the garden. Dozing off, I woke to a quiet, uncluttered moment between sleep and waking, and there before me stood my garden. In the nearest bed, on the south-facing bank, I could see all the gradations of blues and lavenders—*Perovskia, Caryopteris, Nepeta,* and *Eryngium*—mixed with the silver-grays of *Artemisia, Santolina,* and *Achillea.*

There was a time when that bank was sandy and eroding. Now it was full, the plants mature and well blended. I let out a deep sigh of satisfaction before looking further.

In the upper bed, the *Nepeta* was making babies everywhere, crowding out the agapanthus. I watched as my nine-year-old Hanae made a path with her body through the dense foliage to smell a newly opened Heritage rose.

"Mom, there are white lilies hiding in here. You can't even see them from the house."

I had overplanted, and now I was going to have to dig out and transplant to make room for the larger plants so they could spread and drape the way they were meant to. I was going to have to go backwards. For a moment I was frustrated with this insight; then I laughed. I realized that the garden reflects my impulsive side. That's who I am. I remembered my mother telling me that if we approach gardening without the guidance of a designer or landscape architect, it will show us what we are made of.

R ecently, Hanae was helping me to prune the clematis and honeysuckle that were strangling a patch of lavender. I was using my Felco pruners, which always make me feel capable, and wearing my high rubber boots. Hanae was in her bare feet, wielding a pair of scissors. I had a sudden glimpse of her as separate from me, my seed-child growing up. In our garden I could somehow see her more clearly, her color and shape, the way her body comfortably mingled with the plants.

For Hanae, the garden is a place for observing and gathering. Unlike me, she doesn't care about tidiness; it's more important that the dogs have a place to run, that there's grass for rolling and picnicking. When we look through the gardening catalogue in the fall, she chooses the bright pinks and deep reds, colors that I avoid. She is already preparing a cutting garden with hyacinths and tulips for the spring, dahlias and peonies for the summer.

One Saturday morning we went to our favorite nursery. Hanae took her own wagon and meandered through the rows, considering, bending down to get a better look, then gathering. When she returned to me with her wagon full, I looked at the plants she had chosen. They were small mounds, little islands with delicate pink and white flowers, tiny foliage in silvery green. We read together the nature of each plant, how large it grows, whether it likes sun or shade. I saw that she was already learning to tend her own garden.

I called my mother that day and asked her, "How would you define a plantswoman?"

"You know," she said, "it doesn't matter how you're connected to the plants, it's the connection that makes you a plantswoman. If you go out into your garden and it lights up your face, or your whole body, then you're a woman who loves plants."

I walked through my yard at dusk. The oriental lilies my mother had sent had opened. I held the fullness of a pale-orange rose in my hands and finally understood why she loves roses. But I could see in the way I had planted that spring that I was shifting away from flowers toward foliage. I sat on a stone step and listened to the waterfall. I was growing and changing with my garden.

Hanae's tree had grown tall, like her, the deep-plum clematis "Niobe" climbing through her Japanese snowbell. Her placenta had become part of the earth, part of the roots of that tree.

"I am a plantswoman," I told myself. I stood over a newly planted maidenhair fern, lifted my watering can, and began to pour.

Alice Walker

The Nature of This Flower Is to Bloom

Rebellious. Living.
Against the Elemental Crush.
A Song of Color
Blooming
For Deserving Eyes.
Blooming Gloriously
For its Self.

Revolutionary Petunia.

Molly Peacock

State of Grace

range poppies lolled in a great pride, like lionesses, beside the apple trees. Huge and real, they leapt to life from a book I had stowed in my suitcase that summer, the *Lilac Fairy Book*. I'd finally come to visit my grandmother by myself, old enough to be sent the mere hundred miles that separated my prim suburbia from her ramshackle house. She'd placed the perennial beds in a remnant of an apple orchard that still had a few gnarled trees, just to make her garden even more of a fairy tale. Forces I felt responsible for but did not understand were the cause of my prolonged visit: the death throes of my parents' marriage, and my grandmother's insistence that I go to summer Bible school. But the religion she gave me was her garden.

It was a place of grace, a sanctuary I spent hours in, where flowers had personalities, including the queen, a recalcitrant French lilac who had gotten her seasons turned around and insisted on producing blossoms in September. In my parents' house I was never free of the tasks that helplessly fell to me as their lives disintegrated: the care of the house and meals and my younger sister. I had two selves, really: a robot self to dispense my obligations, and a true self that was dangerously buried or, as gardeners say, "caught in the bulb." But in that garden, where I was able to act dreamy, my true self was released.

A Buddhist might call it mindfulness. A Quaker might call it connecting with the light inside you. To be able to look an orange poppy in its chartreuse eye and simply be doing nothing other than looking at that blowsy-headed flower, feeling only one experience without competing subsidiary ones, is my idea of grace. To be fully inside the looking moment is to be fully in your true self, not the one you have created for others' demands. This grace is a kind of blooming.

Because the garden is so deeply connected with the true self, it is also deeply sensual, and intensely so for women because flowers, so shockingly sexual, are identified with women. That summer I became a seed-catalogue junkie, entranced with pictures of flowers. I was riveted and embarrassed by the close-ups of orchids. Each orchid was me, it was every girl, turned inside out for all to see.

My grandmother's poppies and apple trees are long gone, but, just the way we sometimes feel that someone whom we loved and lost is not gone entirely, yet transformed somehow into another type of energy, that garden is inside me. It has become a portable state of grace.

And I need it, because I live a portable life. Having lost each other for decades, my high-school boyfriend and I met again and married. Since we both had well-established lives in two countries, we decided not to dismantle them, but to enlarge—and compli-cate—our lives by keeping both. Now we live in London, Ontario, full of stately trees and tiny backyard gardens; and in New York City, where the flowers are in tin buckets at the fruit markets and in the unexpected gardens one discovers inside stately buildings like the Frick mansion.

Although I don't always feel it, I carry that dreamy flower state within me as I lug my suitcases through customs. Tucked inside, like the *Lilac Fairy Book* in my first suitcase, it insists on its pres-ence, just like the Lilac Queen in my grandmother's garden, who bloomed when she wanted to, turning everybody else's fall into her spring. My attention to a flower can help me rediscover my true self, the self I lose to forces I'm responsible for but often do not completely understand. That centered staring helps erase the robot self of Lists, Calls, Chores, Duties, Dampened Desires.

The frailest of nature's objects, these most female emblems, have staying power. Staying power has healing power, too. You can stand in front of flowers and look them in their many eyes and see *just them,* and for a moment you are doing only one thing fully, being in the presence of their tart soil and tender personalities, and connecting with the tart and tender within yourself.

The Science
of Green

Rachel Carson

Earth's Green Mantle

 ater, soil, and the earth's green mantle of plants make up the world that supports the animal life of the earth. Although modern man seldom remembers the fact, he could not exist without the plants that harness the sun's energy and manufacture the basic foodstuffs he depends upon for life. Our attitude toward plants is a singularly narrow one. If we see any immediate utility in a plant we foster it. If for any reason we find its presence undesirable or merely a matter of indifference, we may condemn it to destruction forthwith. Besides the various plants that are poisonous to man or his livestock, or crowd out food plants, many are marked for destruction merely because, according to our narrow view, they happen to be in the wrong place at the wrong time. Many others are destroyed merely because they happen to be associates of the unwanted plants.

The earth's vegetation is part of a web of life in which there are intimate and essential relations between plants and the earth, between plants and other plants, between plants and animals. Sometimes we have no choice but to disturb these relationships, but we should do so thoughtfully, with full awareness that what we do may have consequences remote in time and place. But no such humility marks the booming "weed-killer" business of the present day, in which soaring sales and expanding uses mark the production of plant-killing chemicals.

One of the most tragic examples of our unthinking bludgeoning of the landscape is to be seen in the sagebrush lands of the West, where a vast campaign is on to destroy the sage and to substitute grasslands. If ever an enterprise needed to be illuminated with a sense of the history and meaning of the landscape, it is this. For here the natural landscape is eloquent of the interplay of forces that have created it. It is spread before us like the pages of an open book in which we can read why the land is what it is, and why we should preserve its integrity. But the pages lie unread.

The land of the sage is the land of the high Western plains and the lower slopes of the mountains that rise above them, a land born of the great uplift of the Rocky Mountain system many millions of years ago. It is a place of harsh extremes of climate: of long winters when blizzards drive down from the mountains and snow lies deep on the plains, of summers whose heat is relieved by only scanty rains, with drought biting deep into the soil, and drying winds stealing moisture from leaf and stem.

As the landscape evolved, there must have been a long period of trial and error in which plants attempted the colonization of this high and windswept land. One after another must have failed. At last one group of plants evolved which combined all the qualities needed to survive. The sage—low-growing and shrubby—could hold its place on the mountain slopes and on the plains, and within its small gray leaves it could hold moisture enough to defy the thieving winds. It was no accident, but, rather, the result of long ages of experimentation by nature, that the great plains of the West became the land of the sage.

Along with the plants, animal life, too, was evolving in harmony with the searching requirements of the land. In time there were two as perfectly adjusted to their habitat as the sage. One was a mammal, the fleet and graceful pronghorn antelope. The other was a bird, the sage grouse—the "cock of the plains" of Lewis and Clark.

The sage and the grouse seem made for each other. The original range of the bird coincided with the range of the sage, and as the sagelands have been reduced, so the populations of grouse have dwindled. The sage is all things to these birds of the plains. The low sage of the foothill ranges shelters their nests and their young; the denser growths are loafing and roosting areas; at all times the sage provides the staple food of the grouse. Yet it is a two-way relationship. The spectacular courtship displays of the cocks help loosen the soil beneath and around the sage, aiding invasion by grasses which grow in the shelter of sagebrush.

The antelope, too, have adjusted their lives to the sage. They are primarily animals of the plains, and in winter, when the first snows come, those that have summered in the mountains move down to the lower elevations. There the sage provides the food that tides them over the winter. Where all other plants have shed their leaves, the sage remains evergreen, the gray-green leaves—bitter, aromatic, rich in proteins, fats, and needed minerals—clinging to the stems of the dense and shrubby plants. Though the snows pile up, the tops of the sage remain exposed, or can be reached by the sharp, pawing hoofs of the antelope. Then grouse feed on them, too, finding them on bare and windswept ledges or following the antelope to feed where they have scratched away the snow.

And other life looks to the sage. Mule deer often feed on it. Sage may mean survival for winter-grazing livestock. Sheep graze many winter ranges where the big sagebrush forms almost pure stands. For half the year it is their principal forage, a plant of higher energy value than even alfalfa hay.

The bitter upland plains, the purple wastes of sage, the wild, swift antelope, and the grouse are, then, a natural system in perfect balance. Are? The verb must be changed—at least in those already vast and growing areas where man is attempting to improve on nature's way. In the name of progress the land-management agencies have set about to satisfy the insatiable demands of the cattlemen for more grazing land. By this they mean grassland—grass without sage. So, in a land which nature found suited to grass-growing mixed with and under the shelter of sage, it is now proposed to eliminate the sage and create unbroken grassland. Few seem to have asked whether grasslands are a stable and desirable goal in this region. Certainly nature's own answer was otherwise. The annual precipitation in this land where the rains seldom fall is not enough to support good sod-forming grass; it favors, rather, the perennial bunchgrass that grows in the shelter of the sage.

Yet the program of sage eradication has been under way for a number of years. Several government agencies are active in it; industry has joined with enthusiasm to promote and encourage an enterprise which creates expanded markets not only for grass seed but for a large assortment of machines for cutting and plowing and seeding. The newest addition to the weapons is the use of chemical sprays. Now millions of acres of sagebrush lands are sprayed each year.

What are the results? The eventual effects of eliminating sage and seeding with grass are largely conjectural. Men of long experience with the ways of the land say that in this country there is better growth of grass between and under the sage than can possibly be had in pure stands, once the moisture-holding sage is gone.

But even if the program succeeds in its immediate objective, it is clear that the whole closely knit fabric of life has been ripped apart. The antelope and the grouse will disappear along with the sage. The deer will suffer, too, and the land will be poorer for the destruction of the wild things that belong to it. Even the livestock which are the intended beneficiaries will suffer; no amount of lush green grass in summer can help the sheep starving in the winter storms for lack of the sage and bitterbrush and other wild vegetation of the plains.

These are the first and obvious effects. The second is of a kind that is always associated with the shotgun approach to nature: the spraying also eliminates a great many plants that were not its intended target. Justice William O. Douglas, in his recent book *My Wilderness: East to Katahdin*, has told of an appalling example of ecological destruction wrought by the United States Forest Service in the Bridger National Forest in Wyoming. Some ten thousand acres of sagelands were sprayed by the Service, yielding to pressure of cattlemen for more grasslands. The sage was killed, as intended.

But so was the green, life-giving ribbon of willows that traced its way across these plains, following the meandering streams. Moose had lived in these willow thickets, for willow is to the moose what sage is to the antelope. Beaver had lived there, too, feeding on the willows, felling them and making a strong dam across the tiny stream. Through the labor of the beavers, a lake backed up. Trout in the mountain streams seldom were more than six inches long; in the lake they thrived so prodigiously that many grew to five pounds. Waterfowl were attracted to the lake, also. Merely because of the presence of the willows and the beavers that depended on them, the region was an attractive recreational area with excellent fishing and hunting.

But with the "improvement" instituted by the Forest Service, the willows went the way of the sagebrush, killed by the same impartial spray. When Justice Douglas visited the area in 1959, the year of the spraying, he was shocked to see the shriveled and dying willows—the "vast, incredible damage." What would become of the moose? Of the beavers and the little world they had constructed? A year later he returned to read the answers in the devastated landscape. The moose were gone and so were the beaver. Their principal dam had gone out for want of attention by its skilled architects, and the lake had drained away. None of the large trout were left. None could live in the tiny creek that remained, threading its way through a bare, hot land where no shade remained. The living world was shattered.

Besides the more than four million acres of rangelands sprayed each year, tremendous areas of other types of land are also potential or actual recipients of chemical treatments for weed control. For example, an area larger than all of New England—some fifty million acres—is under management by utility corporations, and much of it is routinely treated for "brush control." In the Southwest an estimated seventy-five million acres of mesquite lands require management by some means, and chemical spraying is the method most actively pushed. An unknown but very large acreage of timber-producing lands is now aerially sprayed in order to "weed out" the hardwoods from the more spray-resistant conifers. Treatment of agricultural lands with herbicides doubled in the decade following 1949, totaling fifty-three million acres in 1959. And the combined acreage of private lawns, parks, and golf courses now being treated must reach an astronomical figure.

The chemical weed-killers are a bright new toy. They work in a spectacular way; they give a giddy sense of power over nature to those who wield them, and as for the long-range and less obvious effects—these are easily brushed aside as the baseless imaginings of pessimists. The "agricultural engineers" speak blithely of "chemical plowing" in a world that is urged to beat its plowshares into spray guns. The town fathers of a thousand communities lend willing ears to the chemical salesman and the eager contractors who will rid the roadsides of "brush"—for a price. It is cheaper than mowing, is the cry. So, perhaps, it appears in the neat rows of figures in the official books; but, were the true costs entered, the costs not only in dollars but in the many equally valid debits we shall presently consider, the wholesale broadcasting of chemicals would be seen to be more costly in dollars as well as infinitely damaging to the long-range health of the landscape and to all the varied interests that depend on it.

Take, for instance, that commodity prized by every chamber of commerce throughout the land—the good will of vacationing tourists. There is a steadily growing chorus of outraged protest about the disfigurement of once beautiful roadsides by chemical sprays, which substitute a sere expanse of brown, withered vegetation for the beauty of fern and wildflower, of native shrubs adorned with blossom or berry. "We are making a dirty, brown, dying-looking mess along the sides of our roads," a New England woman wrote angrily to her newspaper. "This is not what the tourists expect, with all the money we are spending advertising the beautiful scenery."

In the summer of 1960, conservationists from many states converged on a peaceful Maine island to witness its presentation to the National Audubon Society by its owner, Millicent Todd Bingham. The focus that day was on the preservation of the natural landscape and of the intricate web of life, whose interwoven strands lead from microbes to man. But in the background of all the conversations among the visitors to the island was indignation at the despoiling of the roads they had traveled. Once it had been a joy to follow those roads through the evergreen forests, roads lined with bayberry and sweet fern, alder and huckleberry. Now all was brown desolation. One of the conservationists wrote of that August pilgrimage to a Maine island: "I returned . . . angry at the desecration of the Maine roadsides. Where, in previous years, the highways were bordered with wildflowers and attractive shrubs, there were only the scars of dead vegetation for mile after mile. . . . As an economic proposition, can Maine afford the loss of tourist goodwill that such sights induce?"

Maine roadsides are merely one example, though a particularly sad one for those of us who have a deep love for the beauty of that state, of the senseless destruction that is going on in the name of roadside brush control throughout the nation.

Botanists at the Connecticut Arboretum declare that the elimination of beautiful native shrubs and wildflowers has reached the proportions of a "roadside crisis." Azaleas, mountain laurel, blueberries, huckleberries, viburnums, dogwood, bayberry, sweet fern, low shadbush, winterberry, chokecherry, and wild plum are dying before the chemical barrage. So are the daisies, black-eyed Susans, Queen Anne's lace, goldenrods, and fall asters, which lend grace and beauty to the landscape.

The spraying is not only improperly planned but studded with abuses such as these. In a southern New England town, one contractor finished his work with some chemical remaining in his tank. He discharged this along woodland roadsides where no spraying had been authorized. As a result the community lost the blue-and-golden beauty of its autumn roads, where asters and goldenrod would have made a display worth traveling far to see. In another New England community, a contractor changed the state specifications for town spraying without the knowledge of the highway department and sprayed roadside vegetation to a height of eight feet instead of the specified maximum of four feet, leaving a broad, disfiguring, brown swath. In a Massachusetts community, the town officials purchased a weed-killer from a zealous chemical salesman, unaware that it contained arsenic. One result of the subsequent roadside spraying was the death of a dozen cows from arsenic poisoning.

Trees within the Connecticut Arboretum Natural Area were seriously injured when the town of Waterford sprayed the roadsides with chemical weed-killers in 1957. Even large trees not directly sprayed were affected. The leaves of the oaks began to curl and turn brown, although it was the season for spring growth. Then new shoots began to be put forth and grew with abnormal rapidity, giving a weeping appearance to the trees. Two seasons later, large branches on these trees had died, others were without leaves, and the deformed, weeping effect of whole trees persisted.

I know well a stretch of road where nature's own landscaping has provided a border of alder, viburnum, sweet fern, and juniper with seasonally changing accents of bright flowers, or of fruits hanging in jeweled clusters in the fall. The road had no heavy load of traffic to support; there were few sharp curves or intersections where brush could obstruct the driver's vision. But the sprayers took over and the miles along that road became something to be traversed quickly, a sight to be endured with one's mind closed to thoughts of the sterile and hideous world we are letting our technicians make. But here and there authority had somehow faltered and by an unaccountable oversight there were oases of beauty in the midst of austere and regimented control—oases that made the desecration of the greater part of the road the more unbearable. In such places my spirit lifted to the sight of the drifts of white clover or the clouds of purple vetch with here and there the flaming cup of a wood lily.

Such plants are "weeds" only to those who make a business of selling and applying chemicals. In a volume of *Proceedings* of one of the weed-control conferences that are now regular institutions, I once read an extraordinary statement of a weed-killer's philosophy. The author defended the killing of good plants "simply because they are in bad company." Those who complain about killing wildflowers along roadsides reminded him, he said, of antivivisectionists, "to whom, if one were to judge by their actions, the life of a stray dog is more sacred than the lives of children."

To the author of this paper, many of us would unquestionably be suspect, convicted of some deep perversion of character because we prefer the sight of the vetch and the clover and the wood lily in all their delicate and transient beauty to that of roadsides scorched as by fire, the shrubs brown and brittle, the bracken that once lifted high its proud lacework now withered and drooping. We would seem deplorably weak that we can tolerate the sight of such "weeds," that we do not rejoice in their eradication, that we are not filled with exultation that man has once more triumphed over miscreant nature.

Justice Douglas tells of attending a meeting of federal field men who were discussing protests by citizens against plans for the spraying of sagebrush that I mentioned earlier. . . . These men considered it hilariously funny that an old lady had opposed the plan because the wildflowers would be destroyed. "Yet, was not her right to search out a banded cup or a tiger lily as inalienable as the right of stockmen to search out grass or of a lumberman to claim a tree?" asks this humane and perceptive jurist. "The esthetic values of the wilderness are as much our inheritance as the veins of copper and gold in our hills and the forests in our mountains."

There is of course more to the wish to preserve our roadside vegetation than even such esthetic considerations. In the economy of nature the natural vegetation has its essential place. Hedgerows along country roads and bordering fields provide food, cover, and nesting areas for birds and homes for many small animals. Of some seventy species of shrubs and vines that are typical roadside species in the Eastern states alone, about sixty-five are important to wildlife as food.

Such vegetation is also the habitat of wild bees and other pollinating insects. Man is more dependent on these wild pollinators than he usually realizes. Even the farmer himself seldom understands the value of wild bees and often participates in the very measures that rob him of their services. Some agricultural crops and many wild plants are partly or wholly dependent on the services of the native pollinating insects. Several hundred species of wild bees take part in the pollination of cultivated crops—one hundred species visiting the flowers of alfalfa alone. Without insect pollination, most of the soil-holding and soil-enriching plants of uncultivated areas would die out, with far-reaching consequences to the ecology of the whole region. Many herbs, shrubs, and trees of forests and range depend on native insects for their reproduction; without these plants, many wild animals and range stock would find little food. Now clean cultivation and the chemical destruction of hedgerows and weeds are eliminating the last sanctuaries of these pollinating insects and breaking the threads that bind life to life.

These insects, so essential to our agriculture and indeed to our landscape as we know it, deserve something better from us than the senseless destruction of their habitat. Honeybees and wild bees depend heavily on such "weeds" as goldenrod, mustard, and dandelions for pollen that serves as the food of their young. Vetch furnishes essential spring forage for bees before the alfalfa is in bloom, tiding them over this early season so that they are ready to pollinate the alfalfa. In the fall they depend on goldenrod at a season when no other food is available, to stock up for the winter. By the precise and delicate timing that is nature's own, the emergence of one species of wild bees takes place on the very day of the opening of the willow blossoms. There is no dearth of men who understand these things, but these are not the men who order the wholesale drenching of the landscape with chemicals.

And where are the men who supposedly understand the value of proper habitat for the preservation of wildlife? Too many of them are to be found defending herbicides as "harmless" to wildlife because they are thought to be less toxic than insecticides. Therefore, it is said, no harm is done. But as the herbicides rain down on forest and field, on marsh and rangeland, they are bringing about marked changes and even permanent destruction of wildlife habitat. To destroy the homes and the food of wildlife is perhaps worse in the long run than direct killing.

The irony of this all-out chemical assault on roadsides and utility rights-of-way is twofold. It is perpetuating the problem it seeks to correct, for, as experience has clearly shown, the blanket application of herbicides does not permanently control roadside "brush" and the spraying has to be repeated year after year. And as a further irony, we persist in doing this despite the fact that a perfectly sound method of *selective* spraying is known, which can achieve long-term vegetational control and eliminate repeated spraying in most types of vegetation.

The object of brush control along roads and rights-of-way is not to sweep the land clear of everything but grass; it is, rather, to eliminate plants ultimately tall enough to present an obstruction to drivers' vision or interference with wires on rights-of-way. This means, in general, trees. Most shrubs are low enough to present no hazard; so, certainly, are ferns and wildflowers.

Selective spraying was developed by Dr. Frank Egler during a period of years at the American Museum of Natural History as director of a Committee for Brush Control Recommendations for Rights-of-Way. It took advantage of the inherent stability of nature, building on the fact that most communities of shrubs are strongly resistant to invasion by trees. By comparison, grasslands are easily invaded by tree seedlings. The object of selective spraying is not to produce grass on roadsides and rights-of-way but to eliminate the tall woody plants by direct treatment and to preserve all other vegetation. One treatment may be sufficient, with a possible follow-up for extremely resistant species; thereafter the shrubs assert control and the trees do not return. The best and cheapest controls for vegetation are not chemicals but other plants.

The method has been tested in research areas scattered throughout the eastern United States. Results show that, once properly treated, an area becomes stabilized, *requiring no respraying for at least twenty years.* The spraying can often be done by men on foot, using knapsack sprayers, and having complete control over their material. Sometimes compressor pumps and material can be mounted on truck chassis, but there is no blanket spraying. Treatment is directed only to trees and any exceptionally tall shrubs that must be eliminated. The integrity of the environment is thereby preserved, the enormous value of the wildlife habitat remains intact, and the beauty of shrub and fern and wildflower has not been sacrificed.

Here and there the method of vegetation management by selective spraying has been adopted. For the most part, entrenched custom dies hard and blanket spraying continues to thrive, to exact its heavy annual costs from the taxpayer, and to inflict its damage on the ecological web of life. It thrives, surely, only because the facts are not known. When taxpayers understand that the bill for spraying the town roads should come due only once a generation instead of once a year, they will surely rise up and demand a change of method.

Among the many advantages of selective spraying is the fact that it minimizes the amount of chemical applied to the landscape. There is no broadcasting of material but, rather, concentrated application to the base of the trees. The potential harm to wildlife is therefore kept to a minimum.

The most widely used herbicides are 2,4-D, 2,4,5-T, and related compounds. Whether or not these are actually toxic is a matter of controversy. People spraying their lawns with 2,4-D and becoming wet with spray have occasionally developed severe neuritis and even paralysis. Although such incidents are apparently uncommon, medical authorities advise caution in use of such compounds. Other hazards, more obscure, may also attend the use of 2,4-D. It has been shown experimentally to disturb the basic physiological process of respiration in the cell, and to imitate X-rays in damaging the chromosomes. Some very recent work indicates that reproduction of birds may be adversely affected by these and certain other herbicides at levels far below those that cause death.

Apart from any directly toxic effects, curious indirect results follow the use of certain herbicides. It has been found that animals, both wild herbivores and livestock, are sometimes strangely attracted to a plant that has been sprayed, even though it is not one of their natural foods. If a highly poisonous herbicide such as arsenic has been used, this intense desire to reach the wilting vegetation inevitably has disastrous results. Fatal results may follow, also, from less toxic herbicides if the plant itself happens to be poisonous or perhaps to possess thorns or burs. Poisonous range weeds, for example, have suddenly become attractive to livestock after spraying, and the animals have died from indulging this unnatural appetite. The literature of veterinary medicine abounds in similar examples: swine eating sprayed cockleburs with consequent severe illness, lambs eating sprayed thistles, bees poisoned by pasturing on mustard sprayed after it came into bloom. Wild cherry, the leaves of which are highly poisonous, has exerted a fatal attraction for cattle once its foliage has been sprayed with 2,4-D. Apparently the wilting that follows spraying (or cutting) makes the plant attractive. Ragwort has provided other examples. Livestock ordinarily avoid this plant unless forced to turn to it in late winter and early spring by lack of other forage. However, the animals eagerly feed on it after its foliage has been sprayed with 2,4-D.

The explanation of this peculiar behavior sometimes appears to lie in the changes which the chemical brings about in the metabolism of the plant itself. There is temporarily a marked increase in sugar content, making the plant more attractive to many animals.

Another curious effect of 2,4-D has important effects for livestock, wildlife, and apparently for men as well. Experiments carried out about a decade ago showed that after treatment with this chemical there is a sharp increase in the nitrate content of corn and of sugar beets. The same effect was suspected in sorghum, sunflower, spiderwort, lambs quarters, pigweed, and smartweed. Some of these are normally ignored by cattle, but are eaten with relish after treatment with 2,4-D. A number of deaths among cattle have been traced to sprayed weeds, according to some agricultural specialists. The danger lies in the increase in nitrates, for the peculiar physiology of the ruminant at once poses a critical problem. Most such animals have a digestive system of extraordinary complexity, including a stomach divided into four chambers. The digestion of cellulose is accomplished through the action of micro-organisms (rumen bacteria) in one of the chambers. When the animal feeds on vegetation containing an abnormally high level of nitrates, the micro-organisms in the rumen act on the nitrates to change them into highly toxic nitrites. Thereafter a fatal chain of events ensues: the nitrites act on the blood pigment to form a chocolate-brown substance in which the oxygen is so firmly held that it cannot take part in respiration; hence oxygen is not transferred from the lungs to the tissues. Death occurs within a few hours from anoxia, or lack of oxygen. The various reports of livestock losses after grazing on certain weeds treated with 2,4-D therefore have a logical explanation. The same danger exists for wild animals, belonging to the group of ruminants, such as deer, antelope, sheep, and goats.

Although various factors (such as exceptionally dry weather) can cause an increase in nitrate content, the effect of the soaring sales and applications of 2,4-D cannot be ignored. The situation was considered important enough by the University of Wisconsin Agricultural Experiment Station to justify a warning in 1957 that "plants killed by 2,4-D may contain large amounts of nitrate." The hazard extends to human beings as well as animals and may help to explain the recent mysterious increase in "silo deaths." When corn, oats, or sorghum containing large amounts of nitrates are ensiled they release poisonous nitrogen-oxide gases, creating a deadly hazard to anyone entering the silo. Only a few breaths of one of these gases can cause a diffuse chemical pneumonia. In a series of such cases studied by the University of Minnesota Medical School, all but one terminated fatally.

Once again we are walking in nature like an elephant in the china cabinet." So C. J. Briejèr, a Dutch scientist of rare understanding, sums up our use of weed-killers. "In my opinion too much is taken for granted. We do not know whether all weeds in crops are harmful or whether some of them are useful," says Dr. Briejèr.

Seldom is the question asked, What is the relation between the weed and the soil? Perhaps, even from our narrow standpoint of direct self-interest, the relation is a useful one. As we have seen, soil and the living things in and upon it exist in a relation of interdependence and mutual benefit. Presumably the weed is taking something from the soil; perhaps it is also contributing something to it. A practical example was provided recently by the parks in a city in Holland. The roses were doing badly. Soil samples showed heavy infestations by tiny nematode worms. Scientists of the Dutch Plant Protection Service did not recommend chemical sprays or soil treatments; instead, they suggested that marigolds be planted among the roses. This plant, which the purist would doubtless consider a weed in any rosebed, releases an excretion from its roots that kills the soil nematodes. The advice was taken; some beds were planted with marigolds, some left without as controls. The results were striking. With the aid of the marigolds the roses flourished; in the control beds they were sickly and drooping. Marigolds are now used in many places for combating nematodes.

In the same way, and perhaps quite unknown to us, other plants that we ruthlessly eradicate may be performing a function that is necessary to the health of the soil. One very useful function of natural plant communities—now pretty generally stigmatized as "weeds"—is to serve as an indicator of the condition of the soil. This useful function is of course lost where chemical weed-killers have been used.

Those who find an answer to all problems in spraying also overlook a matter of great scientific importance—the need to preserve some natural plant communities. We need these as a standard against which we can measure the changes our own activities bring about. We need them as wild habitats in which original populations of insects and other organisms can be maintained, for . . . the development of resistance to insecticides is changing the genetic factors of insects and perhaps other organisms. One scientist has even suggested that some sort of "zoo" should be established to preserve insects, mites, and the like, before their genetic composition is further changed.

Some experts warn of subtle but far-reaching vegetational shifts as a result of the growing use of herbicides. The chemical 2,4-D, by killing out the broad-leaved plants, allows the grasses to thrive in the reduced competition—now some of the grasses themselves have become "weeds," presenting a new problem in control and giving the cycle another turn. This strange situation is acknowledged in a recent issue of a journal devoted to crop problems: "With the widespread use of 2,4-D to control broad-leaved weeds, grass weeds in particular have increasingly become a threat to corn and soybean yields."

Ragweed, the bane of hay-fever sufferers, offers an interesting example of the way efforts to control nature sometimes boomerang. Many thousands of gallons of chemicals have been discharged along roadsides in the name of ragweed control. But the unfortunate truth is that blanket spraying is resulting in more ragweed, not less. Ragweed is an annual; its seedlings require open soil to become established each year. Our best protection against this plant is therefore the maintenance of dense shrubs, ferns, and other perennial vegetation. Spraying frequently destroys this protective vegetation and creates open, barren areas which the ragweed hastens to fill. It is probable, moreover, that the pollen content of the atmosphere is not related to roadside ragweed, but to the ragweed of city lots and fallow fields.

The booming sales of chemical crabgrass-killers are another example of how readily unsound methods catch on. There is a cheaper and better way to remove crabgrass than to attempt year after year to kill it out with chemicals. This is to give it competition of a kind it cannot survive, the competition of other grass. Crabgrass exists only in an unhealthy lawn. It is a symptom, not a disease in itself. By providing a fertile soil and giving the desired grasses a good start, it is possible to create an environment in which crabgrass cannot grow, for it requires open space in which it can start from seed year after year.

Instead of treating the basic condition, suburbanites—advised by nurserymen who in turn have been advised by the chemical manufacturers—continue to apply truly astonishing amounts of crabgrass-killers to their lawns each year. Marketed under trade names which give no hint of their nature, many of these preparations contain such poisons as mercury, arsenic, and chlordane. Application at the recommended rates leaves tremendous amounts of these chemicals on the lawn. Users of one product, for example, apply sixty pounds of technical chlordane to the acre if they follow directions. If they use another of the many available products, they are applying 175 pounds of metallic arsenic to the acre. The toll of dead birds ... is distressing. How lethal these lawns may be for human beings is unknown.

The success of selective spraying for roadside and right-of-way vegetation, where it has been practiced, offers hope that equally sound ecological methods may be developed for other vegetation programs for farms, forests, and ranges—methods aimed not at destroying a particular species but at managing vegetation as a living community.

Other solid achievements show what can be done. Biological control has achieved some of its most spectacular successes in the area of curbing unwanted vegetation. Nature herself has met many of the problems that now beset us, and she has usually solved them in her own successful way. Where man has been intelligent enough to observe and to emulate Nature he, too, is often rewarded with success.

An outstanding example in the field of controlling unwanted plants is the handling of the Klamath-weed problem in California. Although the Klamath weed, or goatweed, is a native of Europe (where it is called Saint-John's-wort), it accompanied man in his westward migrations, first appearing in the United States in 1793 near Lancaster, Pennsylvania. By 1900, it had reached California in the vicinity of the Klamath River, hence the name locally given to it. By 1929, it had occupied about a hundred thousand acres of rangeland, and by 1952 it had invaded some two and one half million acres.

Klamath weed, quite unlike such native plants as sagebrush, has no place in the ecology of the region, and no animals or other plants require its presence. On the contrary, wherever it appeared, livestock became "scabby, sore-mouthed, and unthrifty" from feeding on this toxic plant. Land values declined accordingly, for the Klamath weed was considered to hold the first mortgage.

In Europe, the Klamath weed . . . has never become a problem, because along with the plant there have developed various species of insects; these feed on it so extensively that its abundance is severely limited. In particular, two species of beetles in southern France, pea-sized and of metallic color, have their whole beings so adapted to the presence of the weed that they feed and reproduce only upon it.

It was an event of historic importance when the first shipments of these beetles were brought to the United States in 1944, for this was the first attempt in North America to control a plant with a plant-eating insect. By 1948, both species had become so well established that no further importations were needed. Their spread was accomplished by collecting beetles from the original colonies and redistributing them at the rate of millions a year. Within small areas the beetles accomplish their own dispersion, moving on as soon as the Klamath weed dies out and locating new stands with great precision. And as the beetles thin out the weed, desirable range plants that have been crowded out are able to return.

A ten-year survey completed in 1959 showed that control of the Klamath weed had been "more effective than hoped for even by enthusiasts," with the weed reduced to a mere 1 percent of its former abundance. This token infestation is harmless and is actually needed in order to maintain a population of beetles as protection against a future increase in the weed.

Another extraordinarily successful and economical example of weed control may be found in Australia. With the colonists' usual taste for carrying plants or animals into a new country, a Captain Arthur Phillip had brought various species of cactus into Australia about 1787, intending to use them in culturing cochineal insects for dye. Some of the cacti or prickly pears escaped from his gardens, and by 1925 about twenty species could be found growing wild. Having no natural controls in this new territory, they spread prodigiously, eventually occupying about sixty million acres. At least half of this land was so densely covered as to be useless.

In 1920, Australian entomologists were sent to North and South America to study insect enemies of the prickly pears in their native habitat. After trials of several species, three billion eggs of an Argentine moth were released in Australia in 1930. Seven years later, the last dense growth of the prickly pear had been destroyed and the once uninhabitable areas reopened to settlement and grazing. The whole operation had cost less than a penny per acre. In contrast, the unsatisfactory attempts at chemical control in earlier years had cost about ten pounds per acre.

Both of these examples suggest that extremely effective control of many kinds of unwanted vegetation might be achieved by paying more attention to the role of plant-eating insects. The science of range management has largely ignored this possibility, although these insects are perhaps the most selective of all grazers and their highly restricted diets could easily be turned to man's advantage.

Sharon Bertsch McGrayne

Barbara McClintock

hen a Miss Barbara McClintock of St. Louis announced her 1936 engagement in the newspapers, the chairman of the University of Missouri's botany department was horrified. Mistaking his new thirty-four-year-old assistant professor for the woman in the newspaper, he summoned Dr. Barbara McClintock to his office. Then he threatened her, "If you get married, you'll be fired."

The University of Missouri was "awful, awful, awful," McClintock complained years later. "The situation for women was unbelievable, it was so bad."

Eventually, she marched into the dean's office and asked pointblank whether she would ever get on the university's permanent staff. He shook his head no. In fact, he confided, when her mentor left she would probably be fired.

McClintock retorted that she was taking an immediate leave of absence without pay and that she would never return. Then she packed her Model A Ford with all her belongings and drove off, without a job or even any prospect of a job. Toying with the idea of becoming a weather forecaster, she finally decided that she never wanted a job of any kind again. It was years before she changed her mind.

McClintock was at the top of American science when she quit it. She had revolutionized maize genetics; one of her early experiments still ranks among the twentieth century's most important biological experiments. She was the vice-president of the Genetics Society of America and was about to become its president. She had not yet done her Nobel Prize–winning project, but she had already received an honorary doctorate from a well-known university and would soon be elected to the National Academy of Sciences, then the nation's highest scientific honor.

McClintock's vigor, intensity, and enthusiasm marked her as special, and by the time she graduated in 1923, she was already deep in graduate work. So were many other young American women. Between 30 and 40 percent of all graduate students in the United States during the 1920s were women. In fact, women accounted for approximately 12 percent of the science and engineering Ph.D.'s awarded in the United States—a proportion they would not reach again until the 1970s. Most studied biology, and almost one in five was a botanist. A goodly number of them specialized in genetics. Most of the rest were in zoology and psychology, which required little mathematics.

Getting a good science education, however, was much easier than getting a research job. Industry, government, and most colleges and universities refused to hire women. Most women scientists taught in women's colleges, where teaching loads were heavy and research time was short. Only 4 percent of women scientists in the United States were employed by coeducational colleges and universities, and they were concentrated in home economics and physical education and in low-ranking positions as assistants, instructors, and assistant professors.

Genetics, however, was a wide-open field. McClintock and genetics were born and raised together. Gregor Mendel's studies of heredity in garden peas were rediscovered in 1900, just two years before McClintock's birth. By the 1920s, genetics was America's first world-class science and biology's most abstract specialty. When McClintock entered graduate school in 1923, many biologists still did not accept Mendelian genetics. The word "gene" had been coined but it had no clear definition or physical reality. It was just an abstract concept and controversial theory describing the way inherited traits are passed from one generation to another. As Thomas Hunt Morgan put it, geneticists assumed "there is something in the egg that is responsible for every detail of character that later develops out of the egg."

As McClintock began her career, fruit flies and corn were vying as genetics' leading research tool. Cornell geneticists worked with corn, however. Scientifically known as *Zea mays*, corn is an economically important crop. It was an ideal research tool, too. The variegated colors of its kernels functioned like a Technicolor spread sheet of genetic data; genetic changes were as plain as the kernels on the cob. Furthermore, maize could be self-fertilized, inbred to produce tightly controlled extremes of genetic behavior. Each maize plant produces both male and female flowers: female flowers, borne on the ear, contain egg cells; male flowers, produced in the tassel at the top of the stalk, contain sperm cells, known as pollen.

When spring-planted corn reached sexual maturity in July, Cornell's geneticists began working from dawn to dark seven days a week to control the mating. Normally, wind wafts pollen from the tassel of one plant to the silk of another. There a pollen grain germinates, growing a long phallic tube down through a silk to carry the sperm to the egg at the bottom of the cob. Sperm and egg cells fuse, starting the next generation's seed, a kernel on the cob. Each fertilization produces one kernel.

To prevent random promiscuity, geneticists cover the ears and tassels with paper bags and transfer the pollen to the silk by hand. To self-fertilize a plant and inbreed exotic strains, they fertilize the silk of one plant with its own pollen.

Despite the attractions of maize as a research tool, Cornell's geneticists had not studied its chromosomes. They had no way to identify which chromosomes carried which inherited traits. Working in the botany department because Cornell's plant breeders refused to have women in their department, McClintock devised a system.

Using new staining techniques, she discovered that each of the ten chromosomes in maize could be distinguished under a microscope by their tiny knobs, extensions, and constrictions. Then she went on to identify each chromosome with a group of visible traits that are generally inherited together. By plotting the probability of these traits' appearing together, she mapped the position of the genes on the chromosomes, just as Morgan had done with the fruit fly.

At first, none of her Cornell colleagues understood her project. Then Marcus Rhoades, who had earned his Ph.D. with Morgan, came to Cornell. Rhoades immediately realized how good McClintock was. "Hell," he said, "it was so damn obvious. She was something special." Immediately, he asked McClintock, "Can I join you?" Then Rhoades—her champion, interpreter, and soulmate for decades to come—explained the importance of McClintock's work to Cornell.

From then on, McClintock was the enthusiastic leader of a little band of professors and young men who already had their Ph.D.'s. "It was quite a remarkable thing that this woman who hadn't gotten her Ph.D. yet, or probably even her master's, had these postdocs trailing around after her, just lapping up the stimulation that she provided," recalled Ernest Abbe, later a University of Minnesota professor. "Lester G. Sharp was a prominent geneticist, but she was telling him what the answers were. It was very cute," Abbe said with a laugh. McClintock even interviewed prospective graduate students for faculty members, because she noticed so much more than anyone else. Later, during the late 1920s and early 1930s, Sharp propagated McClintock's research to the genetics community at large in his authoritative textbook *An Introduction to Cytology.* "His textbook was very important in getting her recognition early on," Abbe emphasized.

As she recalled, McClintock and her little band "did very powerful work with chromosomes. It began to put cytogenetics, working with chromosomes, on the map in the late 1920s—early 1930s. . . . It was just a little group of young people. The older people couldn't join; they just didn't understand. The young people were the ones who really got the subject going, because they worked intensely with each other. It was group activity, because they discussed everything and were constantly thinking about what they could do to show this, that, or the other thing." Two members of the group, McClintock and George Beadle, would later win Nobel Prizes, Beadle for his "one gene, one enzyme" hypothesis. Following McClintock's lead, the Cornell maize group entered its golden age.

McClintock's enthusiasm and intensity swept her ahead of the others. She worked in spurts, night and day for weeks, to solve a problem. During a long drought, she saved her corn by laying water pipes up to her hilltop patch; standing in the hot sun, she watered her plants with tears of fatigue coursing down her cheeks. During a late-night flood, she replanted her washed-out corn by the light of car headlights. To Beadle's dismay, McClintock could interpret his experimental data faster than he. He complained to the department chairman, the eminent geneticist Rollins A. Emerson. "Emerson told him that he should be grateful there was someone around who could explain it," McClintock commented dryly. "The fun was solving problems, like a game. It was entertaining."

McClintock earned her Ph.D. degree in 1927 at age twenty-five and stayed on as botany instructor. Over the next few years, she published nine papers on maize chromosomes. Rhoades considered each one a milestone in genetics and thought that she already deserved a Nobel Prize.

In the meantime, McClintock's mother still hoped her daughter would quit work and get married. "Every time I went home at vacation time, she'd try to persuade me to let somebody go up and get my things and not go back. It was a real fear on her part that I'd be a professor." But McClintock finally decided that she was too independent for close emotional relationships. She had a faithful beau, her undergraduate chemistry instructor Arthur Sherburne, but she concluded that "marriage would have been a disaster. Men weren't strong enough . . . and I knew I was a dominant person. I *knew* they would want to lean against you. . . . They're not decisive. They may be very sweet and gentle, and I knew that I'd become very intolerant, that I'd make their lives miserable." Eventually, she told Sherburne "not to stay in touch with me."

Instead of marrying, she managed her life with "a fastidious spareness, an aesthetic of order and functionality," as her biographer

Evelyn Fox Keller expressed it. Highly organized, McClintock arranged her data on cards, the cobs neatly tagged and cross-referenced to tables. She scheduled her time so that she could play a fast tennis game each day at five o'clock and still drive to her friend Dr. Esther Parker's cottage for supper before dark. Dr. Parker, a physician, had been an ambulance driver during World War I for the American Friends Service Committee. Her house was McClintock's home away from home.

Late in the summer of 1929, Harriet Creighton came to Cornell as a botany graduate student from Wellesley College. Within minutes of their meeting, McClintock had organized Creighton's academic career, too, steering her to the right courses and advisers. Technically, instructors were too low-level to advise graduate students, but, practically speaking, McClintock was in charge. McClintock gave Creighton her best research project as a thesis topic. In the late 1920s, there was circumstantial evidence, but no hard proof, that chromosomes carried and exchanged genetic information to produce new combinations of physical traits. McClintock wanted the proof.

She had bred a special strain of corn with an easily identifiable ninth chromosome that usually produced waxy purple kernels. Under her microscope, she could see an elongated tip on one end of the ninth chromosome and a knob that readily absorbed stain at the other end. According to her mathematical analysis, the elongated tip was located near the region of the chromosome that determined whether the plant would produce waxy kernels. She suspected that the region near the knob was responsible for supplying purple pigment.

That spring, Creighton and McClintock planted waxy purple kernels from the strain. In July, they fertilized the silks with pollen from a plant of the same strain whose kernels were exactly opposite types—that is, they were neither waxy nor purple.

That fall, when McClintock and Creighton harvested the ears, some of them had the usual waxy purple kernels and some kernels were the opposite, neither waxy nor purple. But some ears were different: they had inherited one trait—but not both. Thus, they were either waxy or purple, but not both. When McClintock and Creighton examined the chromosomes of these new kernels under their microscopes, they could see that their structure had changed markedly. Physical bits of the ninth chromosome—either the knob or the elongated tip—had actually exchanged places. Where every elongated chromosome in the parent plants had a knob, they now found a mix: elongated chromosomes without knobs, and knobby chromosomes without tips.

McClintock and Creighton had proved that genes for physical traits are carried on the chromosomes. They had produced the first physical proof that exchanging chromosomal parts helps create the amazing variety of forms present in the biological universe.

Normally, McClintock liked to publish enormous amounts of supporting data in her papers; today, each one of her reports would make several separate articles. So she was waiting for a second crop before publishing the data. Luckily, Thomas Hunt Morgan visited Cornell and heard about the experiment. He urged them to publish immediately. In his excitement, he wrote a journal editor that an important article would arrive in two weeks. Thanks to Morgan, McClintock's article was published in August 1931. A few months later, a German geneticist, Curt Stern, published parallel data on fruit flies. Had McClintock waited for another crop, Stern would have been first.

The paper made McClintock's reputation. "Beyond any question, this is one of the truly great experiments of modern biology," Mordecai L. Gabriel and Seymour Fogel declared in their book *Great Experiments in Biology.* James A. Peters, editor of *Classic Papers in Genetics,* wrote, "This paper has been called a landmark in experimental genetics. It is more than that—it is a cornerstone." Then he warned, "It is not an easy paper to follow, for the items that require retention throughout the analysis are many and it is fatal to one's understanding to lose track of any of them. Mastery of this paper, however, can give one the strong feeling of being able to master almost anything else he might have to wrestle with in biology." James Shapiro, a University of Chicago microbiologist, told the *New Scientist* magazine that the experiment should have won a Nobel Prize by itself.

When Marcus Rhoades asked McClintock how she learned so much from a microscope, she replied, "Well, you know, when I look at a cell, I get down in that cell and look around." Explaining the remark later, she said, "You're not conscious of anything else. . . . You are so absorbed that even small things get big. . . . Nothing else matters. You're noticing more and more things that most people couldn't see because they didn't go intently over each part, slowly but with great intensity. . . . It's the intensity of your absorption. I'm sure painters have the same thing happen right along."

"When you're doing something like this, the depth of your thinking is very penetrating. You can feel the intensity of it," she added. Many scientists believe that the thrill of discovery is unique to science. But McClintock contended that engineers, historians, and writers—"anyone who must think intensely and integrate vast amounts of information to solve a problem"—must feel it, too. "The thrill comes from being intensely absorbed in the material."

By this time, McClintock knew she would have to leave Cornell. Emerson, the department chairman, was one of her greatest fans, but he could not override the faculty, who were strongly opposed to giving permanent faculty positions to women.

For the next five years, from 1931 to 1936, McClintock crisscrossed the country in her beloved Model A Ford. At the top of her profession, she was at the bottom of the career ladder. While her friends worked frantically to find her a permanent job, she won a series of short-term fellowships to do research at various universities. The fellowships were highly prestigious stepping-stones for men on the way to professorships. For the few women who received them, however, they were stopgaps intended to tide them over.

Years later, McClintock explained in a speech to the American Association of University Women what those fellowships meant to her: "For the young person, fellowships are of the greatest importance. The freedom they allow for concentrated study and research cannot be duplicated by any other known method. They come at a time when one's energies are greatest and when one's courage and capacity to enter new fields and utilize new techniques are at their height."

Of all the advances in genetics during the 1920s, one of the greatest was the discovery that X-rays enormously speed up the rate of mutations, fifteen-hundred-fold in fruit flies, for example.

Instead of waiting for spontaneous mutations, scientists now could produce them at will. Lewis Stadler had a Rockefeller grant to build a genetics center at the University of Missouri to study X-ray-induced mutations. Stadler planted a field with kernels from X-ray-irradiated pollen and asked McClintock to figure out how the mutations had occurred.

Studying Stadler's fields, McClintock discovered that X-rays actually break a plant's chromosomes and leave them with damaged, frayed ends. Then she was surprised to see the chromosomes mend themselves: their frayed ends fuse with the frayed ends of other damaged chromosomes. She even found that some damaged chromosomes fuse together in rings. Often, two fragments fuse in such a way that the ends of the repaired chromosome pull in opposite directions during cell division and make the chromosome break *again*. As a chromosome breaks, repairs itself, and rebreaks, its ends lose more and more genetic material. She called the entire process the breakage-fusion-bridge cycle.

Many scientists would have been content to have discovered ring chromosomes, but McClintock was always interested in maize for the clues it offered to nature as a whole. She constantly tried to integrate her specialized studies with broad questions regarding heredity in other species. Thus, when she discovered ring chromosomes, she immediately asked how the frayed ends of the damaged chromosomes find each other and repair themselves. If the genetic process includes emergency repairs, it must be able to recognize and process information. As she pointed out, "The conclusion seems inescapable that cells are able to sense the presence in their nuclei of ruptured ends of chromosomes and then to activate a mechanism that will bring together and then unite these ends, one with another. . . . The ability of a cell to sense these broken ends, to direct them toward each other, and then to unite them so that the union of two DNA strands is correctly oriented is a particularly revealing example of the sensitivity of cells to all that is going on within them."

McClintock's insight came a good fifteen years before other scientists, like Evelyn Witkin, began work on DNA-repair processes in the 1950s. McClintock was already poking holes in the standard picture of the chromosome as a rigid string of stable genes, arranged like pearls along a necklace chromosome. She was starting to think of the genetic process as responsive to signals, processing information, and receiving and interpreting signals from inside and outside the cell. She was looking at nature afresh, free of the conceptual constraints that most scientists work within, observed Witkin, who, until her retirement, was the Barbara McClintock Professor of Genetics at Rutgers University. Eventually, McClintock's unbiased approach would meet head-on with those who still believed in the stable chromosome.

When McClintock and her Model A Ford moved on to Caltech in 1931, she was the first woman postdoctoral fellow to work at the men's school. Although McClintock was paying her own way with her fellowship, Caltech's board of trustees had to give its approval before she could come. Her first day there, a colleague took her to lunch at Caltech's elegant faculty club. As she walked the length of the dining room to an empty table, everyone stopped eating and stared at the tiny thirty-year-old woman with her boyish figure, tousled hair, and practical clothes. To Warren Weaver of the Rockefeller Foundation, she seemed "more boy than girl."

Alarmed at the stares, McClintock demanded, "What's wrong with me?"

"Oh, everyone's heard about the trustees' meeting, and they're looking you over," her host replied cheerily.

Caltech's practice was to make visiting researchers with fellowships automatic members of the faculty club, but McClintock was never allowed in the building again. Nor did she visit any labs other than her own and that of Linus Pauling, the politically liberal chemist who later won two Nobel Prizes. Scientifically, however, her visits to Caltech were productive. Two summers later, she discovered the nucleolar organizer there. The nucleolar-organizer region of the chromosome helps form the nucleolus, the cell's factory for synthesizing ribosomes. Although Caltech would not hire her full-time, she did not mind helping men who were hired there. When Charles Burnham, one of her old gang at Cornell, asked her what he should teach in his cytology-techniques class at Caltech, she laid the course out for him. It was 1971 before Caltech hired its first woman professor.

Using her Guggenheim fellowship, McClintock visited Germany in 1933, the traumatic year in which Hitler became chancellor and fired the Jews from German universities. Science laboratories were in chaos, and her student residence was empty except for herself and a Chinese gentleman, who dined in silence. Loneliness, the politicizing of genetics, and the persecution of Jews appalled her. In December, she fled back to Cornell.

She returned at a bad time. The Depression was worsening and universities were cutting back. Few could afford a pure researcher. As Warren Weaver observed at Cornell, "The Dept. of Botany does not wish to reappoint her, chiefly because they realize that her interest is entirely in research and that she will leave Ithaca as soon as she can obtain suitable employment elsewhere; and partly because she is not entirely successful as a teacher of undergraduate work. The Botany Dept. obviously prefers a less gifted person who will be content to accept a large amount of routine duty."

Friends interceded with the Rockefeller Foundation, however, and arranged eighteen hundred dollars a year for McClintock to spend two more years at Cornell. Morgan wrote the foundation that "she is highly specialized, her genius being restricted to the cytology of maize genetics, but she is definitely the best person in the world in this narrow category." The eighteen hundred dollars was the largest income McClintock had ever earned.

Testifying in her behalf, Morgan also confided that "she is sore at the world because of her conviction that she would have a much freer scientific opportunity if she were a man." But McClintock denies that she was ever bitter. Realistic at recognizing prejudice, yes, but never bitter. "If you want to do something, you have to pay the price and never take it seriously. I never worried. I couldn't compete with men, so I didn't try."

When McClintock left Cornell for good in 1936, Cornell's golden age of maize genetics ended. After years of trying to get her a permanent position, friends had finally found her a job with Lewis Stadler at the University of Missouri starting in 1936. She would be only an assistant professor—far below the rank and pay of a man with comparable attainments—but it was her first faculty position. Her wandering years were over. Or so she thought.

For several years, McClintock worked in Columbia, Missouri, during the winter and raised her corn plants at Cornell during the summer. She grew only a few thousand plants each year, but they were highly selected, so she had no waste. "I wanted to know each plant well, so I carefully organized what I was going to need and why, and how many samples I needed in each case. I was highly organized . . . so that it was manageable. It had to be manageable. The recording was equally foolproof. I didn't want to have anything come up that seemed irrational and not right, and if I did it myself I would know, because my memory would tell me where to look . . . and how to find the error."

Helen Crouse, who had read McClintock's nucleolus paper as an undergraduate at Goucher College, visited Ithaca the summer of 1938. When she asked a timid young man how to find McClintock's lab, he replied, "Oh, well, she's up under the roof, and she doesn't want to see anybody." But he took Crouse up anyway. McClintock came to the door with a green, opaque visor over her eyes and a cigarette in a long filter holder in her hand. "What do you want?" she demanded. Crouse turned around, but her companion had vanished. After Crouse introduced herself, McClintock answered, "I heard you were coming. I was expecting you. Let's go home for lunch."

Home was Dr. Parker's house. When they got to the porch, McClintock sprayed their ankles well with flea repellent because Parker kept three large Irish setters. "We had a great lunch with Dr. Parker, who never knew whether her dress was right- or wrong-side out and didn't care. She was a wonderful vigorous sort of person. And I must have stayed a week," Crouse said. A few weeks later, McClintock invited Crouse to the Genetics Society meeting in Woods Hole, Massachusetts. "I didn't have fifty cents; but she said she'd pay all my expenses to go, that she'd like to have someone to go with her," Crouse said. "I had a glorious time."

After Crouse's sun-filled visits in Cornell and Woods Hole, she started graduate studies at the University of Missouri. There she was surprised to discover that McClintock's position was not only clouded over but downright stormy. As a teacher, McClintock was intense, inspiring, and so full of ideas and fast talk that it was hard to keep up. She had insisted on proper equipment, and the university bought her new microscopes for a lab course. She installed them late on Friday night, putting a slide in each and delicately adjusting their lights and lenses to highlight the important feature in each demonstration. The next morning, the students gave a passing glance to the demonstrations on their way to pollinate their fields. McClintock was crushed. On the way to lunch with Crouse, she burst into tears—because the "corn boys" had skipped some of the slides. "She took it all so intensely," Crouse realized.

As usual, McClintock was way ahead of everyone else. Taking a quick look through Crouse's microscope one day, she discovered more than Crouse had found in her own material. Crouse had not adjusted her microscope's light and lens properly, and McClintock stalked out of the lab, slamming the door behind her. "You had to have a pretty sturdy constitution to survive," Crouse decided. McClintock was not about to waste her time on inept students, especially when jobs were scarce for even the best.

McClintock reigned over a spacious third-floor lab like "the Queen Bee. Everyone was scared of her," according to Crouse. Technically, Crouse was not McClintock's graduate student, so there was little tension between them. But McClintock's sharp tongue so terrified one of her official graduate students that he fled by the back greenhouse door whenever she entered the front. Another young man escaped to Berkeley.

Although the Rockefeller Foundation regarded Stadler and McClintock as the leaders of the genetics center at Missouri, university administrators thought that McClintock was a troublemaker and hoped she would leave. Everyone wore knickers for field research, but McClintock wore pants *all* the time. She even let her students work in the lab past the 11:00 P.M. campus curfew. Then, one Sunday, she forgot her keys, climbed into her lab through a ground-floor window, and totally scandalized the locals. The culture shock was reciprocal. Crouse was appalled that agriculture students practiced their hog-calling on campus. She was even more upset to learn that wildlife students hunted at night by blinding animals with their car headlights before they shot them.

McClintock was in a no-win situation. Excluded from faculty meetings, she was not part of the department. The authorities would not accommodate her research needs; she arranged for substitute lecturers each fall so that she could harvest her plants in Cornell, but the administration disapproved. At the same time, she could not get another job. She was expected to recommend male colleagues for the likes of Yale, Harvard, and elsewhere—"jobs that would have been just right for me, with my experience"—but she was never considered for those jobs herself. Finally, in 1941, she had it out with the dean and hit the road.

"I just quit the whole business," McClintock declared. She had no job, no means of support, no place to work, and no prospects.

She did not care about her career, but she did care about her corn. Writing Marcus Rhoades, then at Columbia University, she inquired where he grew his plants. "Cold Spring Harbor" was the reply.

Cold Spring Harbor had been founded on rural Long Island in 1890 as a summer center for the study of Darwin's evolution theory. In 1941, a handful of researchers worked there year-round, financed by the Carnegie Institution of Washington. In summertime, as many as sixty geneticists, including Harriet Creighton, Marcus Rhoades, Max Delbrück, and Salvador Luria, flocked there.

McClintock wangled an invitation to plant her corn at Cold Spring Harbor that summer. In the fall, she stayed on in a summer house until the weather turned cold and Marcus Rhoades lent her a spare room in his New York apartment. Finally, a friend, Milislav Demerec, became genetics director at the lab and offered her a temporary position.

Before she could get permanent status from the Carnegie Institution, she had to go to Washington, D.C., to be interviewed by its president, Vannevar Bush. Demerec nagged McClintock to go, but she kept postponing the trip. Finally, he ordered her to take a plane.

Not caring whether she was hired or fired, McClintock went to see Bush "with complete freedom from any nervousness. And, as a consequence, we had a very good time talking, because I simply didn't care what his opinion would be. It took three or four years before I realized that I could stay in a job, that this was more like no job at all. I had complete freedom. . . . I could do what I wanted to do, and there were no comments. It was simply perfect."

The decade that had started so disastrously in Missouri ended gloriously at Cold Spring Harbor. It was Barbara McClintock's kind of place. Everyone wore blue jeans, worked seventy to eighty hours a week, and loved biological research. Teaching was not required, and there were no restrictions on research.

McClintock settled into a routine undisturbed by passing decades. She alternated quiet winters analyzing data with busy summers filled with visitors and corn-growing. For exercise, she ran, swam, and played tennis. Loaded with field guides, she took long nature walks, gathering black walnuts for brownies or checking the spots on ladybug beetles.

In addition to her cornfield, she had a spacious laboratory within a stone's throw of Long Island Sound. Seven days a week she worked from early morning until late evening on a long surface made of several desks pushed together. In a small side room she stored boxes of dried corncobs, each carefully tagged and cross-referenced so that when colleagues asked for seed of a particular strain she could explain its lineage.

Life at Cold Spring Harbor became both McClintock's strength and her weakness. Thanks to the support of the Carnegie Institution, she could work without interruption, even on unpopular projects. But isolation also left her without colleagues to popularize her research to the scientific community at large. For the first time in her career, McClintock would have to explain her own work.

She began reaping the benefits of her international reputation during her early years at Cold Spring. In 1944, she was elected the first woman president of the Genetics Society of America. That same year, she was named to the prestigious National Academy of Sciences, which had admitted only two other women in eighty-one years. Surprisingly, when McClintock heard about the honor, she burst into bitter tears. Had she been a man, she said, she would have been delighted by the honor. But as a woman, she felt trapped. She wanted to be free to walk out on genetics if she ever got bored.

Now she would never be able to leave it. "It was awful because of the responsibility to women," she explained. "I couldn't let them down." As she wrote a friend, "Jews, women, and Negroes are accustomed to discrimination and don't expect much. I am not a feminist, but I am always gratified when illogical barriers are broken—for Jews, women, Negroes, etc. It helps all of us."

World War II had put women to work in unprecedented numbers. In its wake, McClintock felt buoyant and self-confident enough in 1947 to declare, "Opportunities for women have never been greater than they are at the present time. There is no question in my mind that these opportunities will become increasingly better and at a very rapid rate. The restrictions in opportunity . . . are being steadily removed."

Challenging her maize plants with broken-chromosome problems at Cold Spring Harbor, McClintock was fascinated by their response. During the winter of 1944–1945, she planted a greenhouse with self-pollinated kernels. Each was the heir to a long traumatic history of inbreeding and self-fertilization that had resulted in broken arms at the end of their ninth chromosome. When the seedlings sprouted, she was astounded. The leaves had broken out with quirky patches of curiously colored patterns. Moreover, the bizarre patches occurred in pairs. The left of one plant, for example, had two albino splotches of similar size side by side: one patch contained many fine green streaks but its complementary twin patch contained only a few green streaks. The results, McClintock thought, were startlingly conspicuous and totally unexpected. Generations of breaking, healing, and rebreaking the chromosomes had created a crisis in the plant's genetic system. Every time a cell divided, chromosomes broke and some genes were lost.

Because the complementary patches sat side by side, McClintock immediately realized that some bizarre event had struck the plant's cells as they had divided. "One cell had gained something that the other cell had lost," she told herself. "I set about to find out what it was." Eventually, she realized that, when a chromosome that has broken and re-fused breaks in two again, one of its parts may gain some genetic material while the other part may lose some.

From the beginning, she knew she had discovered a basic genetic phenomenon, not just an event unique to maize. Long before scientists knew that genes are made of DNA, she asked the next question: How are genes controlled?

Comparing chromosomes of both the plants and their parents under her microscope, she deduced that parts of their chromosomes had changed positions. Six years of painstaking research later, she would be able to prove that a gene need not have a fixed position on a chromosome. She would conclude that genes are not stable pearls laid out along a chromosome string. Instead, they can move around and turn on and off at various times during a cell's development.

Eventually, McClintock described and characterized two new kinds of genetic elements. The first is a controlling element, a switch to turn on and off the genes that express physical characteristics like color or size. The second type is an activator that can make the on-and-off switch jump around from one part of a chromosome to another. Today, McClintock's discovery is called genetic transposition, and the moving chromosome parts are called transposable elements, transposons, or "jumping" genes.

Thus, an activator gene can cause the off-switch gene to jump next to a pigment gene and turn off the color. If the off-switch turns off the pigment gene early in a plant's development, a large region of the plant gets no pigment. If the pigment gene is turned off partway through development, parts of the plant are streaked or spotted with color. When the activator makes the off-switch turn back on, the pigment gene resumes work.

As a result, not only are genes unstable, but their mutation effects are, too. Geneticists had assumed that a mutated gene was dead and could not be reactivated. But McClintock showed that environmental conditions could reverse some mutations and turn the genes back on. Her experiments provided a radically fluid picture of genetics, in contrast to the old view of stable mutations and immovable genes.

The implications of transposable elements fascinated McClintock even more than the discovery itself. She saw immediately that transposons are a fundamental phenomenon that helps explain the incredible variety of organisms produced by nature. In 1951, she noted, "The same mechanisms may well be responsible for the origins of many of the observed mutations in plants and animals." In a famous 1955 statement, McClintock prophesied that it "would be surprising indeed if controlling elements were not found in other organisms."

For six years, McClintock collected evidence, stuffing cards, tables, filing cabinets, and shelves with data. She was so excited that she often called Evelyn Witkin down from her lab to see the latest wonder. "It was a great thing to see. She was getting such really intense joy out of it," Witkin remembered. "She was so very sure of what she was seeing, and her evidence was absolutely convincing."

While McClintock was studying transposons, the world of genetics was changing. Chemists and physicists had joined the hunt for the physical basis of heredity. Trained in Cold Spring Harbor summer schools, they applied the principles of physics to biological problems. In their excitement, these new molecular biologists ignored previous work by crystallographers, biochemists, bacterial experts, chemists, and geneticists, including McClintock. The molecular biologists' softball games became a symbol of their disregard. As the codiscoverer of DNA's structure James Watson told the story, the softball "all too often" wound up in McClintock's cornfield.

In an hour-long talk at a major Cold Spring Harbor symposium in 1951, McClintock summarized her findings before a group of leading scientists. The report was long, complicated, and dense with statistics and proofs. When she finished, there was dead silence, Witkin remembered. "It fell like a lead balloon," recalled Harriet Creighton. McClintock felt as if she had "collided with the stable chromosome."

Scientists scrambling to learn molecular biology wanted it simple; they did not like a genetic system that was fluid, moving, changing, and intricately regulated. They reacted with puzzlement, frustration, even hostility. "I don't want to hear a thing about what you're doing. It may be interesting, but I understand it's kind of mad," a biologist told her. A leading molecular biologist called her "just an old bag who'd been hanging around Cold Spring Harbor for years."

Understandably, McClintock was upset and disappointed. She summarized her work in a longer article published in 1953. Maize geneticists understood and accepted the data, but she wanted the science community at large to realize the wider significance of her work. Only three scientists outside her field, however, requested copies of the article. McClintock concluded that publishing was a waste of time. From then on, she wrote up her work in large notebooks, all tabulated, documented, and analyzed, and filed the notebooks on a shelf. She submitted only brief summaries of her work for publication in the annual reports of the Carnegie Institution of Washington—which only a few libraries purchased. "I don't know of any other scientist who would have had the discipline or self-confidence to do that," observed a friend of her later years, molecular biologist Bruce Alberts of the University of California at San Francisco. She stopped giving seminars at Cold Spring Harbor, too. Twenty years ahead of her time, McClintock went into "internal exile" at the lab, waiting for the scientific community to catch up with her.

McClintock so enjoyed ideas and thinking that the pain of being ignored soon slipped away. "I was startled when I found they didn't understand it, didn't take it seriously," she explained. "But it didn't bother me. I just knew I was right. People get the idea that your ego gets in the way a lot of time—ego in the sense of wanting returns. But you don't care about those returns. You have the enormous pleasure of working on it. The returns are not what you're after."

Being ignored gave McClintock more time to work and learn about other fields of biology. She was one of the few non–molecular specialists who kept up with molecular biology. "Despite her age and her coming from a very specialized area of biology, she's on top of everything," Alberts noted while McClintock was still alive. She devoured nonfiction—from biographies to monographs on offbeat biological subjects. Keeping an open mind about anything she could not understand, she viewed nature's oddities as windows onto fundamental phenomena in nature. She read up on stick insects, animal mimicry, plant galls, midwife toads, extrasensory perception, and the methods by which Tibetan Buddhists control their body temperature. She regularly scanned twenty biological journals of

widely differing specialties; one year she spent a month reading all
the literature on insect evolution.

Finding transposable elements everywhere in nature, McClintock photographed them for her own pleasure and for teaching her
friends. She would stop her car to walk through a field of Queen
Anne's lace. Each flower consists of a cluster of florets, each formed
from the progeny of a single cell. Normally, the white florets on the
outside rim of the blossom open first and the center floret opens
last, to reveal a spot of pink, green, or purple pigment. But on closer
examination, McClintock found blossoms where the colored floret
was not confined to the center. The activator gene had turned the
pigment gene on too soon. "It was the right pattern in the wrong
place at the wrong time," she realized, her face lighting up at the
memory.

Still, McClintock became discouraged enough to write Marcus
Rhoades and Helen Crouse during the 1960s and 1970s to ask about
jobs elsewhere. For two winters in the late 1950s, she even suspended her research entirely and trained Latin American cytolo-
gists to identify maize strains for the National Academy of Sciences.
The adoption of modern seed was destroying indigenous maize
strains. Studying the geographic distribution of particular chromosomes, McClintock realized that they revealed ancient migration
and trade routes. Corn seeds are so tightly enclosed in their husks
that the plants cannot travel without people. Her insights led to a
major study of ancient migrations based on the chromosomes of
present-day maize plants.

During the 1960s, when McClintock could have considered
retirement, she collected awards from Cornell University, the National Academy of Sciences, and the National Science Foundation.
None of these honors was given for her transposable-element work.
Nevertheless, a parade of pilgrims began to line up outside her door
to learn from her. Many remained her friends. As always, to save
time for activities she loved, she concentrated on her family and on
close friends who interested her; she ignored casual acquaintances
who bored her.

With friends, she was warm, charming, and open—far from the
recluse that the media made her out to be. In fact, she studied

human nature the way she studied corn—carefully, precisely, and with absorbing interest. An enthusiastic teacher one-on-one, she moved instinctively to the age and intellectual level of the person she was talking to, Guenter Albrecht-Buhler discovered. Speaking before McClintock's death, he said, "She's far ahead of her time and tries not to startle you with it. I think it's a defense mechanism from the time when it was important for women not to be brighter than others. . . . She enjoys making things clearer. She's a passionate teacher. The passion of her existence is removing the fog. . . ."

Often, the highlight of a visit with McClintock was a nature walk, during which she showed these professional biologists things they had never seen before. For example, "I'm *very* interested in galls. When an insect injects a chemical into a plant, the plant grows an elaborate, highly specific home that fits that particular kind of insect perfectly. And one grape plant may have many different types of galls. This tells me that organisms have all the necessary machinery, the potential, to make any kind of organism. All around you, there is so much pleasure, if you think about it."

Molecular biology finally caught up with McClintock during the late 1960s, when James Shapiro and others discovered transposable elements in bacteria. Suddenly, molecular biologists started finding mobile genetic elements in all kinds of organisms, including people. Transposable elements are used in much of today's genetic engineering. They are responsible for many mutations and play an important role in evolution, inherited birth defects, resistance to antibiotics, and perhaps the incidence of cancer. The movement of genes and gene segments on chromosomes helps to explain how cells produce antibodies to combat a host of different viral and bacterial threats, how bacteria retaliate by acquiring immunities to human defenses, and how certain cancer cells develop. These genetic elements, cloned by recombinant-DNA techniques, are used to carry desired genes to new hosts. Scientists today make mutations with transposable elements, instead of with chemicals and X-rays.

Contemporary scientists regard the inheritance process as a fluid information-processing system, much like a computer. "We now think of a dynamic storage system subject to constant monitoring, correction, and change by dedicated biochemical complexes," Shapiro explained in an article in *Genetica*. "We can now think about integrated, multigenic systems that can be turned on and off in a coordinated fashion according to the needs of the organism."

By the late 1970s, McClintock's honors were piling up in glorious profusion, this time for transposable elements. In 1980–1981, she received eight major awards, three of them in one week: the Albert Lasker Basic Medical Research Award, the hundred-thousand-dollar Wolf Prize in Medicine from the Wolf Foundation in Israel, and a MacArthur Foundation Fellowship, sixty thousand dollars a year tax-free for life. As McClintock noted, she made her money late in life.

Her reaction? "Rather upset. I'm not a person who likes to accumulate things," she explained, squirming miserably in her chair during a press conference. "I don't like publicity at all. . . . It's too much at once." Her biographer, Evelyn Fox Keller, conducted five interviews before McClintock broke off discussions. Keller wrote about McClintock as a brilliant recluse, a mystic whose "passion is for the individual, for the difference," not in broad fundamental issues common to all of biology. When *A Feeling for the Organism* was published in 1983, McClintock announced tersely, "I want nothing to do with a book about me. I do not like publicity." She never read the book. She even refused to autograph it for a colleague.

McClintock's friends reacted to the book in a variety of ways. But virtually all stressed that McClintock was neither a recluse nor a mystic. And they argued that she had always been interested in maize as a window on fundamental biological phenomena and not just as a study in and for itself. McClintock herself denied that she was a mystic, if being a mystic meant believing in something she knew little about. She said she did not dismiss phenomena that she did not understand, but she did not believe in them either. "You just don't know," she declared flatly.

Early in the morning of October 10, 1983, McClintock was listening to her apartment radio when she learned that she had been awarded the Nobel Prize for Medicine and Physiology. The Nobel Committee called her work "one of the two great discoveries of our times in genetics," the other being the structure of DNA. The prize was remarkable in many respects. Only once before had the Nobel Committee waited so long to award a researcher. She shared the award with no one; in the past several decades, all but a handful of the medical and physiology prizes have been shared by two or three winners. She was the seventh woman to receive a science Nobel. And, finally, the prize, which is generally given for medical or animal biology, had never been awarded for studies of higher plants. McClintock won only after it was clear that her work had implications beyond botany.

Overwhelmed at the news, McClintock took a walk in the institute woods, collecting black walnuts and her thoughts. "I knew I was going to be in for something," she explained. "I had to psych myself up. I had to think of the significance of it all; to react. I had to know what approach I would take."

Then she told the lab's administrative director, "I will do what I have to do." She issued a press release noting how unfair it seemed "to reward a person for having so much pleasure, over the years, asking the maize plant to solve specific problems and then watching its responses." Then she held a press conference, sitting on a stool in her carefully pressed dunagrees and shirt, whispering courteously. At eighty-three, her brown hair was graying, her skin was sun-wrinkled, and her eyes were bright.

"I don't even know what the award brings in," she admitted.

"It's approximately $190,000," a reporter replied.

"Oh, it is," she whispered. The reporters laughed. Then, with characteristic objectivity, she spelled out how her mind was working. "No, I didn't know, and I'll just have to get to one side and think about this."

Asked if she was bitter at having to wait so long for recognition, she took pains to explain, "No, no, no. You're having a good time. You don't need public recognition, and I mean this quite seriously. You don't need it. You need the respect of your colleagues. . . . When you know you're right, you don't care. You can't be hurt. You just know, sooner or later, it will come out in the wash, but you may have to wait some time. But . . . anybody who had had that evidence thrown at them with such abandon couldn't help but come to the conclusions I did about it."

The announcement that Barbara McClintock had won the Nobel Prize electrified the scientific community like no other recent prize—as much for the beauty of her motivation and dedication as for her scientific tour de force. When McClintock accepted her award from King Carl Gustaf in Stockholm, the ovation from the normally reserved and formal audience was so loud that it made the concert-hall floor vibrate. Her solitary excellence, her quiet thoughtfulness, and her perseverance in the face of male prejudice and scientific rejection had captured their imaginations.

Yet the Nobel Prize, with its competition, publicity, fawning hangers-on, and name-droppers, was a burden for McClintock. "You put up with it," she remarked tersely. "It's a good thing it happened so late in life," she told a friend. Otherwise, it would have interfered with her work. Overall, she said, "it's been very, very difficult on a person. It hasn't been easy or pleasant."

Despite the Nobel, McClintock continued with her research. In her eighties, she switched her exercise program from running to aerobic dancing. She ate a chocolate a day; traveled twice yearly to South America, where much of today's maize research is conducted; and worked twelve-hour days. Her reading was as encyclopedic as ever. She spent much of her time helping molecular scientists analyze her material.

The tiger in McClintock mellowed, and there were fewer blasts of impatience. As she neared ninety, she began to slow down to an eight- or nine-hour workday. Minor health problems irritated her. "I'm almost ninety," she told a caller. "And in my family ninety is the end, and I'm beginning to feel it."

She still passionately resisted anything that bored or distracted her from the main joys of life. As she protested, "I want to be free."

On September 2, 1992, Barbara McClintock died. At age ninety, she was free.

Sandra Steingraber

Living Downstream

hen I was a young woman, I was diagnosed with bladder cancer. One of my aunts died of this same cancer. My mother was diagnosed with breast cancer at the age of forty-four, and several other relatives died of colon cancer.

You could say that cancer runs in my family, and it does—and yet I was adopted. None of the people I mention here are related to me genetically. Furthermore, bladder cancer, as I learned, is a disease with deep connections to environmental contamination.

My personal history made urgent my scientific need to understand the connections between cancer and the environment; and my professional training as an ecologist helped me to make sense of my unchosen identity as a cancer patient. I began to use my research skills to explore the toxic contamination in my hometown in Illinois, which, as in so many other communities around the country, is considerable.

On a clear night after the harvest, central Illinois becomes a vast and splendid planetarium. This transformation amazed me as a child. In one of my earliest memories, I wake up in the back seat of the car on just such a night. When I look out the window, the black sky is so inseparable from the plowed, black earth—which dots are stars and which are farmhouse lights?—that it seems I am floating in a great, dark, glittering bowl.

Rural central Illinois still amazes me. Buried under the initial appearance of ordinariness are great mysteries. At least, this is what I attempt to convince newcomers.

What you do see, of course, are soybean fields and cornfields. About 89 percent of Illinois is cropland, meaning that, if you fell to earth in Illinois, nine times out of ten you would land in a farm field. Illinois grows more soybeans than any other state in the country, and produces more corn than any state but Iowa. Read any supermarket label. Corn syrup, corn gluten, cornstarch, dextrose, soy oil, and soy proteins are found in almost every processed food from soft drinks to sliced bread to salad dressing. These are also the ingredients of the food we feed to the animals we eat. Thus, you could say that we are standing at the beginning of a human food chain. The molecules of water, earth, and air that rearrange themselves to form these beans and kernels are the molecules that eventually become the tissues of our own bodies. You have eaten food that was grown here. You *are* the food that is grown here.

What remains of the twenty-two million acres of tall-grass prairie that once covered this state is the deep-black dirt that those grasses produced from layers of sterile rock, clay, and silt dumped here by wind and glaciers. The molecules of earth contained in each plowed clod are the same molecules that once formed the roots and runners of countless species unfamiliar to me now. Touching Illinois soil, I am touching prairie grass.

Illinois soil holds darker secrets as well. To the 89 percent of Illinois that is farmland, an estimated fifty-four million pounds of synthetic pesticides are applied each year. Introduced into Illinois at the end of World War II, these chemical poisons quietly familiarized themselves with the landscape. In 1950, less than 10 percent of cornfields were sprayed with pesticides. In 1993, 99 percent were chemically treated.

Pesticides do not stay on the fields where they are sprayed. They evaporate and drift in the jet stream. They dissolve in water and flow downhill into streams and creeks. They bind to soil particles and rise into the air as dust. They sink into the glacial aquifers and buried river valleys and thereby enter groundwater. They fall in the rain. They are detectable in fog. Little is known about how much goes where. In 1993, 91 percent of Illinois's rivers and streams showed pesticide contamination. These chemicals travel in pulses: pesticide levels in surface water during the months of spring planting—April through June—are seven times the winter levels, although detections never fall to zero. Even less is known about pesticides in groundwater. A recent pilot study showed that one-quarter of private wells tested in central Illinois contained agricultural chemicals. Those sampled in the Havana Lowlands region of Mason County, at the confluence of two ancient rivers, show some of the most severe contamination.

Some of the pesticides inscribed into the Illinois landscape cause cancer in laboratory animals. Some, including the most commonly used pesticide, atrazine, are suspected of causing breast and ovarian cancer in humans. Other probable carcinogens, such as DDT and chlordane, were banned from use years ago, but their presence endures.

I was born in 1959 and so share a birthdate with atrazine, which was first registered for market that year. In the same year, DDT—dichlorodiphenyltrichloroethane—reached its peak usage in the United States. The 1950s were also banner years for the manufacture of PCBs, oily fluids used in electrical transformers, pesticides, carbonless copy paper, and small electronic parts.

I have no memories of DDT. Instead, my images come from archival photographs and old film clips. In one shot, children splash in a swimming pool while DDT is sprayed above the water. In another, a picnicking family eats sandwiches, their heads engulfed in clouds of DDT fog. Old magazine ads are even more surreal: an aproned housewife in stiletto heels and a pith helmet aims a spray gun at two giant cockroaches standing on her kitchen counter. They raise their front legs in surrender. The caption reads, "Super Ammunition for the Continued Battle on the Home Front." In another ad, the aproned woman appears in a chorus line of dancing farm animals who sing "DDT is good for me!"

Fellow baby-boomers just a few years older do not rely on old magazine ads to recall DDT. From memory, they can describe the fogging trucks that rolled through their suburban neighborhoods as part of mosquito or gypsy-moth control programs. Some can even describe childhood games that involved chasing these trucks. "Whoever could stay in the fog the longest was the winner," remembers one friend. "You had to drop back when you got too dizzy. I was good at it. I was almost always the winner." Says another, "When the pesticide trucks used to come through our neighborhood, the guys would haul their hoses into our backyards and spray our apple trees. Mostly we kids would throw the apples at each other. Sometimes we would eat them."

For those of us born in the 1940s, '50s, and '60s, the time period between the widespread dissemination of these pesticides and their subsequent prohibition represents our prenatal periods, infancies, childhoods, and teenage years. We were certainly the first generation of babies to eat synthetic pesticides in our pureed vegetables.

Banned pesticides, like fugitives from justice, have not entirely disappeared. They frequent foreign ports. They languish underground. But they are beginning to surface again in the tissues of women with breast cancer, sometimes under different names— DDT is metabolized in the human body into a chemical called DDE—and sometimes along with banned industrial chemicals belonging to the same chemical clan.

Four years after DDT was banned, researchers reported that women with breast cancer had significantly higher levels of DDE and PCBs in their tumors than in the surrounding healthy tissues of their breasts. Similar but weaker trends held for lindane, heptachlor, and dieldrin. The study was small—involving only fourteen women—but the findings were provocative, because DDT and PCBs were already linked to breast cancer in rodents.

In 1993, biochemist Mary Wolff and her colleagues conducted the first carefully designed major study on this issue. They analyzed DDE and PCB levels in the stored blood specimens of 14,290 New York City women who had attended a mammography screening clinic. Within six months, fifty-eight of these women were diagnosed with breast cancer. The most stunning discovery was that women with the highest levels of DDE in their blood were four times more likely to have breast cancer than women with the lowest levels. The authors concluded that residues of DDE "are strongly associated with breast cancer risk." Subsequent studies have not always confirmed these results, and the ensuing debate over pesticides and breast cancer clamors on.

Perhaps the matter would seem less urgent if women born in the United States between 1947 and 1958 did not now have almost three times the rates of breast cancer than their great-grandmothers did when they were the same age. Or if pesticide use in the United States had not doubled since Rachel Carson wrote *Silent Spring*. But we do. And it has.

The development of industrial chemistry in this century has been driven by the exigencies of war. Out of this crucible came new chemicals of all sorts. Some, such as organophosphate poisons used in Europe's gas chambers, seem to have been born from truly evil intentions; others from admirable ones. Because many of these new chemicals were developed under emergency conditions and within the secretive atmosphere of wartime, they had not been fully tested for safety. After the war, private markets were quickly developed for these products, and yet their long-term effects on humans or the environment were not known. In addition, because wartime attitudes accompanied these products onto the market, the goals of conquest and annihilation were transferred from the battlefield to our kitchens, gardens, forests, and farm fields. The Seek, Strike, and Destroy maxim of the war was brought home and turned against the natural world. All life was caught in the crossfire.

World War II is mentioned throughout the chapters of *Silent Spring*. Carson's references are casual, and they seem designed to remind already aware readers that the technologies developed for wartime purposes had changed chemistry and physics forever. The atomic bomb was only the most arresting example. More intimate aspects of the human economy were also changed. The multitude of new synthetic products made available after the war altered how food was grown and packaged, homes were constructed and furnished, bathrooms disinfected, children deloused, and pets de-flea'd.

Taped above my desk are graphs showing the U.S. annual production of synthetic chemicals. I keep them here to make visible a phenomenon I was born in the midst of but am too young to recall firsthand. The first consists of several lines, each representing the manufacture of a single substance. One line is benzene, the human carcinogen known to cause leukemia and suspected of playing a role in multiple myeloma and non-Hodgkin's lymphoma. Another is perchloroethylene, the probable human carcinogen used to dry-clean clothes. A third represents production of vinyl chloride—a known cause of angiosarcoma and a possible breast carcinogen. They all look like ski slopes. After 1940, the lines for all three begin to rise significantly, and then they shoot upward after 1960.

A second graph shows the annual production of all synthetic organic chemicals combined. It resembles a child's drawing of a cliff face. The line extending from 1920 to 1940 is essentially horizontal, hovering at a few billion pounds per year. After 1940, however, the line shoots skyward, becoming almost vertical after 1960. Production of synthetic organic chemicals increased a hundredfold between the time my mother was born and the year I finished graduate school. Two human generations.

Agriculture consumes the lion's share of the synthetic organic chemicals called pesticides, but family pesticide use is emerging as an important source of exposure for those of us not living on farms. Yard and garden weed-killers are used by about one-half of American families, as are insecticidal flea collars, sprays, dusts, shampoos, and dips for household pets. These kinds of uses place us in intimate contact with pesticide residues, which can easily find their way into bedding, clothing, carpet, and food. Pesticide residues persist much longer indoors than outdoors, where sunlight, flowing water, and soil microbes help break them down or carry them away. Yard chemicals tracked indoors on the bottoms of shoes can remain impregnated in carpet fibers for years. Some researchers now believe that crawling on carpets and ingesting house dust constitute significant routes of exposure for infants and toddlers—perhaps exceeding those from pesticide residues on food.

From an ecological point of view, World War II was a catalyst for the transformation from a carbohydrate-based economy—as it had been called by some analysts—to a petrochemical-based economy. I found myself amazed at how many products, now derived from a barrel of oil, were once manufactured from vegetation.

You may be excited to learn, as I was, that plastic existed before it was synthesized from petroleum. It was derived from plants, invented in the 1870s, and called celluloid. Clear plastic film derived from wood pulp with adhesive on one side was introduced in the 1920s as cellophane tape. Plant-derived substances were once used to make steering wheels, instrument panels, and spray paint for cars. Thus, although the carcinogen vinyl chloride was actually first synthesized in 1913, its production did not begin to skyrocket until after World War II, when research on the industrial uses of plant matter was replaced by an emphasis on petrochemistry. Automobile interiors would no longer come from cotton fibers or wood pulp but from oil.

Other plant-based oils also played leading roles in industry before the war. Oils extracted from corn, olives, rice, grape seeds, and other plant parts were used to make paint, inks, soaps, emulsifiers, and even floor covering. The word "linoleum" echoes the name of its original key ingredient: linseed oil. Castor oil—from the tropical castor-bean tree—was used to lubricate machine parts.

Countless examples of synthetic substitutions have occurred in the last half-century and have provided us with new exposures to known or suspected carcinogens. And the rapid birthrate of new synthetic products that began in 1945 far surpassed the ability of government to regulate their use and disposal. There are now between forty-five thousand and a hundred thousand chemicals in common commercial use; of these, only between 1.5 and 3 percent have been tested for carcinogenicity. Only 10 percent of pesticides in common use have been adequately assessed for hazards; for 38 percent, nothing useful is known; the remaining 52 percent fall somewhere in between.

Of all the unexpected consequences of World War II, perhaps the most ironic is the discovery that a remarkable number of the new chemicals it ushered in are estrogenic—that is, at low levels inside the human body, they mimic the female hormone estrogen. Many of the hypermasculine weapons of conquest and progress are, biologically speaking, emasculating.

This effect occurs through a variety of biochemical mechanisms. Some chemicals imitate the hormone directly; others interfere with the various systems that regulate the body's production and metabolism of natural estrogens. Still others seem to work by blocking the receptor sites for male hormones, the androgens. In 1995, fifty years after its triumphant return from the war and entry into civilian life, DDT again made headlines when new animal studies showed that DDT's metabolic breakdown product, DDE, is an androgen-blocker.

Our enzymes quickly convert DDT into DDE. But because the next step is much slower (DDT has a half-life of seven years), we accumulate DDE as we age. Molecules of DDE can cross the human placenta and can also accumulate in breast milk. For boys and men, the consequences may include physical deformities such as undescended testicles, lowered sperm counts, and testicular cancer. No one knows what effect DDE exposure has on the reproductive development of girls or women. No research has been done.

Much of the concern about hormone-disrupting contaminants has focused on their possible role in contributing to birth defects, reproductive failures in wildlife, and infertility in humans. At times, these discussions seem nearly to eclipse the quieter but longer-running conversations about the possible contributions of estrogen-mimicking contaminants to cancer. Certain breast cancers, for example, are notorious for growing faster in the presence of estrogen. Many other cancers are also known to be, or suspected to be, hormonally mediated. These include cancers of the ovary, uterus, testicle, and prostate. Thus, identifying pollutants that interfere with hormones is important to public dialogues about human cancers of all kinds.

When *Silent Spring* was published, the Victory Days of the Second World War had not yet reached their twentieth anniversary. Compared with Carson's generation, those of us born after World War II are not so aware of the domestic changes wrought by this war. We have inherited its many inventions—as well as the waste produced in their manufacture—but we do not have a keen sense of their origins.

As the daughter of a World War II veteran, I am grateful that my father returned home safely from Naples, Italy, where DDT was first used to halt a typhus epidemic. But as a survivor of cancer, as a native of a badly polluted region of the country, and as a member of the most poisoned generation to come of adult age, I am sorry that cooler heads did not prevail in the calm prosperity of peacetime, when careful consideration and a longer view on public health were once again permissible and necessary. I am sorry that no one asked, "Is this the industrial path we want to continue along? Is this the most reasonable way to rid our dogs of fleas and our trees of gypsy moths? Is this the safest material for a baby's pacifier or for a tub of margarine?" Or that those who did ask such questions were not heard.

It is not my contention that all synthetic organic chemicals be immediately banned. Nor do I advocate a return to the days of celluloid and castor oil. From what I understand, celluloid was flammable and brittle. I'm sure that castor oil had its problems too. However, I am convinced that human inventiveness is not restricted to acts of war. The path that chemistry has taken in the last half of this century is only one path. It is not even a particularly imaginative one.

Some solutions may indeed be found through the rescue of chemical processes abandoned years before—as in the quiet decision of many daily newspapers to switch to soy-based inks—but others may be sought through altogether new applications of knowledge. Chlorine-free methods of bleaching paper are possible and are already in small-scale commercial use both here and in Europe. Special soaps and computerized control over humidity, agitation, and heat, for example, allow many dry-cleanables to be wet-cleaned. Citrus-based solvents, ultrasonics, and old-fashioned soap and water can often replace chlorinated solvents used for degreasing operations and precision cleaning of electronic parts. New methods of embalming and different attitudes about the role of funeral services can reduce the use of formaldehyde in mortuaries.

It is time to start looking for alternative paths. From the right to know flows the duty to inquire—and the obligation to act.

Lesa Quale

Radioactive Tumbleweeds

igrating seeds, like migrating people, have tales to tell. The story of the tumbleweed begins in Russia, from which, between 1870 and 1874, Mennonites began to flee. Catherine the Great's pact exempting Mennonite men from military service had been rescinded by Czar Alexander II. Emissaries from Kansas, eager for hardworking homesteaders, secured military exemption along with acreage for the pacifist sect of farmers. Before their journey, Mennonite women sewed winter wheat seeds known as Turkey red into clothing, basting the seeds into hems, linings, and pockets. The Mennonites' clothing was a hope chest, packed with the bounty of their homeland and their plan for the future, but another seed hitched along for the ride, transforming the hope chest into a Pandora's box. Accidentally stuffed into the folds and pockets along with the Turkey red was *Salsola kali*, also known as the Russian thistle, also known as the tumbleweed.

The Russian thistle seeds tucked into Mennonite clothing were not the first of these to tumble onto U.S. soil. The first had arrived with an import of flax to South Dakota from Russia, but the shipment had not harbored enough stowaway tumbleweed seeds to populate the landscape and become an American metaphor for rugged individualism and the Old West. The Mennonites spawned tumbleweed success. One spring following the Mennonite immigration, a Biblical number of crickets descended on Kansas farms and fields, blighting a year's worth of crops, all except the Mennonites' winter-harvested wheat. A mass import of the wheat followed, and strains of Turkey red became the cash crop of Kansas. Once again, the Russian thistle hitched along for the ride and was inadvertently sown with the wheat.

Salsola kali shoots up green sprouts, blooms flowers hidden in clusters of burnt-red spines, dries a hay color, breaks off its main stem, and tumbles with the wind, dispersing its two hundred thousand seeds before it decomposes. *Salsola kali*'s life cycle repeated again and again across the West. If the wind did not offer a lift to new frontiers, then trains, farm machinery, ranch animals, petticoats, or a pair of Levi's did.

As humans expanded westward, tumbleweeds pinwheeled along in their wake. The species' success depended on expansion. Given pristine land, tumbleweeds faltered. The traveling bundle stalled against the prairie grass or sage or yarrow; the seedlings piled and competed for limited space—not enough elbow room. Tumbleweed thrived where land had been tilled and cleared, the native species plowed under, the soil depleted with overdevelopment. Tumbleweed reaped the fruits of human endeavor. After U.S. atomic-weapons testing in the Utah desert during the Cold War, it was the first plant life to recover from impact, to sprout and to bloom.

Now tumbleweed thrives again in a postatomic landscape at the Hanford nuclear project in eastern Washington State, where for seventeen years it has been the job of Jill Molenaa to keep it from escaping.

I had read about the tumbleweed in the *Seattle Times*, which had reported that it had been escaping the highly toxic areas inside Hanford. In the winter of 1999 I drove out to meet Jill, who allowed me to ride along in her truck as she went about her work. She was in her forties, tall and thin, dressed in a blue workman's jumpsuit. A badge hanging around her neck gave her job description as "teamster," but her looks belied her trade: lipstick, cropped blond hair, blush on her high-boned cheeks, lilac nail polish. She wore a second pendant, a small black box—a dosimeter, she explained, that blinked and beeped if she entered a contaminated area.

A patchwork of dried sage and yarrow crested the gentle curve of hills beside the road to the plant. Beds of tumbleweeds snuggled in ditches between the small road bluffs and the concrete. I considered how these vagabond plants that once signified the romance of the Old West were on the move again, this time telling tales of contamination.

Jill stopped her truck at the entrance booth and flashed her badge. The man in the booth nodded and waved us in.

In 1943, the U.S. government purchased these 560 square miles for the development and construction of the atomic bomb. The population of what was then called White Bluffs was relocated, along with the Wanapum tribe, to the other side of the Columbia River. The water of the Columbia River had been chosen as a plentiful and natural coolant for the hot materials used in making the bomb that eventually dropped on Nagasaki. Following World War II, Hanford continued as a nuclear-weapons manufacturing site with the addition of breeder plants in the 1960s to combine weapons and nuclear-power services. At the end of the Cold War, Hanford's utility dwindled with cuts in military expenditure and the high cost of nuclear power. Hanford devolved into a dump, a repository for nuclear waste. Ghost-town remnants—a crumbling brick high school, a hollowed-out bank, parched fruit orchards—still stood on the property, shadowing the span of Hanford's history. Jill's family—both grandfathers, her father, and her mother—actively participated in Hanford's evolution, as everything from atomic engineers to construction workers.

The cleanup fell to Jill. It was her job to dispose of the tumbleweeds, the ones that clutched fences, nested in cracks of concrete, and piled and stacked against buildings. "They could grow out of a rock," she said. Their proliferation was a menace. From the fields surrounding the power plants, tumbleweeds had blown into the

Hanford Reach, an area preserved as a natural habitat. Halted in their windy travels by the slope of hills, the tumbleweeds clumped together, suffocating the native vegetation. They had sprouted in toxic soil, snapped, and taken off. Jill once worked on the road crew that hauled away the snag of weeds lining the roads and burned them, but then came the burn bans, so the weeds were now mulched and buried.

The accouterments of Jill's job were a pitchfork and a truck. A "hazard protection technician" accompanied the cleanup crew. When we arrived at an area where tumbleweeds had collected behind barrels and fence lines, the HPT waved his Geiger counter like a wand and checked the mass of tumbleweeds. The monitor beeped, but not with the spastic stutter meaning radioactivity. He stepped back and gave Jill the go-ahead.

Jill thrust a pitchfork into a clump. Airy bits of spine shed off the tines. She raised the cluster over the guardrails at the back of the truck, slid it off, and went back for another load. Only a small portion could be hauled at one time, lest the weeds fly off the pickup truck.

We drove to a gravel-lined crater. A mound of tumbleweeds huddled in the crater's core. Jill popped the latch that upended the back of the truck and the tumbleweeds spilled. She swept out the rest. Eventually, the contents of the crater would be buried. Stockpiled farther down the road, awaiting their turn for burial, were casings from nuclear-submarine engines, huge canisters that had been transported to the site from elsewhere in the country.

The tank farm was our next destination. Plutonium waste from the weapons-manufacturing and power plants was buried there. It had already leaked from containment and seeped into the river and soil. One company proposed storing the waste in a mesa—the idea was that the rock would keep the waste from leaching—but the project was abandoned. The latest storage technique was to convert the waste into a solid similar to glass before burying it.

Along a straight road, a yellow tape cut us off, the same bright yellow as on the "Radioactive" signs, the same tape that is used to mark crime scenes. Jill stopped the truck and pointed. On the right-hand side were a trailer and a large pink tank with knobs and pipes attached to it. A tangle of wire, knotted around stakes, prevented access to the tank farm, but a larger fence was on the left-hand side. It was as if the fence were blocking off the safe countryside rather than containing the hot spot.

Tumbleweeds scattered across the road, and some gripped the fence, awaiting a good wind. Jill said, "These are the radioactive tumbleweeds."

They were the same hay color as ordinary tumbleweeds. They did not glow, nor had they grown in size or in diabolic intelligence, as they might in a sci-fi film. Without an HPT and a Geiger counter, these tumbleweeds could pass as any other. Their ordinary appearance spooked me.

Jill attempted to reassure me. "These tumbleweeds will be bagged, tagged, and buried with other low-level radioactive waste— gloves and shoes and other equipment. You'd have to eat twenty of these tumbleweeds to get even mildly sick." Though I believed her, there was no way of knowing, without her expertise to inform me, about their safety or danger. Radioactivity cannot be perceived with the senses. Whenever people connected to Hanford spoke to me about radioactivity, they used similes: "as radioactive as a day in the sun," or "as radioactive as an airplane taking off." Similes could be used to measure what I could not sense.

The day after I met with Jill, I visited the Columbia River Exhibition of History, Science and Technology. A Geiger counter was attached to a display of objects—a pendant, a nugget of plutonium, a watch, a change purse. I enacted the role of HPT. I passed the Geiger counter over the objects. At first there was a stutter of beeps and the needle rested at the low end. Over plutonium, the needle went spastic and the high-pitched beeps accelerated. When I took the Geiger counter away from the display, the instrument settled. I waved the Geiger counter over my body—a beep and the needle made a slight jump, maybe from the change in my pocket, maybe from something else. *As radioactive as a human body as radioactive as plutonium as radioactive as a tumbleweed.*

———

During the agricultural booms of the 1890s, the tumbleweed became a blight. It outgrew the agriculture. Its spines scratched cattle, ranchers, and horses, twisted into gears of farm equipment, plugged up sewage and drainage. A South Dakota legislator and farmer once proposed a bill to fence in the whole state to keep the tumbleweed out. How does one contain what must flee to survive?

In the Columbia River Exhibition center, there were pictures of nuclear waste. Rust stained a wall of carbon steel. A dense brown liquid, foamy, almost like a salt marsh, swished below the stain. Next to the picture was a placard informing me that one million gallons of waste were speculated to have leaked into the soil and the Columbia River. I wondered about the goal for Hanford, the assurance that this property would one day be returned to the public—for what use? Who would want to build a home or mall or business over a tank farm? The possibilities seemed absurd. This land was tapped out. What thrives best in Hanford are the tumbleweeds.

While Jill was giving me her tour, pointing out Rattlesnake Mountain, the location of World War II bunkers, and a perfect picnic spot along the Columbia River, she had been as gracious as a host showing off her home. Her family story—another familiar tale of migration, this time to a place in which to work and raise a family, taking root there for generations—was the same as any other immigrants' tale, imbued with the requisite hope and tenacity that I, as a great-granddaughter of immigrants, can share. Our history. But in our wake another story unfolded: the effect of human history on the land. What we have brought with us, the Turkey red and the tumbleweed, the promise as well as the peril, still seems tucked in a Pandora's box. The seeds of our history are germinating.

Linda Jean Shepherd

My Life with Weed

What is a weed? A plant whose virtues have not yet been
discovered.

—RALPH WALDO EMERSON

y love affair with plants began on my sixteenth
birthday, when my friend Joyce gave me a phil-
odendron. I admired the seven glossy, heart-
shaped leaves trailing from the little white pot
and reverently placed her on the windowsill
above my bed. As I poured water into her rich black soil, I whimsi-
cally baptized her "Weed." I imagined her birth in the steamy jungles of tropical America, where she attached herself to a tree and
climbed to prodigious heights.

Weed was the first nonplastic plant to enter my family's home in
Pennsylvania. Unlike the Japanese dolls and ceramic animals on my
bookshelves, Weed was alive. I celebrated each new leaf. By the
time I graduated from high school, she covered my bedroom window in a luminous green weaving. She has been a more constant
companion than any family member, lover, husband, friend, or pet. I

keep marveling at how she creates so much green beauty from the meager dirt in her pot.

Weed accompanied me to college. When I needed to decide on a major, I sought inspiration in my tree-house refuge. There I decided that what I most wanted to know was how plants work— how the xylem and phloem transport nutrients, how chloroplasts capture light and make food. It felt as if the knowing would bring me closer to them, and so I majored in biology. But in the process of my training, I was waylaid onto the path of science that looks at smaller and smaller parts of nature. I earned a doctorate in biochemistry, with a minor in physical chemistry.

Daughter-of-Weed sought out light amid the reagent bottles and experiments on my lab bench, while Weed presided over my studies at home. By now, she had many cousins, including an unruly purple-passion plant and a cascading spider plant. Various shades of green pervaded all my living and working spaces. Weed witnessed my marriage and accompanied me to my first job.

When my husband and I separated, and I took a job with a biotechnology company clear across the country, I carefully boxed up my plant family—despite the dire predictions and disclaimers of the movers. I couldn't leave my green sisters behind. While I flew to Seattle and found a place to live, they traveled in a moving van through the winter cold of Montana. They arrived in Seattle with blackened leaves, almost dead and certainly unattractive. But they were my family. So, holding on to hope, I patiently tended them. They had always given me solace. Now it was my turn to talk to them, encourage them, and cheer them on when I saw the first glimmers of green. Over the weeks and months, their beauty gradually returned, and Weed's heart-shaped leaves unfurled. Again she thrived.

One day the director of quality control asked me to remove Daughter-of-Weed and her cousins from my office. She feared they might harbor fruit flies, which could contaminate the monoclonal antibody products in the manufacturing rooms across the hall. Somewhat to my surprise, the first thought that sprang to mind was: *If my plants go, I go.* I dug in my heels in silent passive resistance. We both stayed.

At that point, I realized I needed plants around me as much as I need air to breathe. Though I rarely talk about my feelings for plants, they are intrinsic to my nature—as much a part of who I am as my long hair. My bond with them is a given, a foundation for my life. I require their beauty and tranquillity for inspiration—in all senses of the word, since plants literally give me my life breath, oxygen.

While I was developing biotech health-care devices, I read about a new Weyerhaeuser product: Inscape Interiorized plants and trees—real plants that had been fed a liquid plastic that polymerized inside the plant and essentially embalmed it. "No mess, no maintenance," the advertisement said. "A revolution in interior landscaping. This forest thrives without light, water, or even soil." I read the advertisement over and over, unable to believe my eyes. Was this better living through chemistry? What could motivate anyone to undertake such research? Why would anyone want a plant that could not offer the joy of watching it grow? "They're still beautiful," a friend said. "Human skin makes lovely lampshades," I replied.

Without Weed's growth, her abundance and generosity—her messiness—I never would have had the pleasure of sharing her with other humans. She and her green cousins have made a living bridge to many friends' homes, offices, massage studios, and dojos. At the same time, I know that plants themselves thrive on companionship with their green cousins. For example, Russian peasants appreciated the value of the "noxious weed" cornflower (also known as bachelor's buttons) growing in a field of waving rye. They had observed that rye grew better with her blue-blossomed cousin than alone. To honor this companionship, Russian peasants decorated the first sheaf of rye harvest with a cornflower wreath and placed it in front of an icon. Similarly, one oxeye daisy amid a hundred wheat plants promotes growth of the wheat. Further experiments have shown that a ratio of twenty daisies or cornflowers to a hundred crop plants crowds out the sprouting crop. But in limited numbers, such "weeds" bring minerals up from the subsoil and create root highways that enable crop-plant roots to dive deep to otherwise unavailable food.

Weeds are usually undervalued—or seen as the enemy. In the competitive worldview of agribusiness, herbicides eliminate weeds that compete with crops. As a woman scientist, I love to learn about research that demonstrates how weeds *cooperate* with crops and form community. Researchers at the University of California at Santa Cruz studied the traditional Mexican farming practice of pruning back, rather than pulling, a weed that commonly sprouts between rows of corn. They found that the roots of the weed *Bidens pilosa* secrete compounds lethal to fungi and nematodes that destroy corn. Instead of competing with the corn, the weed controls the pests without significantly stealing soil nutrients from the corn. The practice protects the soil and provides more wholesome food. The weed gets to express its nature. That, I believe, is what Earth asks of us: for each of her creatures to express her unique nature joyfully and exuberantly.

From my sunny condominium in Seattle, Weed and I moved to a house in an acre of young forest on Tiger Mountain to be with Paul, who became my second husband. We suspended Weed from the beam of the cathedral ceiling in our living room. Her scant six-inch yellow pot disappeared behind her shiny leaves. Abundant leafy tendrils climbed up twine macramé to the skylight, while others trailed down the wall to wander amid a Navajo wedding basket and Hopi kachina dolls on a shelf before cascading to the floor.

Paul and I had selected the house partly so we'd have minimal outside upkeep. Then I discovered that I could not resist planting and co-creating with the plants. Over the past ten years, my garden has become a conversation with nature about living beauty. When a huge decaying cedar stump fell on its side, I filled the depression with dirt and planted a weeping Japanese maple and fuchsias in it. When an ice storm felled hundreds of fir, alder, and hemlock branches, I wove them together to create a long flowerbed along the side of the road.

My gardening style is to respond, rather than to bulldoze plants and impose an abstract landscaping plan. I'm happiest when I'm making use of what's around. I heap together weeds and fallen leaves until, over the years, they magically become the rich black dirt of a new bed. Split logs edge trails filled with chipped branches. I build rock walls from stones uncovered in planting shrubs. Reveling in a sense of abundance and resourcefulness, I feel the satisfaction of nurturing and bringing order to all the forms of life in the garden.

When a space in the garden opens up, I'm led by desire. Plant lust. Pictures in seed catalogues seduce me with their promise of beauty. I imagine lush colors attracting bees, butterflies, and hummingbirds. Emerald temptresses in nurseries lure me with their fragrance of lilac and lavender, honeysuckle and spice. I'm captivated by descriptions of fruit that can't be found at the supermarket, such as native American pawpaws, which produce yellow fruit whose pulp tastes like vanilla custard.

Hesitant to force my will, I'm reluctant to prune. I'm too curious to see what the plant will do on her own. I want to learn about her habits. Yet browsing—pruning—stimulates growth in plants such as sage or rosemary.

I'm still coming to terms with weeding. "A weed is a plant out of place," I learned in ninth-grade biology. Usually, "weed" carries a negative connotation, implying a plant that is unsightly or a nuisance. But, ecologically, weeds are pioneers, colonizers of open habitats—healers of land disturbed by mankind. "Very successful life forms," as *Star Trek*'s Spock would say. It is only our egotistical human point of view that labels a weed a weed.

When viewed as a functioning part of nature, weeds have much to teach. They are excellent indicators of soil conditions. Sorrels, docks, and horsetails are a sign that the soil is becoming too acidic. Far from being harmful, plants such as ragweed, pigweeds, purslane, and nettles bring up minerals from the subsoil, especially those that have been depleted from the topsoil. As companion crops, they help domesticated plants get their roots down to food that would otherwise be beyond their reach. Dandelions actually heal the soil by transporting minerals, especially calcium, upward from deep layers, even from hardpan.

Having grown up feeling like an outsider, I have an affinity for weeds—which is how Weed got her name. I've admired their robustness, their ability to thrive in harsh conditions. They are wild, uncivilized, untamed—free—the American ideal of rugged individualism. Old-growth forests, on the other hand, are the climax of a community of wild plants who have learned to live together.

As I grow older and seek more intimacy and community, I realize that many weeds are symptomatic of imbalance. Some weeds act to heal the soil, but others haven't yet learned to live in their new communities. Like rats, cockroaches, and starlings, they are uninvited guests in niches carved by humankind. Most Northwestern weeds were brought intentionally or accidentally from Europe or Asia. For example, purple loosestrife is a valued wildflower in her native Eurasian habitats, where her patches are kept small by a complex society of insects and animals feeding on her leaves and seeds. But in North America, she crowds out native species and chokes waterways.

And so I pull wild geraniums and blackberry vines that run rampant over more delicate trilliums and bleeding hearts because I love diversity. I want to create a balanced community in my garden. Now, to my delight, I'm finding uses for some overly rambunctious—generous—plants. I've perfected a recipe for dandelion-chive quiche. Sweet woodruff scents my living room. I keep lemon balm and comfrey in check by harvesting leaves for tea. And Weed travels to ever more friends—an ambassador of the plant world.

Since plants are sessile, peaceful—undramatic—they rarely make breaking news. They set boundaries with thick skins and thorns. They infuse their leaves with unappetizing tannins to protect themselves from overgrazing. They protect themselves, but they don't intentionally cause harm.

As a child, I always sought out the comfort of plants after a family dispute. I sat high on an old log in the woods and felt the forest embrace me. As I entered the contemplation of trees, I felt soothed. My perspective broadened and deepened like the branches and roots of the trees around me.

In fact, I'm not alone in seeking the solace of trees. Recently, researchers at the University of Illinois found a correlation between safety and trees, which appear to have a calming effect on city dwellers. At tree-lined housing projects, children play more creatively, parents are more sociable, and adults report dramatically fewer incidents of domestic violence. The researchers concluded that trees are as necessary to urban life as streets, sewers, and electricity.

I was not surprised to learn that, in contrast to the prevailing competitive, survival-of-the-fittest, Darwinian conception of nature, plants also practice charity. A study done by a group of researchers in British Columbia showed that well-fed birches shared their bounty of sugar with nearby undernourished birches. Underground fungi transfer nutrients between plants via their roots.

Disconnection from plants and the natural world can lead to everyday evil, usually with the best of intentions. "Clearing the land" is equated with progress, with civilizing. A gardener cuts down hemlocks and cedars to grow lettuce. Ancient forests left uncut are deemed "wasted." Trees mean lumber. In mankind's narcissism, a view is worth more than a living tree. *How do we arbitrate such divergent value systems?* I wonder. *Who speaks for the plant world? How can I become a better guardian?*

When I hear accounts of war, battles, and bombings, I mourn the slaughter of innocent plants and animals as well as I do the people who die. Napalm denuded the jungles of Vietnam. Meadows of wildflowers decimated by tanks and grenades leave rabbits and foxes to starve in the muddy wastelands left behind. Atomic testing obliterates every plant, every seed, within range. The Gulf War killed even the most tenacious desert vegetation. Yet few mention the cost of war to the land. Even in times of peace, the violence continues. I look away when I drive past clear-cuts; sometimes it feels easier to deny the sacredness of all parts of the natural world than to feel the distress of its ruin.

Recently, I was shocked to read a report by the World Conservation Union that said that 12.5 percent of the world's seed-producing plants and ferns—nearly thirty-four thousand species—are endangered. In the United States, some 29 percent of plants, or sixteen thousand species, are at risk of extinction because of loss of habitat and competition from nonnative species. In a statement to the press, a representative of the New York Botanical Garden observed,

"Every nation understands and appreciates its biotic wealth much less than it does its material and cultural wealth. Ironically, it is precisely the biological assets that are most at risk."

The rate of extinction is being exacerbated by agribusiness. Philip Abelson, editor of *Science* magazine, contends that "the greatest ultimate global impact of genomics will result from manipulation of the DNA of plants." He predicts that most of the world's food, fuel, fiber, and chemical feedstocks, and some pharmaceuticals, will be obtained from genetically altered vegetation and trees. Major companies including Dow Chemical, DuPont, and Monsanto are now spending billions of dollars annually on genetic engineering. Already, they have succeeded in their highest priority—creating crops resistant to their proprietary herbicides. With research financed and motivated by sales of the highly profitable herbicide Roundup, Monsanto has genetically altered soybeans, cotton, potatoes, corn, and other plants. Sale of these seeds has been expanding rapidly since the federal government approved the first biotech crop for commercial planting in 1992. Over 50 percent of the soybeans planted in 1999 were herbicide-resistant. Such Roundup Ready varieties mean that farmers can apply more herbicide to their crops— our food.

This continuing trend toward chemically intensive agriculture degrades our soil, water, air, and health. As more herbicides find their way into our bodies, our health declines—even as it fosters the economy, since we then spend more money on pharmaceuticals, doctors, and hospitals. We now eat "virtual" food, devoid of nourishment—and then buy bottled water, vitamins, mineral supplements, fruit-ceutical and vegi-ceutical caplets, and additive-packed Ensure drinks and energy bars.

With increased reliance on genetically engineered seeds, the diversity of naturally growing varieties is being lost. Fortunately, devoted gardeners are striving to maintain viable banks of heirloom seeds, sponsoring seed exchanges and even expeditions to collect and preserve vanishing varieties. In contrast to seeds from plant hybrids, which are unpredictable and sometimes sterile, heirloom varieties can be pollinated through insects, wind, and water to produce offspring with reliable characteristics, allowing seeds to be saved and grown out year after year, generation after generation, without herbicides, fungicides, or pesticides.

In April 2000, a National Academy of Sciences report confirmed that crops engineered to contain pesticides might produce unexpected allergens and toxicants in food. In addition, they have the potential to create far-reaching environmental effects, including harm to beneficial insects, the creation of super-weeds, and possibly adverse effects on soil organisms. Yet these environmental side effects have been virtually unstudied. In response to consumer protest, 130 nations signed a treaty that would allow any country to ban the import of genetically altered foods. Now many food-processing plants and farmers are shunning genetically engineered crops, and Monsanto is considering abandoning the part of its business model that combines pharmaceuticals and agricultural products.

As I work in my garden, I continually ask myself: How can we, as humans, help our plant companions to express themselves most fully? How can we create *more* life by cooperating with weeds and bugs—by allowing them to do what they do best—rather than killing them with herbicides, pesticides, and fungicides?

During a three-week herbal apprenticeship in wise-woman tradition, I saw how much life could be woven together on less than an acre of land. Chickens scratched the ground, trimmed and fertilized the grass, ate kitchen scraps, and laid eggs. Ducks grazed on slugs and fertilized the strawberry patch. Rabbits ate dandelion greens and provided meat. Goats ate invasive blackberry bushes and gave milk. Worms, bugs, fungi, and bacteria filled the soil with life. We humans harvested weeds—chickweed, bittercress, shepherd's purse, and lamb's-quarters—for our salad, and prepared medicinal tinctures from cleavers, yarrow, and Saint-John's-wort. We invited bacteria and fungi into our bodies by eating foods such as goat cheese, yogurt, miso, fermented tea, and dandelion wine. Now that I was better able to see the interconnections within the web of life, it made perfect sense to me that research shows that high-frequency sound—in the range of birdsong—opens the stomata, the pores, of plants and increases the flow of nutrients.

I began to learn about the wise-woman tradition of healing, which honors a bond between women and plants that spans millennia. Often the medicinal plants were what we call weeds. Women used Saint-John's-wort oil for healing burns, and her tea for a diarrhea remedy; calcium-rich horsetail healed bone fractures and cleansed the urinary tract; plantain made a poultice to soothe bee stings, and her seeds provided a laxative. Since each plant treated a variety of ailments, the forests and meadows provided an entire pharmacy.

Only in the past year have I experimented with eating wild plants. Mineral-rich stinging nettles and deep-rooted burdock are deemed impractical for mass cultivation, but are freely available in wild places. By narrowing our experience to sweet and salty tastes, we miss the tonifying bitterness of dandelion leaves that wakes up our digestive system. We forget the pungent zip of gingerroot and anise seeds. In isolating (and patenting for profit) single "active ingredients" of plants, we lose the ameliorating and balancing effects of the plant's multiple components. For example, meadowsweet, whose "active ingredient" is methyl salicylate, heals damage to the stomach wall because of the combination of mucilages and tannins in the whole plant. Yet salicylates alone, such as aspirin (named for the old botanical name for meadowsweet), are known to cause stomach bleeding as a side effect.

In our commercial culture, gathering dinner from the wild has somehow become associated with poverty. Yet to me it provides joy, grounding, and an intimate connection to the earth and her seasons. During the salad days of spring I watch to catch peppery bittercress before she goes to seed, and nutrient-rich lamb's-quarters while she is tender. I eagerly await the blooming of calendula, impatiens, and red clover to adorn my summer salads. I graze on plantain, chickweed, and miner's lettuce as I garden. When the nip of fall crisps the air, I notice my body asking for root stews.

Surrounded by the bounty of the forests and fields, we no longer know how to survive without a supermarket. We've forgotten that honeysuckle flowers are sweet and delicious, plantain is palatable and nutritious, and Oregon grape leaves and flowers are lemon-tart. Wild foods bring wildness into our bodies.

Through my connection to Weed, I have grown sensitive to other plants as well. While Paul notices the Jaguars and Ferraris on the road, I relish the first blush of willow green and the spare winter skeleton of a maple. Watching for patches of yellow Saint-John's-wort to harvest, I practice my sixty-miles-per-hour botany. I try to remember when and where I saw a linden tree's fairy blossoms last summer. I wonder if the bankers will chase me away if I harvest leaves from the ginkgo tree in their parking lot.

We take plants for granted; yet they give us life. Weed and her cousins give me the air I breathe; they give me their fruits, seeds, and bodies to nourish my body. Their beauty nourishes my soul; their flesh becomes my flesh. They fill me with a sense of abundance. From next to nothing—simple carbon dioxide, water, nitrogen, and minerals—they alchemize huge, beautiful, complex, intricately adapted structures. The cathedral hush of a redwood forest. The sensuous cinnamon bark of madrona. The voluptuous iris. I marvel at their mystery. I am grateful for their generosity.

The Forest for
the Trees

Kathleen Norris

Dreaming of Trees

> I have noticed in my life that all men have a liking for some
> special animal, tree, plant, or spot of earth. If men would pay
> more attention to these preferences and seek what is best to
> do in order to make themselves worthy . . . they might have
> dreams which would purify their lives. . . .
>
> —BRAVE BUFFALO, Sioux,
> in *By the Power of Their Dreams*

im Burden, the narrator of Willa Cather's *My Ánto-
nia*, says of the Nebraska prairie to which he has
moved from Virginia that "trees were so rare in
that country, and they had to make such a hard
fight to grow, that we used to feel anxious about
them, and visit them as if they were persons." He adds, "It must
have been the scarcity of detail in that tawny landscape that made
detail so precious."

Burden is speaking of the American frontier at the end of the
nineteenth century, but his words ring true for a prairie dweller one
hundred years later. The small town where I live, like most towns in

the western Dakotas, was plunked down on a treeless plain. Settlement followed the path of railroad lines, not rivers, and nearly all of the trees, like all the buildings, had to be planted. Photographs of our backyard taken in the 1920s, when my mother was a child, offer a view of buttes, a stark horizon. No houses. No trees. Even now, standing in the dirt alley to the east of our house, I can look north, down a three-block length of hedges and trees, to open country.

My mother can remember when most of the trees on our street, and in the town itself, were mere saplings. My husband and I had to take down a lovely cottonwood a few years ago—it was crowding a basement wall—and a neighbor came by to mourn with us. He was five years old when that tree was planted; he's now in his seventies. It was strange to think that we were erasing a part of his childhood. My husband says that destroying that tree still makes him sad, that he imagined it to be like killing an elephant, something larger, wiser, and more mysterious than himself. I miss the tree for the marvelous ray of light and shade it made on our kitchen windows in the late afternoon.

But it's folly to miss trees here, where, as one friend says, out of a hundred things that can happen to a tree, ninety-nine of them are bad. A lengthy drought in the 1980s killed off many of the aging shelter belts around farmhouses, as well as windbreaks in cropland that were first planted, with government assistance, in the 1930s. Though it's been a good conservation practice, I doubt that there will be money available to replant them. Like so many human institutions on the Western plains, these rows of trees will simply fade away.

Even the monks at a nearby monastery, who have planted and tended trees here for nearly a hundred years, tend to be fatalistic about it. They work hard—one monk I know says that in his nineteen years at the monastery he's planted nearly a hundred trees—and on hot summer days it's a common sight to see a monk on a small tractor hauling a home-rigged tank that holds thirteen hundred gallons to water trees in the cemetery, the orchard, the western ridge. But the monks also know that to care for a tree in western Dakota is to transcend work; it becomes a form of prayer, or, as Saint

Paul said, a "hope in things unseen." Maybe that's why they're so good at it, so persistent in their efforts.

I marvel at the fecundity of a crabapple tree that my grandmother planted at the north edge of our backyard that has drawn four generations of children to its branches and tart, rosy fruit. I worry about the two elms just south of the garden plot, weakened by drought and then disease. Will we have the energy, the hope, to replace them? Maybe with cottonwoods, the Siouxland variety developed for this harsh climate. But most of all, when I dream of trees here, when I visit them, they are the trees out in the open, trees I can take no responsibility for but consider to be my friends.

One of my favorites stands at the edge of a large pasture on the outskirts of Mandan, North Dakota. A young, small tree—what kind I don't even know, but from the highway it looks like a burr oak—nudges a fence, its branches straddling the barbed wire. There it has persisted for God knows how long with one half of it in vigorous leaf, the other rubbed bare by cattle. There are no other trees in that pasture. This tree—like a tough little juniper that emerges from the lodgepole pines of the Slim Buttes, far to the south, to stand alone on a limestone outcropping—reminds me of an elegantly carved figurehead on a sailing ship's prow, riding magnificently the dry prairie winds that will one day help to tear it down.

Many such glimpses abide: a tall, leafy locust split down the middle by a lightning strike; a lone Russian olive standing like a sentry near a pasture gate, its black branches vivid beneath the shimmery leaves. I picture the large burr oak in a ranch family's yard; it's been pruned and shaped to a striking perfection, and is the one tree I know of here that would not look out of place on a New England village common. And I mourn what I think of as the political trees, an eerie landscape of waterlogged dead and dying trees just west of Mobridge and the Missouri River, casualties of the Oahe Dam. They make me treasure all the more the profusion of trees—willow, box elder, elm, cottonwood, wild plums—in the vast Missouri bottomland at Fort Yates, Cannonball, and Bismarck.

The immensity of land and sky in the western Dakotas allows for few trees, and I love the way that treelessness reveals the contours of the land, the way that each tree that remains seems a message bearer. I love what trees signify in the open country. The Audubon field book describes the burr oak as "a pioneer tree, invading the prairie grassland," and I try to listen to what these "volunteers" have to say about persistence, the strength of water, seeds, and roots, the awesome whimsy of birds scattering seed in their excrement, casting not only oak but small groves of Russian olive in their wake. Cottonwoods need more water; their presence signifies groundwater, or the meanderings of a creek. Sometimes, in the distance, you glimpse what looks like a stand of scrub brush or chokecherry bushes. But if you turn off the asphalt two-lane highway onto a gravel road, you find that what you've seen is the tops of tall cottonwoods standing in glory along a creek bottom, accompanied by willows.

Nearly every morning I pass by a young tree—some sort of locust—that signifies survival against all odds. Most likely it was stripped bare in its earliest years, when every summer a farmer mowed the roadside ditch for hay. But it lived on, a leaf or two surviving each year, until the farmer noticed it and decided to mow around it. It's now nearly seven feet tall, a clever tree standing alone at the very bottom of the shallow ditch, catching what moisture it can. It feels natural for me to converse with it, in any season, in the light just before dawn.

I share with this tree years of mornings, a moonset so enormous and red I mistook it for a fire in the distance, an ice storm with winds so sharp I couldn't keep walking westward and had to return home. Years of painterly skies at dawn. Foxes on the run, cats on the hunt. For much of my walk I am as treeless as the land around me, but on my way back into town I pass a large grove, an entrance to a drive-in movie theater, long since gone. If the wind is up, the trees roar like the ocean. Sometimes sheep are grazing there, and even though I expect to see them, they startle me with their cries, which sound remarkably like those of a human infant. This past summer the grove was the haunt of kestrels, and I often watched them maneuvering in the sky, wondering what it would feel like to ride backwards, forwards, sideways on the currents of air.

Our trees, our treelessness, are, as so much in life, a matter of perspective. One summer both my father-in-law and my mother were visiting. He was raised in New York State, and couldn't get over the lack of trees. I think he found it terrifying, as many Easterners do. My mother kept telling him that there were many more trees here now than when she was a girl, so many that the countryside seemed luxuriant. Maybe trees are a luxury here; the question then becomes, how many do we need?

My mother has told me that she first encountered the notion of a forest from the illustrations in Grimms' fairy tales. She wanted so badly to see a forest, any forest, that she would crawl under the lilac bushes that her mother had planted by the front door and pretend she was in the Black Forest. I used to pretend—I can no longer remember what—with the honeysuckle bushes in the first backyard I remember, in Arlington, Virginia. I spent a lot of time with them, watching from my two-seat glider swing. The one great tree in that backyard, an elm, was a powerful symbol for me, a tree of family myth, because, when I was five and my brother nine, he had used it to run away from home. Climbing out his second-story bedroom window to get away from a baby-sitter he disliked, he'd spent an afternoon at a neighborhood drugstore, reading comic books. I remember looking up at that tree, after the great event, trying to imagine that freedom. I also examined the branches from the upstairs window, and doubted that I'd ever have the nerve to make the leap.

We left Virginia when I was seven, and moved to Illinois. I lost the honeysuckle, and the other trees of my early childhood—dogwood, magnolia, sassafras, sycamore, and the enormous weeping willow and white oak of a nursery school in the countryside where my mother had enrolled me. I have only faint memories of the fabled cherry trees of Washington, D.C., and suspect that my memories of the cherry blossoms come mainly from having been told about them, and looking at family photographs.

Beach Park, Illinois, just north of Waukegan, was still rural in 1954; I walked to a four-room country school. We lived in a small, new suburb on acre lots, where the trees were saplings. But across the street was a plowed field with an island of tall trees in the center. Oak, elm, aspen. Although it was good to know that the trees were there, a brooding, comforting presence, I never ventured into them. I much preferred what was close at hand, the stands of pussy willow in the roadside ditch.

The trees of northern Illinois were lost to me when we moved to Honolulu in 1959, and I learned a new vocabulary: Banyan. Hala. Koa. Bamboo. My favorite tree on all of Oahu was (and is) the magnificent spreading monkeypod of Moanalua Gardens. Even the stench and incessant roar of traffic on an encroaching freeway doesn't diminish its beauty. The other tree I came to love in Honolulu is the eucalyptus that stands by the wooden stairway of Old School Hall on my high-school campus, a building erected in the 1860s. It made me happy to study English in a building that had stood when Emily Dickinson was alive, and the stately tree, its bark variegated like a fragile nineteenth-century endpaper, seemed a suitable companion for that happiness.

I recall testing an ancient legend on the slopes of Kilauea, on the Big Island, with some high-school girlfriends. We picked several sassy, fringed blooms of the native lehua tree, and, sure enough, were sprinkled with rain on our hike back to our lodge. I also recall harvesting bananas in our backyard, a process that involved arming myself with a machete and cutting down the entire tree—it is in fact a form of grass, a thick and pulpy weed. I shook out the spiders and let the tiny bananas, over twenty pounds' worth, ripen in a paper sack. They're much sweeter than anything you can buy in a grocery store. Years later, that experience rescued me. At a cocktail party in New York City, a man recently returned from Brazil declared that the trouble with America was that you couldn't buy a decent machete. I had no idea if the family machete was a good one or not, but I was the only person in the group who'd actually used one, and what had been a dreary, sodden literary gathering became more interesting.

By the time I went to college, in Vermont, I had lost the language of deciduous trees. People had to name for me the maple, oak, sumac, and beech. I recognized birches from photographs, and poems. As fine and fabled as it is, now that I've been on the plains for over twenty years, New England foliage seems profligate to me, too showy. Here, in the fall, the groves of ash and poplars planted as windbreaks glow in a golden, Italianate light, and I feel as if I am in a painting by Giotto, or Fra Angelico. A dusty, spare, but lovely place in Tuscany, or western Dakota.

Each December I visit my family in Honolulu, traveling from the wintry plains to what I call the green world. It is profligate to the extreme; in a yard not much bigger than my own is an enormous mango tree, and also lime, tangerine, pomegranate, pomelo, mountain apple, lichee, hibiscus, hala, lehua, plumeria, and Norfolk Island pine. Like many Hawaii residents, we often top a pine to make a Christmas tree.

After all of that, I find it an odd joy to return to winter, to a stark white world. And I dream of trees, wondering if sometimes I would rather dream of trees than have so many close at hand. Even when it means adjusting to a temperature more than a hundred degrees colder than in Hawaii, it's the dryness of the plains that most affects me. My face and hands turn to tree bark. In the heart of winter the green world is dormant, not yet hoped for. Moisture is scarce—even our snow is dry—and the vast space around the bare branches of trees is all the more a presence.

This brings me back to where I began, with Jim Burden's reflection on scarcity. If scarcity makes things more precious, what does it mean to choose the spare world over one in which we are sated with abundance? Is this the spiritual dimension that Brave Buffalo leads us to? Does living in a place with so few trees bring with it certain responsibilities? Gratitude, for example? The painful acceptance that underlies Psalm 16's "Welcome indeed the heritage that falls to me"?

Monastic men and women tell me that one question that bites pretty hard in their early years in the monastery is why anyone would choose to live this way, deprived of the autonomy and abundance of choices that middle-class Americans take for granted. We're taught all our lives to "keep our options open," but a commitment to monastic life puts an end to that. It is not a choice but a call, and often the people who last in a monastery are those who struggle through their early years reminding themselves of that fact. One sister told me that it wasn't until she had entered monastic formation that the words of Jesus in John 15:16 had any significance in her life: "Ye have not chosen me, but I have chosen you. . . ."

Stark words in a stark environment. A monk in his early thirties once told me that he'd come to the monastery not realizing what a shock it would be suddenly not to have to compete for the things that young men are conditioned to compete for in American society—in his words, "a good salary, a cool car, and a pretty girlfriend." "When all of that was suddenly gone," he added, "and held of no account, I felt as if my whole life were a lie. It took me years to find out who God wanted me to be."

What does it mean to become simple? I think of the abbey of New Mellary in Iowa, the walls of its church long plastered over, until the architectural consultant they had hired to help them remodel discovered that underneath the plaster were walls of native stone. The monks themselves did the work of uncovering them, and now the church is a place where one can sit and wait and watch the play of sunlight and shadow, a place made holy by the simple glory of light on stone.

What would I find in my own heart, if the noise of the world were silenced? Who would I be? Who will I be, when loss or crisis or the depredations of time take away the trappings of success, of self-importance, even personality itself? Could the trees of my beloved plains, or the lack of them, help me to know? The first monks read the earth as the work and word of God, a creation that was spoken into being. "Study fish," advises Saint Gregory of Nazianzus. "In the water they fly, and they find the air they need in the water. They would die in our atmosphere, just as we would die in the water. Watch their habits, their way of mating and procreating their kind, their beauty, their permanent homes and their wanderings." Look, Gregory says, "at the bees and the spiders. Where do their love of work and their ingenuity come from? Can you explain it and arrive at an understanding of the wisdom they point to?"

The wisdom of the few, struggling trees on the plains, and the vast spaces around them, are a continual reminder that my life is cluttered by comparison. At home, an abundance of books and papers overlays the heavy furniture I inherited from my grandparents. A perfectly simple room, with one perfect object to meditate on, remains a dream until I step outside, onto the plains. A tree. A butte. The sunrise. It always makes me wonder: What is enough? Are there enough trees here? As always, it seems that, the more I can distinguish my true needs from my wants, the more of a shock it is to realize how little *is* enough.

On a summer night, between 2:00 and 3:00 A.M., a front moves in and I awake. A fierce wind has stirred the trees. It's been hot for so long, I go outdoors to luxuriate in the newly cooled air. A friend from far away is sleeping in my studio, and I want to say the prayers that will protect him, give him needed rest. I want my husband's sleep to help him heal from the pain of recent surgery. The trees that fan me are the fruit of others' labor, planted by an earlier generation of plains dwellers who longed for trees to shelter them. The land resisted, but let them have these few. I am startled by something flashing through the trees—it is the Pleiades, all seven of them plainly visible with the naked eye. This is another's work, and a mystery. And it is enough.

Laura Bowers Foreman

For the Maples

rum, chop, burn!" the professor chanted as he paced the lecture hall. Dutifully I took notes. I was nineteen, a second-year forestry student at a Southeastern university in 1975.

Pounding the lectern with a volume of Gifford Pinchot, the revered father of forest management, my burly, bearded professor repeated, "Drum!" He was referring to the huge drum that is dragged behind a tractor across the forest floor after all the valued wood—the oak, ash, and hickory—has been cut and taken. That drum crushes everything in its path—brush, small trees, and wildlife as well.

"Chop!" His arm flew into the air as if to rev the chainsaw and chipper that would tear apart whatever branches and trees the drum had not crushed.

"Burn!" To him, this fallen forest was worthless slash. Fires would be ignited, incinerating all. Where once a lush forest had flourished, only a charred landscape would remain.

"Rejuvenate to loblolly pine!" Loblolly is revered in the South for its commercial value. The wood is relatively knot-free, which has made it valuable for lumber, plywood, and paper production. Often loblolly is called old-field pine because it is naturally aggressive and forms fast-growing, pure stands on abandoned fields. Tree farms would be planted. Row after row, a battalion of pines would be kept uniform with the abundant application of herbicides. Any new and wild growth would be considered invasive and destroyed.

I stopped taking notes, deeply appalled by the professor's vision. My pulse pounded as I listened to him. To Gifford Pinchot, trees were a crop, like corn, and he convinced Teddy Roosevelt to transfer the national forests to the Department of Agriculture in 1905. Pinchot then announced that this great crop of trees must be managed by "well-trained, vigorous, tough men." Decades later, Richard Nixon promoted this same environmental manifesto: "Old growth timber [must be] converted into new, well-managed stands of trees." I knew that soon these well-managed stands of loblolly would produce great profits for the South. But, like tobacco, the South's other cash crop, they would eclipse other forms of plant and animal life.

I looked around the hall at my classmates and wondered, *Am I the only one who questions this destruction?*

Hundreds of men filled the lecture hall. Some were eighteen-year-old boys masquerading as grizzled loggers in their Redwing boots and flannel shirts, tobacco juice trickling down their sparse beards. Some were suburban boys shod in expensive Italian hiking boots. Raking their soft hands through unkempt morning hair, they yawned and sprawled lazily across the upholstered seats. Some were older, nearing thirty. Shrugging off any hint of costume, having had their fill of uniforms in Vietnam, they wore sneakers, jeans, and T-shirts. They sat together warily, in silence.

Scattered sparsely amid this forest of men, I spied about five other feminine faces. Isolated, we had formed no sorority, yet we were a visible disturbance in Pinchot's vision of "vigorous, tough *men.*" A couple of women opted for a masculine forester look, with Vibram-soled boots and hunting knives looped to their belts. The attire of the rest of us only hinted at our field of study—a thermal shirt here, hiking boots there.

I looked like a hybrid of sorts. Unable to afford costly hiking boots, I wore the slick-soled construction variety. Jeans weren't made to fit my womanly hips, so mine were baggy thrift-shop trophies. I clung to the remnants of my femininity, wearing my mother's delicately embroidered chiffon blouses over leotards. But I wondered at what point during my education I would be expected to conform to Pinchot's ideal.

I had come to forestry with a passionate desire to understand the complexity of the natural world. Throughout my childhood, the forest had provided sanctuary from an often troubled home. Acutely aware of the pollution that threatened the environment, I hoped my education would prepare me to work as a defender of the wild world. The land had nurtured me for eighteen years, and I longed to reciprocate.

I soon sensed that my ideals were considered too "feminine"— yet I could find no other curriculum that embraced my quest to learn about the plants of the forest. Fearing ridicule, I hid my agenda—my spiritual connection with the forest and all things wild. The other women in forestry seemed equally guarded.

Rather than seek the camaraderie of my own sex, I sat with the Vietnam vets. I sensed they sought more than board-foot production from the forest; perhaps they hoped to heal their scarred spirits. Yet rarely did a classmate reveal affection for this, our battered and beloved earth.

As I sat in class, I still remembered the grief I carried for the maples I had loved in my best friend's yard. Mary Ann had lived next door with her grandmother, in a big old white Virginia farmhouse that was surrounded by trees—deeply rooted, lush-leaved Norway maples. Our house was part of a new development which had been built on her grandfather's old farm fields. Unlike her home, my house had no history and looked desolate, as it sat without landscaping. Mary Ann's family seemed serene compared to mine, with the frequent moves my dad's Air Force career had required. My parents showed scant interest in lawn work, and our yard seemed to be the result of what the wind blew in: feral locust trees, scattered helter-skelter, offering only their ratty little stems. I longed for the planned and planted fence line of Mary Ann's sturdy maples.

But those weed trees grew quickly in that open field, and soon the locusts were rooftop-high. Yet they were a disgrace to me, because they offered no low branches for climbing, only lengthy stretches of scratchy furrowed bark. I sought refuge in the land of *real* trees, Mary Ann's maples with their smooth branches. In summertime we invented green treetop apartments, and mine were always on the uppermost floor. We surprised the occasional pedestrian passing under our leafy domain with handfuls of seed-thick samaras, their helicopter wings swirling like drunken green dust devils.

And then, one summer, I was startled to discover black branches clawing the green crowns. A fungus had infected the trees. Mary Ann's grandmother hired a horticulturalist. Infected branches were removed and wounds were salved. But the holes of decay grew larger. Scattered leaves clung to dying branches. One by one, every tree succumbed, until all of those proud maples were cut down. Mary Ann and I walked the fence row listlessly, curling our toes around the lifeless roots. We mourned the death of the trees like the passing of our own childhood.

Down the hill, the feral locust trees in my own yard were thriving, waving in wild glory as they towered over my parents' home. Willow and mulberry had joined the homestead. The trees had jostled one another for elbow room, and each had found a niche. In college I would learn that the rhizomes of locust trees grow nodules filled with nitrogen-fixing bacteria which help to restore nutrients to depleted farmed soil. Together the trees were pioneers, healing and preparing the land for other species. Although I mourned the loss of the maples, their deaths had given me my first lesson in the ways of the natural world.

So now, as I sat in the university auditorium, listening to my professor expound the virtues of monoculture, I was restless and troubled. Nervously, I tapped my pen against my notebook. My heart thundered as my anger grew. At last I stood up, my shaking hands curled into fists. "What if tree farms are attacked by disease or insects?" I asked. "Aren't they a monoculture and therefore vulnerable?"

Stopping his lecture, the professor glared at me in silence. My seatmate, a veteran of two tours in Vietnam, whispered, "You heard the man—long live the loblollies!" I heard the sarcasm in his voice and realized I had at least one ally. Grimly I fell back into my seat.

I had come to forestry because I longed to understand nature's secrets. Where Pinchot and his proponents sought to organize trees into farms, I longed for the diversity of the forest. Where foresters saw only competition, I could also see cooperation. Oaks were not merely *Quercus* but a huge family whose members found a place to thrive within an ecosystem. White oak coveted richly soiled coves, whereas its scrappy sister post oak thrived on rocky ridges. This diverse family lived in communities populated by other, equally complex families—hickories, maples, and sumacs, to name just a few. As with human communities, these tree towns were not without competition, but neighbors also supported each other. They conserved and shared moisture. Each species added its own nutrients to the soil. Together they maintained an exquisite balance.

But in those days foresters ranked trees with a critical eye toward commerce. White oaks were highbrows, sought after for furniture and flooring. Box-elder maple was a lowlife, of no economic importance. On such criteria I would be expected to make life-and-death decisions.

The summer before my senior year, I took a seasonal job as an intern with the Forest Service in Idaho's old-growth forests. On the daily commute to our work sites over twisty, narrow logging roads, we usually spotted a herd of elk, and occasionally a sow bear ambled by. Each step I took into the cool, dark forest disturbed centuries of layered detritus, dusty humus cloying the air with its pine-scented incense. A sunbeam graced a nurse log tending her brood of saplings. Although cedars, six feet in diameter, reigned supreme, the forest also nurtured hemlock, grand fir, Douglas fir, and even an occasional sun-loving Western white pine.

My job was to mark "leave trees" with yellow spray paint. All others would be cut. The "leave trees" would carry the genetic burden of reseeding. Almost exclusively they were to be fast-growing clear-grained Douglas fir. Grand fir was shunned, even though it produced beautiful lumber, because it grew more slowly than Douglas fir. My boss ordered, "Get rid of that hemlock. The lumber is just full of cracks—too much ring shake." I looked at the flat russet scales in the bark of an ancient hemlock and remembered a small stand back east. So few old-growth Eastern hemlock remained, even the professors revered them.

"Don't leave any white pine," he continued. "Blister will just come in after it." I knew the story of white pine. European settlers had clear-cut huge blocks of acreage. This land had previously supported a diversity of species, but because white pine is a pioneer tree, it was the first to seed in. Its ecological role is to cover and protect damaged ground. The species is aggressive and, under natural conditions, covers small and isolated patches. With clear-cuts, hundreds of acres lay open to receive wind-cast white pine seeds. Never before had white pine grown in such large, pure stands. Blister rust, a fungus that attacks the bark and eventually kills the tree, became a problem when pure stands seeded in after earlier rounds of massive clear-cuts.

One by one, my boss dismissed and eliminated tree species. Under his command, Douglas fir, a beautiful tree, was being forced to conquer the wild forest. Months later a co-worker finally fumed, "I used to love Douglas fir. Now I just hate it. I'm sick of it!"

Then, one day, my boss's raspy voice interrupted the deep drumming of a ruffled grouse. "These old-growth forests are just 'biological deserts.' Old cedars and hemlocks block out all the light. We can't get a thirty-year ROI!" In timber production, a thirty-year ROI was the gold standard, meaning that trees should produce harvestable lumber in thirty years. "These mountainsides have to be cleared out. Burn the slash, expose the mineral soil, and Douglas fir will seed in."

I was standing in a cove of healthy grand fir when I heard him. I ran my palm along the smooth gray bark of a trunk. Tiny resin bubbles released their sticky sap, coating my fingers. I stopped and looked at my hand. Stringy resin stretched between my fingers, and soft green fir needles clung to it. Mossy tendrils of grandfather's beard dripped from my wrist, and each fingernail was dusted with black loamy soil. Conscious of my breath, I inhaled great gulps of oxygen the trees offered. I understood then that I was part of the forest. I could no longer deny the destructive reality of my work. The scars of massive clear-cuts pockmarked the Idaho mountainsides.

Standing in that cluster of grand firs, I recalled a recent afternoon when I was picking my way through the blackened bones of a recently burned clear-cut. I watched a coyote digging furiously beneath a mound of strewn logs. Catching my scent, she stopped digging and stared at me, panting heavily in the sunlight. Her fur was matted with gray scabs. She paused only briefly and then returned to her frantic burrowing. Recalling her distress, I realized she must have returned to her den and found it buried beneath the devastation.

What was to become of a world in which only one or two species were allowed? What was to become of foresters who did not conform? Would we too be culled?

I stared at my other hand, which was covered in paint. I took a stand. Throwing back my shoulders, I sprayed a grand fir. I sprayed a hemlock. I sprayed a white pine. I sprayed a cedar. I saved each healthy tree with great swaths of Forest Service yellow.

Each day, I continued my mission. No one examined my work. I was not suspect. By late August, duties were done. Loggers were next on the Forest Service payroll, for they would fell unmarked trees through the winter months. As I packed up the car, it spilled over with the found treasures of summer: pine cones, elk antlers, and wood burls.

During my first years after graduation I continued to work in the forest industry, but my anger with forest-management practices only grew. My long and often painful process of waking up had begun. During those years I lived my life as a battle, yet I could find no allies to instigate change. Isolated and deeply discouraged, I left my work as a forester. I moved to the Northwest, and for a time I continued to fight. For seven years I served on my community's planning policy commission and struggled to protect the salmon-spawning streams and forested mountains from development.

But in contrast to my isolation in the Southeast and Idaho, here in the Northwest I have finally found my allies. Mostly women, these kindred spirits have a new way to voice their commitment to the environment. As members of Catkin Moon, we are a community committed to both learning and teaching about the ecology of plants native to the Northwest. Often we go out to salvage plants from sites destined for development. Frequently the back end of my van is loaded with buckets filled with vine-maple wands, clusters of piggyback plants, and trilliums offering their creamy white lilies. Surrounding my house is a forest—filled with cedars, hemlocks, alders, maples, and Douglas fir. Along my fence I have planted a bountiful hedgerow of native ferns, dogwoods, and maples. Each spring I rejoice with the return of familiar migrating birds to my refuge. Green and violet swallows swoop down for pollinating insects. Tiny rufous hummingbirds flash bejeweled orange chest feathers and boldly claim territory. Shy black-headed grosbeaks flirt among cedar branches.

In 1975 I sat in my forestry lecture hall and began to hide the passion I felt for the natural world. Now, twenty-five years later, I work to honor the love I felt in my young heart. I do this for myself and my children. I do this for trees, for the maples.

Diane Ackerman

Rain Forest

n the rain forest, no niche lies unused. No emptiness goes unfilled. No gasp of sunlight goes untrapped. In a million vest pockets, a million life-forms quietly tick. No other place on earth feels so lush. Sometimes we picture it as an echo of the original Garden of Eden—a realm ancient, serene, and fertile, where pythons slither and jaguars lope. But it is mainly a world of cunning and savage trees. Truant plants will not survive. The meek inherit nothing. Light is a thick yellow vitamin they would kill for, and they do. One of the first truths one learns in the rain forest is that there is nothing fainthearted or wimpy about plants. They are aggressive about self-defense. Some trees protect their circulatory systems by putting a layer of strychnine or quinine under their bark. Others have poisonous sap, leaves, or berries. There are tannins and scents that mimic insect juvenile hormones, and enzymes strong enough to tenderize meat (or your tongue), and agents powerful enough to paralyze a wayward insect or animal. One ingenious plant is the derris vine, whose bark Amazonian Indians crush in the river to poison fish. Some plants develop colorful red-speckled or -streaked leaves so that they appear to be dying or dead and therefore of no interest to hungry mouths. Others evolve long vicious spines. *Strychnos* can stop your heart with its beauty . . . or its curare. And then, of course, there are the hallucinogens, produced by tree and vine bark, flowers, beans, cacti, and fungi. Some of the toads are hallucinogenic, too, which isn't at all surprising when you look at their burst of free-floating hop-and-color squatting on a branch, brazenly daring you to touch. On a rain-forest walk, I found a vibrant aqua-blue-and-yellow arrowhead frog that was covered with a poisonous mucus. Tiny but pungent with death, it sat right out on a felled tree and let me get close enough to breathe on it.

In temperate Northern forests, one finds fewer species of plants in an area, but many of each species; it's not unusual to see large glades of hemlock or maple. But in the rain forest, there are kaleidoscopic numbers of different species, and very few samples of each one. When you look at such a forest, it has depth, texture, variety. Yet the members of each species are spaced far apart. There is not much breeze to carry seeds about. It's hard to have a sex life when you can't move, so jungle plants have become incredible tricksters and manipulators, conning others into performing sex acts with them. In a rain forest, it's no use spilling their seed on the ground beneath them. There would be too much inbreeding, and one of the best aspects of sex, from a plant's point of view, is that it freshens the gene pool. So plants lure hummingbirds, bees, bats, butterflies, moths, insects. Plants are willing to dress up in animal disguises. Some plants are carnivores. They are not mild-mannered, even if they aren't quick-footed. They are promiscuous, and they will stoop to every low-down trick. They would dress up in a gorilla suit if they could.

Some orchids, for example, living high up in the canopies, have learned how to divert bees with their splashy color and blossoms that lure the unsuspecting bee to brush up against their sex organs. Other orchids have evolved to mimic the female tachinid fly, so that males will try to mate with them and end up dusted with pollen. Still other orchids mimic the territorial movements of a male *Centris* bee and need only wait for passing males to take up the fight. Sex or violence will do equally well: whether the orchids are courted or fought with, they rub pollen on the visitor. Some of the best pollinators are male orchid bees, which are bright metallic blue or green and are after not pollen but fragrances, which they use as part of an aphrodisiac brew and store in pockets on their hind legs. Going from flower to flower, they collect a note of fragrance and blend it in their hind-leg pockets; at some magical point, the mix begins to simmer just right, and they become such Adonises that even other males take notice. Soon, a swarm of brightly flashing males dancing in the sunlight attracts female orchid bees, just as the flowers attracted the males. Now the males are the beautiful, fragrant blossoms of the jungle. Who could resist them?

Carolyn Kizer

Index, a Mountain

(Part of the Cascade Range, Washington State)

I.

Early one day a mountain uprose, all cased in silver
Where morning fog caught in the tips of cedars
And a moon-colored sun polished virgin timber.

As Red Freddie, our old new Studebaker,
Steams over the Cascades, Mother says to Father,
"I wanted to bring you here on our honeymoon;
First growth. Never cut over." In my fifth year,
Carsick on hairpin turns, bribed not to chatter
A penny a mile; the black-timbered inn at the summit
Where I roll out and under the bed at night,
Awake, screaming with claustrophobia,
Clawing the bedsprings, having dreamed
Me in my coffin.

Motoring on at dawn, to Index then we came:
A cut muscle. A smoking cinder.

An old bald lumberman had cut God's finger,
Himself missing a limb. (As usual, Retribution
Didn't know when to quit, took the whole arm.)
One day he'll appear, on 16-millimeter film,
Bracing his brassie between one stump
And a tough left arm.
The drive sails down the fairway, hooking slightly.
He gloats; a ghostly hand pinned to his shoulder.
Twenty years have passed, and I, all unknowing,
Have married the grandson of this predator.

O friends and our descendants, what remains?
Banquets of sawdust, hazy leisure bought
From the swink of loggers and the stink of pulp;
Victorian mansions ugly as the mills
Bulldozed for malls, car stalls defined
By rows and rows of scruffy little trees.
Preserve nothing! The simple motto of our frontier
Because men choked on green, were suffocated
By a press of trees, fire was their liberator.
Fire went too far, like Retribution,
Like any Revolution. Revenge has a long finger.

O Pioneers, who stripped the earth so fast,
Who toiled so hard Imagination failed.
How could you dream of the later Marxist
Trailblazers, enshrining worker-heroes
On their plinths of crumbling concrete,
Giant fingers that pierced the ancient ceiling
Scarred with the junk of her astronauts and ours?
Our icons: Lenin, Bunyan: Peter and Paul
Like Barnum pointing, "This way to the Egress,"
To be saved from our follies by fleeing to the stars.

2.
Ours is a world full of finger-worship
As the holy Roman bone-collectors knew:

Keepers of femur and tibia, toenail sniffers,
Their artisans formed silver reliquaries,
Cool tubes, like those that encase a good cigar,
To hold erect the dust of an index finger.

Now, for history, we drive a car
From the empty summit (the old inn long burned down)
Past Troublesome Creek to Goldbar, a mining camp
Where a few Chinese were saved from an early riot
By shipping them out-of-town in slapped-up coffins,
To Sultan, where they lit the lamps at three
In the afternoon, woods were so dense.
Lilacs were as large as fruit trees once;
Houses of pioneers, with weathered siding,
Looked like birds' nests fallen among the cedars,
Such great dark brooding trees they were!

The barren shade of the high Cascades ends here.
It's all burned-over, pocked with stumps that look
Like the old man's arm. The view, as we descend,
Blending to smooth pasture, pastoral landscape
Dotted with cows, gives way to golf-course lawns,
A strident green, bobbed willows, men on carts.
While just outside the gates a sign proclaims,
"The Wages of Sin is Death!" A finger aimed at *you*.

This West! full of crank religions, bleeding atoners,
Raw, shapeless women, stringy men with tracts
On your porch at dawn, wanting to play you a record.
The pulp they press on us with bony fingers
Conceiving us in Sin, had its own conception
In the sawmill's sweet dust—pressed from our trees!

O Index, naked mountain, with your scarred flanks
Still your raw summit points to heaven.
Serve as God's tombstone. Have no green mercy on us.

Stephanie Kaza

House of Wood

 have woken up at the end of a long week of tired-
ness. I am too tired to go anywhere. Too tired to
seek out a tree for comfort. Too tired to walk in
the forest on the mountain. Too full of the sadness
and tenderness that speaks through me as I teach
about how we are living with the environment, how we are dying
with the environment. It is difficult work to be present with the
state of the world. The more I pay attention to the economic and
political forces driving environmental deterioration, the less certain
I am that anything I do will stop it. My heart aches for the thought-
less deaths of so many trees. Sometimes I long for a break from the
destruction and grief.

Here in my home I find some comfort in the beauty and simplicity of this house. I am grateful to be surrounded by wood and by
the memory of trees. Wood walls and ceiling, a beautiful oak floor,
paned glass and wood windows, kitchen cupboards crafted of wood.
From all sides I am embraced by wood. The presence of trees

soothes my eyes and soul. The natural warm brown color is restful. It is just what it is, nothing extra. No decorations, no wallpaper, no paint, no layers of anything masking the wood. The simplicity is refreshing. I appreciate the unevenness and random variation of the wood.

All these trees—the oaks in the floor, the firs and redwoods in the walls, the cedar in the yarn chest—are trees of the Pacific forest, trees of my homeland. But here in the house they are quiet and alone, no longer dancing in the wind or singing with the birds. It feels a bit like a tree cemetery—in elegant form, of course. It is hard to think of the wood as dead. It doesn't feel as if I live in a house of death. The grain of the wood is too alive. Its memory is too vivid, etched from the experience of lifetimes. I feel the histories of individual trees; they resonate in each beam and board.

One thing is wrong, though—the straightness. All of the wood has been cut into straight forms. Trees, however, are not entirely straight, especially the hardwoods. It is convenient to live in this straightness. It makes walking and organizing things easier. It works well with gravity and the desire of the inner ear for balance. But I miss the graceful curves of the living tree. I miss the tangle of branches, the intimate spaces between the twigs and fingers of each limb. Planed surfaces in a house have all the intimacy ironed out of them. They have been flattened, standardized, regulated, cut to conform to human design. In the process the trees' own naturally beautiful shapes have been altered beyond recognition.

So this is the pain of it: in leaving its life-form behind, the wood has become an object for human use. Object—where is the heart in that? An object is something to carry around, to count, to purchase, to collect. It is something separate. The process of objectification begins with the first cut toward straightness. After the trees are felled, the conspiracy of object continues in the timber-sales reports, lumberyard accounts, and architectural plans. The carpenters perhaps cradled the wood in their hands as they built this house, but did they remember the once living trees? I wonder who among the many people who deal with wood as product have walked in the forests of these trees and listened to their voices.

When the memory of tree has vanished and the connection is broken, the wood becomes corpse, or not even corpse, but something that appears never to have been alive.

The wood ceiling here is supported by two big crossbeams and pillars. I look up at these beams often, because the shape and design are compelling. They form a cross. I look at this cross of wood and imagine a person suspended, connected to the wood. The image of Jesus with downcast head and pierced hands and feet evokes a powerful response of compassion. I can't help identifying with the human agony of his experience.

But what about the wood of the cross? I wonder if Jesus was embraced by the spirit of tree in his painful death. He did not die alone. Even in his last moments he was supported by life. The cross served as a link to the ground, touching the common soil of our lives. Jesus on high hung partway between grounded reality and the mysterious unknown. Many have focused on the transcendent theme of his story, but what about his fundamental connection to the earth through the cross? Is this not an equally valid route to spiritual awakening?

But the cross was only a piece of a tree. Why didn't they nail him to a living tree? Perhaps that would have offered too much life force and spiritual strength. Also, the tree represents intimacy; a cross speaks of exposure. This central religious story is about crucifixion of tree as much as crucifixion of person. The curving intimacy of the tree was symbolically replaced by the linear abstraction of the cross. This is the loss I feel—the living tree reduced to objectified pieces, the loss of life as it really is, vivid and unsimplifiable.

In the midst of his own tragic story, I wonder if Jesus noticed the loss of tree life. As a great teacher of compassion and a carpenter himself, I want to believe that he had some care and concern for trees. It seems to me that his gospel of love applies to relationships with trees as well as people. In the story of the crucifixion, the tree did not have any choice in the decision to end its life and to be disfigured in death. The tree did not ask to be sacrificed any more than Jesus did. And the tree could not cry out to others, "My God, my God, why hast Thou forsaken me?" The recorders of history passed on the story of the great wrongdoing to Jesus, but they overlooked the story of the cross.

Gazing at the crossbeams of my house, I am caught by this double crucifixion, and with my culture I carry the pain of both deaths. In studying the story of Jesus, people ask themselves over and over, what does it mean? Theologians, ministers, ordinary people want to know how this suffering speaks to their lives. It encourages the practice of compassion, forgiveness, and the development of spiritual strength. The story is passed on to others, and the search for meaning stays alive.

The story of the tree is another matter. The loss has barely been noticed. The drama of tree death is repeated over and over again, day after day, decade after decade, century after century. As if in a daze, people permit the continual execution of millions of tree martyrs, whose crosses become chopsticks, tables, paper, and buildings. I am as much a part of this web of sacrifice as anyone, and that is painful. I cannot find an easy way to live with integrity in the midst of this confusion. I am weary with wondering how much will be destroyed before we find the tree behind Jesus.

Brenda Peterson

Killing Our Elders

s a small child growing up on a Forest Service lookout station in the High Sierras, I believed the encircling tribe of trees were silent neighbors who protectively held the sky up over our rough cabins. For all their soaring, deep stillness, the ponderosa pines and giant Douglas firs often made noises in the night, a language of whispers and soft whistles that sang through the cabin's walls.

Several summers ago, a friend and I drove through those High Sierra and Cascade forests again on a road trip from Los Angeles to my home in Seattle. In the four-hour drive between the old mining town of Yreka in northern California and Eugene, Oregon, we counted fifty logging trucks, roughly one every four minutes. Many of the flatbeds were loaded with only one or two huge trees each. On the mountainsides surrounding the highway, I was shocked to see so many clear-cuts, where once flourished ancient trees. Thousands of tree stumps bobbed across the barren hills like morning-after champagne corks.

I don't know when I started crying, whether at the sight of crazy-quilt scars of clear-cutting or when I saw the sullen bumper sticker in Drain, Oregon, heart of logging country, that read: WHEN YOU'RE OUT OF TOILET PAPER, USE A SPOTTED OWL! Maybe it was when we called our friend's cabin on Oregon's Snake River, outside of Merced, and he told us that every day, from dawn to dusk, a logging truck had lumbered by every five minutes. "It's like a funeral procession out of the forest," my friend Joe said. "It's panic logging; they're running shifts night and day before the winter or the Congress closes in on them."

As I drove through those once lush mountains, I noticed my fingers went angry-white from clenching the steering wheel every time a logging truck lumbered by me. I wondered about the loggers. They, too, grew up in the forest; their small hands also learned that bark is another kind of skin. Among these generations of logging families, there is a symbiotic love for the trees. Why, then, this desperate slashing of their own old-growth elders until less than 10 percent of these ancient trees still stand?

Amid all the politics of timber and conservation, there is something sorely missing. Who are the trees to us? What is our connection to them on a deeper level than product? In the five hundred thousand years of human history throughout Old Europe, the pagans worshipped trees. The word "pagan" means simply "of the land or country." When we recognized that our fate was directly linked to the land, trees were holy. Cutting down a sacred oak, for example, meant the severest punishment: the offender was gutted at the navel, his intestines wrapped around the tree stump so tree and man died together.

Our pagan ancestors believed that trees were more important than people, because the old forests survived and contributed to the whole for much more than one human lifetime. Between four and five thousand years ago in our own country once stood the giant sequoias in the Sierra Nevadas. Most of these great trees are gone; but in Sequoia National Park the General Sherman Tree still stands. Thousands pay homage to it every year. And no wonder. According to Chris Maser in *Forest Primeval: The Natural History of an Ancient Forest*, the General Sherman Tree "was estimated to be 3,800 years old in 1968. It would have germinated in 1832 B.C. . . . [It] would have been 632 years old when the Trojan War was fought in 1200 B.C. and 1,056 years old when the first Olympic Games were held in 776 B.C. It would have been 1,617 years old when the Great Wall of China was built in 215 B.C. and 1,832 years old when Jesus was born in Bethlehem."

How have we come to lose our awe and reverence for these old trees? Why have we put our short-term needs for two or three generations of jobs before our respect for our own past and our future? As we drove past the Pacific Northwest sawmills, I was startled to see stockpiled logs, enough for two or three years of processing. And still the logging trucks thundered up and down the mountain roads.

To quiet my own rising panic over such a timber rampage, I tried to understand: "What if trees were people?" I asked myself. "Would we treat them differently?" My initial response was "Well, if old trees were old people, of course, we'd preserve them, for their wisdom, their stories, the history they hold for us." But with a shock I realized that the reason we can slash our old-growth forests is the same reason we deny our own human elders a place in our tribe. If an old tree, like our old people, is not perceived as *productive*, it might as well be dead.

Several years ago my grandfather died. An Ozarkian hard-times farmer and ex-sheriff, Granddaddy was larger than life to the gaggle of grandchildren who gathered at his farm almost every summer vacation. Speaking in a dialect so deep it would need subtitles today, he'd rail against the "blaggarts" (blackguards) and "scoundrills" (scoundrels) he sought to jail for every crime from moonshining to murder. One of my earliest memories is playing checkers with a minor scoundrel in Granddaddy's jail. Another is of bouncing in the back of his pickup as he campaigned for re-election, honking his horn at every speakeasy and shouting out, "I'll shut ya down, I will, quicker 'n Christ comin' like a thief in the night!" I also remember Granddaddy sobbing his eyes out over his old hound's death. "It's just that he won't never be alongside me no more," Granddaddy explained to us. Somebody gave him a young hound pup, but Granddad was offended. "You can't replace all that knowin' of an old hound with this pup. That hound, he took care of me. Now I gotta take care of this young'un."

My granddaddy's funeral was the first time I'd ever seen all my kinfolk cry together. Without reserve, some thirty-odd people in a small backwoods church sobbed—bodies bent double, their breathing ragged. It was a grief distinct from the despair I'd heard at the deaths of an infant or a contemporary. At my granddaddy's funeral, we all, no matter what age, cried like lost children. We were not so much sad as lonely. We were not so much bereft as abandoned. Who would tell us stories of our people? Who would offer us the wisdom of the longtime survivor? Our grandfather, this most beloved elder, was no longer alongside us.

When I returned home from the funeral, someone asked me, "How old was he?" When I replied eighty-six, this person visibly lightened. He actually made a small shrug of his shoulders. "Oh, well then . . ." He dismissed the death as if it were less a loss than if it had been of a person in his prime. I wondered if the man might next suggest that I get myself a new hound puppy.

The nowadays notion that people, like parts, are replaceable and that old parts are meant to be cast aside for newer models is a direct result of an industrial age that sees the body and the earth as machines. In the preindustrial pagan or agrarian society, the death of an elder was cause for great sorrow and ceremony.

If, for example, my granddaddy were one of those old Douglas firs I saw in the forest funeral procession, would he really be equaled by a tiny sapling? Old trees, like old people, survive the ravages of middle-age competition for light or limelight; they give back to their generations more oxygen, more stories; they are tall and farsighted enough to see the future because they are so firmly rooted in the past. Old growth, whether tree or person, gives nurturing; the young saplings planted supposedly to replace them *need* nurturing.

As a nation are we still so young, do we still worship what is newborn or newly invented so much that we will be eternal adolescents, rebelling against the old order of trees or people? If our two-hundred-year-old country were a two-hundred-year-old Douglas fir, would we see ourselves as no more than prime timber to cut down and sell to Japan? Maturity teaches us limits and respect for those limits within and around us. This means limiting perhaps our needs, seeing the forest for the timber. If we keep sending all our old trees to the sawmills to die, if we keep shunting off our elders to nursing homes to die, if we keep denying death by believing we can replace it with what's new, we will not only have no past left us, we will have no future.

A Nez Percé Indian woman from Oregon recently told me that in her tradition there was a time when the ancient trees were living burial tombs for her people. Upon the death of a tribal elder, a great tree was scooped out enough to hold the folded, fetuslike body. Then the bark was laid back to grow over the small bones like a rough-hewn skin graft.

"The old trees held our old people for thousands of years," she said softly. "If you cut those ancient trees, you lose all your own ancestors, everyone who came before you. Such loneliness is unbearable."

Losing our old forests is like sacrificing many generations of our grandparents all at once; it's like suffering a collective memory loss. I could not help pondering this vast loss when I read the sad reports of former President Reagan's succumbing to Alzheimer's disease. In an interview, his biographer, Edmund Morris, reported that Mr. Reagan had stopped recognizing him—". . . I did not feel his presence beside me, only his absence." Morris then related a haunting scene: Referring to a set of his own presidential papers, Mr. Reagan told Morris to "move those trees." Morris commented, "Well, if a poet can compare stacked volumes to garners of grain, I guess a retired statesman can call his collected works trees if he wants."

Mr. Reagan was, of course, correct—his presidential papers were originally made from trees. But the eerie coincidence is that he presided over a decade in which vast areas of our old-growth forests were cut down, and he then, like those ancient forests, lost his memory. When I told this story to a South American who has spent many years studying with Brazilian shamans, she said softly, "Oh, your ex-president is like an old tree now, a grandfather who's fallen down and forgotten who he is." She shook her head sadly. "Old trees hold us to the earth by their deep roots. And trees are our memories, like the blueprints of our planet's history. When you cut those ancient trees, the earth loses its memory, its way of knowing who it really is."

Our children's generation is growing up with only the memory of ancient forests; they don't feel the presence of old trees, only their absence. If we continue to cut down the ancient forests, will the earth endure a kind of planetary Alzheimer's? Our forests, those brave and sheltering Standing People, need their ancestor forests, just as we humans need to be firmly rooted to our past generations, the grandparents who hold down our family tree.

I will always be lonely for my grandfather; the child in me will always long for the Standing People who watched over me in my forest birthplace. On some spiritual and physical level our human entrails are still wrapped around the old trees, like an umbilical cord. And every time a great tree is cut, our kind die, too—lost and lonely and longing for what we may someday recognize as ourselves.

Flora for Fauna

Donna Kelleher

Living Medicine for Animals

any of the drugs we use for animals today were originally derived from plants, but in veterinary school I learned only that plants were often toxic to animals. We students were taught to fear many of nature's most powerful medicinal herbs as if they were pathogens, and to place our trust in pharmaceutical drugs instead. By the time I graduated from veterinary school in 1994, amoxicillin (an antibiotic) and prednisone (a steroid) felt as safe and comfortable to me as an old pair of slippers, while lobelia (Indian tobacco), equisetum (horsetail), or even Saint-John's-wort were suspicious.

Gradually, I began to question this distrust of plants. I remembered how my grandmother used woolly-leaved mullein or gel-filled aloe to cure our sore throats or scraped knees. Her medicine cabinet extended to the plants perched precariously on the kitchen windowsill. Her knowledge of leaf poultices and root teas had been handed down through many generations. Once, after a nasty bike accident, she prepared an aloe-and-chamomile poultice for my scuffed elbows. As she simmered the flowers to make my medicine, she told me how her mother had done the same for her when she fell out of a tree. My embarrassment and pain were soothed not only by my grandmother's care, but by the many generations of women before her who had healed with living medicine.

The first patient upon whom I practiced plant medicine, however, was not a child but a frail canary nicknamed Chirpy, for the feeble sounds he made in lieu of singing. He sat at the bottom of his cage, unable to perch or even to walk normally. Large red calluses enveloped the bottom of both his feet, tipping him backward onto his tail when he tried to stand.

For two years my colleague Dr. Tracy Bennett, an experienced and capable avian veterinarian, struggled with the treatment of Chirpy's foot infection, otherwise known as "bumble foot." This condition is caused by a deep bacterial infection, a faulty immune system, and having a round, symmetrical perch instead of one that is bumpy like a real tree branch. Improving a bird's diet usually helps strengthen the body's defenses, so Tracy advised replacing Chirpy's unhealthy all-seed diet with organic pellets and fresh fruits and vegetables. She also prescribed antibiotic injections, oral antibiotics, soaking in antibiotics, and perch changes—to no avail. Chirpy's bumble foot worsened. Tracy had reached the limits of what conventional medicine could accomplish, and the canary's owner, who had given up on ever hearing his song again, donated him to our clinic.

Neither Tracy nor I give up easily. I had just finished doing acupuncture on a Boston terrier with skin problems when Tracy walked in carrying the pink cage. She gently scooped the tiny yellow bird from the bottom of the cage where he had fallen and splayed his red swollen feet, which curled inward. Chirpy's feathers were as dull as stone-ground mustard, and he squawked faintly in protest. Tracy suggested I try some herbs.

My thoughts traveled down two different roads as I compared the conventional approach with the holistic approach I had recently been studying. I decided not to focus so much on the bacteria and instead to concentrate on making the skin itself healthier. After all, it is normal for *Staphylococcus* bacteria to be all over all birds' feet without causing disease. I could think of no better way to heal living tissue than by using living medicine. I went home and sprawled out with all my texts about treating people with herbs, intent on transferring that information to Chirpy.

Birds pose a special problem in treatment. Because their metabolic rate is about twenty times that of a dog or human, drugs have little time to act on them. Most conventional drugs don't work for birds, and they may harm or even kill them. The more I thought about it, the clearer it seemed to me that with birds, safe medicinal herbs should be a treatment of first, not last, resort.

My next task was to find the herbs whose names I had scribbled down. The only herb shop I knew was in downtown Seattle. On the way, I practiced pronouncing the names on my list so I wouldn't embarrass myself when ordering them. Passing under the old wooden beams hung with chimes and crystals that framed the doorway of the shop, I imagined that waves of sandalwood incense were like the hands of Hindu spirits guiding me into an ancient healing cave.

Large dark-amber jars of dried flowers, leaves, and roots were piled to the ceiling on neat shelves behind the counter. I scanned the unfamiliar names, wondering about their origins. Cat's claw, shepherd's purse, yucca—who came up with such strange names in the first place, I wondered. The counter was cluttered with rings, stones, and incense holders in the shapes of elephants and foreign gods. But the herbalist was quiet and knowledgeable, and he weighed the herbs and poured them into little brown-paper bags that he labeled in pencil, smiling when I mispronounced "calendula."

My excitement grew as I drove home, thinking about these dried plants in the little paper bags beside me. I knew that since the beginning of time, animals have evolved with plants, in a symbiotic relationship: animals required the nutrition and restorative properties of plants, while plants needed animals to prune them and to spread their seeds. Animal bodies have long known how to utilize the active components in each plant. And despite my veterinary training, I was convinced that drugs throw off the animal's natural balance, because pharmaceutical chemistry is so foreign to it. The genetic material of animals and that of plants have evolved over thousands of years in response to one another.

When I got home, I opened the bags, touching and sniffing their contents. From my reading, I remembered how each herb had been used by our ancestors. Like my grandmother, and her own grandmother before her, I measured the herbs into a large pot and prepared a tea.

Tiny petals of golden calendula fell into the brew first, followed by rich, dark-green leaves of plantain, both good for healing wounds. Next, the slightly intimate scent of grindelia flowers, which were used by Native Americans to treat rashes from poison ivy and poison oak. Then the bitter-smelling, powerful antimicrobial herb goldenseal, which was renamed by Samuel Thomson in the early nineteenth century because he didn't like the Indian name, "yellow root." Salvia, from the Latin meaning "to heal," or sage, came next, with its antibiotic properties. I saw my grandmother in the kitchen again when I added the fresh, gelatinous pulp of an aloe plant—or "kumari," the Ayurvedic name—to soothe Chirpy's burning feet. Chamomile flowers smelled like sweet, freshly cut clover on a dewy summer morning, and they calmed my anxiety about trying this new form of medicine. After all, Peter Rabbit's mother had made him chamomile tea to settle him down after Mr. McGregor chased him with the business end of a rake.

I brewed the concoction, then left it to cool overnight. In the morning, I strained out the herbs. The tea looked like dirty dishwater, but it smelled like chamomile. It was hard to believe it was powerful enough to help my feathered friend, who had been sick for so long. Now I had to figure out a way to apply the herbs to the canary's feet. Cotton ball? Spray bottle? At a loss, I called Tracy. As she suggested, I poured some herbal tea in the bottom of a plastic container, poked holes in the lid, and placed Chirpy inside. To my surprise, he squatted comfortably on the bottom and did not struggle. I placed the container on the counter and Chirpy watched me closely through the sides as I did kitchen chores.

We repeated the treatments for the next few days, at home and at the clinic. Each day the bird's reflexes seemed faster and his eyes were more alert. On the fourth morning, Tracy called me at home with an anxious tone in her voice. "Chirpy's feet are sloughing off!" she exclaimed.

"What do you mean, 'sloughing'?" I asked. This didn't sound like especially good news.

"The big gnarls are peeling off," she said, "and it looks like healthy skin underneath."

I rushed over to the clinic to see for myself. For the first time, Chirpy's eyes were bright, and he walked with determination to a snack of fresh broccoli and carrots, ate heartily, and flew up to his madrona branch, where he perched proudly. Though the skin was still red and raw, I could make out each tiny toe. A few days later, the red calluses were gone entirely.

It seemed like a miracle until I realized that in nature, regular bathing in algae-laden rainwater would have been a daily event for Chirpy. He would have eaten a constant diet of fresh plants, and instead of perching all day, he would have been flying, as birds are supposed to do. All I had done was attempt to restore some of the bird's natural routine.

I adopted Chirpy, who lived two more years, free of ailments. He began to sing again, providing inspiration as I immersed myself in the study of holistic animal care. Now, years later, I use only holistic medicine on animals with long-term diseases. I've used herbs for many patients who are taking conventional therapies, too: dogs with epileptic seizures, itchy skin, or gastrointestinal problems, cats with urinary tract infections, feather-picking birds, paralyzed ferrets, horses with swollen joints.

I visited my grandmother soon after Chirpy's feet were restored to health. I told her about the herb store, the treatment, and the miraculous recovery.

"Not surprised," she murmured. "You know, I think herbs could cure just about anything."

And then I watched as she watered some seemingly empty pots out on the deck—they were filled with calendula seeds—and helped her settle them in the sun.

Jane Goodall and Dale Peterson

Visions of Caliban

himpanzees are practical botanists, but their botanical knowledge and traditions vary from one community to the next. In Gombe, scientists have found that chimps recognize and eat a minimum of 201 plant types. Chimps in Tanzania's Mahale Mountains, some one hundred miles south of Gombe, contend with a different pattern of vegetation, and their diet includes at least 328 different plant species and subspecies. But the chimpanzees' traditional knowledge extends beyond merely recognizing what is good food and what is not.

Anthropologist Richard Wrangham, while studying the eating habits of chimpanzees at Gombe in the early 1970s, discovered another dimension to chimpanzee tradition that had previously been considered unique to humans. Wrangham's curiosity was aroused when he noticed that some chimps sometimes, upon leaving their sleeping nests at dawn, would directly seek out certain plants. The plants were of a single species, *Aspilia pluriseta*, growing in six-foot-high bushes with bristly, spear-shaped leaves and yellow flowers. The chimps almost always sought the bristly leaves of this species at dawn, before 8:15 A.M.

The seeming purposefulness of their pursuit of these plants in itself was unusual. More remarkable was the fashion in which the apes selected and then ingested the bristly leaves of *Aspilia*. With elaborate care they selected only young leaves of a certain length, visually inspecting them and even, on occasion, touching and tasting without finally consuming them. (Wrangham observed chimps closing their lips around a leaf still on the bush, holding leaf in mouth for a few seconds as if tasting it, then sometimes abandoning the leaf without removing it from the plant.) When an *Aspilia* leaf was chosen, the chimpanzee would ingest it, again in remarkable fashion. "They picked each leaf individually," Wrangham told me one rainy afternoon in Uganda, "and took it into the mouth on the tongue, left the jaw slack while the mouth was closed, and then rolled it round and eventually swallowed it. Well, these are hairy leaves, and can you imagine just swallowing them?" Chimpanzees ordinarily eat leaves by chewing them, as one would expect. In this case the apes were not chewing at all—they were swallowing the leaves whole, with some deliberation. Normally, when Gombe chimps eat leaves, they ingest them rapidly (approximately thirty-seven per minute for comparable-sized leaves of another genus), but Wrangham found their ingestion of the *Aspilia* leaves to be remarkably slow (about five per minute). That they were swallowing them whole rather than chewing them became even more apparent when Wrangham examined the apes' dung and found *Aspilia* leaves still intact, even retaining their original color, the surface damaged only slightly by minor folds. Further investigation turned up a total of five *Aspilia* species in the Gombe habitat; the apes seemed to be selecting and ingesting two of the five. (When Wrangham later contacted scientists in the Mahale Mountains of Tanzania, he discovered that the chimpanzees there were also swallowing certain *Aspilia* leaves whole, including those from at least one species not occurring in the Gombe habitat.)

The fact that the leaves were not chewed like ordinary food strongly suggests that their value was not strictly nutritional. That the leaves were folded, a process that ruptured some surface cells sufficiently to release surface chemicals, suggests that the chimps were seeking medicinal or euphoric benefits—to get well or high. We now recognize that many animals, in surprising ways, take advantage of nonnutritional chemistry around them. Monarch butterflies eat cardiac glycosides and thus become noxious to potential predators. Starlings weave into their nests green leaves with high concentrations of phenolics, thereby discouraging various pathogens. Yet such activities do not necessarily require reflection, self-awareness, or self-diagnosis. In the cases Wrangham was noticing, it seemed that the few chimpanzees who on rare occasions were forgoing their ordinary routines to seek out an extraordinary leaf and consume it in an extraordinary fashion were doing so very deliberately. They were, it appeared, diagnosing and then treating themselves, doctoring themselves.

Wrangham was unable to find a plant chemist with sufficient expertise to analyze samples of the *Aspilia* leaves until 1985, when he became acquainted with Eloy Rodriguez of the University of California at Davis. Rodriguez found a sulfurous red oil in the leaves; the oil yielded a chemical he identified as thiarubrine-A. This chemical had been noted previously to occur in plant roots, but never in leaves; Rodriguez was astonished. "It was like finding water on the moon," he subsequently told a journalist.

He had isolated thiarubrine-A on a Friday, April Fools' Day. That weekend Rodriguez was visited by a colleague and friend, biochemist Neil Towers of the University of British Columbia. In casual conversation Rodriguez asked Towers what he was up to. Towers was sorry, but he couldn't say. His lab had just discovered something so exciting that they were all pledged to secrecy, in writing. But, Towers wanted to know, what was Rodriguez up to? Well, Rodriguez said, this fellow Wrangham has sent some plants. He thinks there's something funny inside. I've just extracted this red oil, and here's the formula for it.

Towers couldn't believe it! Rodriguez's thiarubrine-A was identical to the chemical that Towers's group had just extracted from the roots of a plant, *Chaenactis douglasii*, used as a medicine by native Canadians.

Mary Troychak

Miriam Rothschild:
Through the Eyes of a Butterfly

A woman stands beneath a tree at dusk in Washington, D.C. Hidden in the leaves above her head is a flock of migrating butterflies, monarchs making their way south to winter in the mountains of Mexico. She knows they are there, but to the eyes of most people the wings of roosting monarchs are indistinguishable from the canopy of a tree—until, with a rustling sound and startling motion, they rise in a mass to the sky. Suddenly the orange-and-black butterflies strike her as sinister, like a hostile crowd. She recalls old Chinese paintings that show butterflies with menacing faces, protruding eyes, and beaklike mouths. Many years later, she will discover that in order to intimidate potential predators, monarchs secrete an aromatic substance, a pyrazine, that has a strange, evocative quality—a warning of danger. "In retrospect I wonder if a faint odor of pyrazines accounted for my desire to leave the roost,"

she would write in *Butterfly Cooing like a Dove,* "instead of watching the phenomenon spellbound—as indeed I would today."

An avid butterfly gardener devoted to making Britain aware of its vanishing wildflower heritage, Miriam Rothschild went on to publish more than 350 scientific papers on entomology, neurophysiology, chemistry, and zoology, as well as books for the general reader including *Fleas, Flukes, and Cuckoos* and *The Butterfly Gardener.* Born in 1908 to a distinguished British family of naturalists and bankers, Rothschild was encouraged in her childhood curiosity and passion by her father, Charles, who discovered the flea that causes bubonic plague, and by her eccentric uncle Walter, who posed for a family portrait, in top hat and tails, on the back of his Galápagos turtle, and whose collection, now a part of the British Museum, ranges from starfish to gorillas and includes two and a quarter million butterflies.

In *The Rothschild Gardens,* she presents the history of her family through the gardens they created in Europe and Israel. The story begins in 1773, in a house on Jew Street in the Frankfurt Ghetto, where ten children shared one tiny bedroom and the garden consisted of potted plants on a terrace. By the time Miriam was born, the family owned thousand-acre English estates with formal Victorian gardens and exotic plants in greenhouses. At her uncle Walter's, imported kangaroos, emus, and cassowaries wandered the grounds.

Two World Wars and the Holocaust had a devastating effect upon the Rothschild family. Miriam's husband, a pilot in the Royal Air Force, spent time in a POW camp; most of her mother's family was killed during the Nazi regime. Aerial bombs and occupying armies destroyed family homes and altered the face of the landscape she loved. Her house was taken over by the Red Cross; looters pillaged the outbuildings and grounds. "Even the swans on the lake were shot," she recalls. "No invading army could have achieved more wanton destruction."

Like her family's, the story of Rothschild's life and work is one of regeneration through gardening. The war, she writes, changed her from a lover of flowers and an appreciative onlooker into a practical gardener. At first, she would bicycle up from the village, where she stayed during the war, to try and save the rare plants. She watered, weeded, and learned how to grow vegetables—something her parents had relied on gardeners to do. "I also discovered how beautiful asparagus ferns are when they are spangled with scarlet berries," she writes. "Sometimes, trying to keep pace with weeds and cope with nagging war worry, I worked at night if there was a bright moon."

Known among entomologists as "Queen of the Fleas," Rothschild went on to focus on parasites for much of her career. She wrote a six-volume treatise on the structure and habits of fleas and, in a 1965 *Scientific American* article, showed how the reproductive cycle of a parasite is synchronized with that of its host. She discovered that rabbit fleas, which subsist entirely on their host's blood, will breed only when stimulated by sex hormones in the blood of a pregnant rabbit. As soon as the newborn rabbits emerge, the fleas jump down and copulate on their bodies, infesting the next generation. Like her later work with plants and insects, Rothschild's research on parasites revealed the interdependency of different life-forms.

Butterflies and flowers need one another not just for pollination but for other matters critical to their survival, which Rothschild has illuminated. "Flowers and insects have traveled down the ages together, bound up in a kaleidoscopic rainbow relationship of mutual benefit and exploitation," she writes. Working with Nobel Prize–winning chemist Tadeus Reichstein, she demonstrated that the monarch butterfly protects itself from spiders and birds with toxins drawn from the leaves of the milkweed plant, which is its sole food source as a caterpillar. If a bird attempts to swallow a monarch, it becomes ill and learns to avoid such prey in the future. Monarchs also obtain pyrazines from the milkweed plant, which Rothschild thinks serve to warn away predators. A whiff of their persistent smell reminds birds of the consequences of eating the butterfly, Rothschild suggests, and they fly off—just as she was inclined to when she stood beneath the monarch roost in Washington.

Rothschild's intimate knowledge of insect chemistry and perceptions inspired her to design a garden that would be attractive from a butterfly's point of view as it flies overhead, searching for shelter and food. "In the garden we should plan to please the small copper and the blues as well as ourselves," she wrote, "but what do the butterflies see?" A butterfly's eyes bulge out from its head, she explains, and have thousands of separate lenses. It can see all around itself without turning its head, making the sky appear, she imagines, like a well-lit bowl. Unlike humans, butterflies see polarized light—light waves vibrating at right angles to the direction in which they are traveling. These light rays could indicate the position of the sun, for example, and act as a compass in navigating flight.

Butterflies can also see into the ultraviolet range, which means they perceive flowers differently from the way humans do. Under ultraviolet light, some flowers reveal lines on their petals that lead pollinators to the center of the flower, where nectar is stored. Ultraviolet is also used by male butterflies in signaling to females. As they flap their wings, Rothschild explains, ultraviolet "glances off their specially structured scales like tiny flashes of lightning." Poppies, in addition to appearing red, also reflect ultraviolet. "The effect must be greatly accentuated by the crinkled petals," she imagines, "so that, presumably, they shine and flash as they shake in the breeze." Rothschild's ability to see her garden through a butterfly's eyes enables her to select plants with the colors and shapes most likely to attract them.

To Rothschild, nature does not revolve around human beings. A garden is not a lifeless canvas on which we impose a human design, but a living drama in which the attentive observer can see plants and insects enacting the cycles of sex, birth, battle, and death. In *The Butterfly Gardener*, Rothschild reveals the microcosmos in our own backyards and declares a commitment that has been her consuming passion ever since—preventing the extinction of butterflies and wildflowers by recreating their habitats on private and public lands.

Wildflowers are rapidly disappearing from the countryside, and the loss is not just one of beauty, Rothschild has pointed out in a *Smithsonian* profile. "You're losing the gene pool and that's something . . . you can never get back. That's millions of years of evolution down the drain." Wildflowers provide valuable pharmaceutical substances, like the heart medication digitalis, which is derived from the foxglove plant.

Pollination is another example of the tremendous benefits humans derive from mere flowers, and the intricate and manifold ways in which insects and plants depend upon one another. The process is critical to 90 percent of the world's flowering plants, and to the stability of the world's food supply. In *The Forgotten Pollinators*, Steve Buchmann and Gary Paul Nabhan point out that we owe one out of every three bites we eat to bees or other pollinators, including wasps, moths, beetles, butterflies, birds, and bats. The honeybee, a European import managed by humans, is succumbing to exotic pests and diseases. This has increased our dependence on wild pollinators at a time when pesticide use, habitat fragmentation and destruction, and the loss of nectar sources and larval-host plants have resulted in their decline. In order to reverse the trend of fewer flowers and fruits and lower crop yields, Buchmann and Nabhan recommend setting aside sizable tracts of pesticide-free habitat and restoring the flowering plants required by migratory pollinators such as monarch butterflies. Rothschild proposes that people reintroduce native wildflowers along highways and rivers and in parks, backyards, and vacant city lots, creating "butterfly highways" instead of the usual "dreary mono-crop of coarse grasses."

As a gardener, Rothschild puts what she learns into practice. Her farm of several thousand acres includes a butterfly garden and ninety acres of wildflower meadows, from which she harvests and sells the seeds of plants previously threatened with extinction or discarded as weeds. It's a profitable business, which has supported her scientific research for years. Her own seed packet, which she dubbed "Farmer's Nightmare," includes mayweeds, poppies, cornflowers, corn cockles, feverfew, marigolds, oats, and flax. A friend of hers has described the results as "Claude Monet come to life."

Like Buchmann and Nabhan, conservationist Robert Michael Pyle believes butterfly gardening has profound implications for conservation:

> I am very concerned about what I call the *extinction of experience*— the loss of everyday species within our own radius of reach. When we lose the common wildlife in our immediate surroundings, we run the risk of becoming inured to nature's absence, blind to

delight, and, eventually, alienated from the land. This is where butterfly gardeners come in—they create and maintain diverse habitats for species that need not become endangered, bolster the numbers of species in our midst, and collectively engage themselves in the rewarding nearness of nature.

In *Butterfly Gardening*, Rothschild recommends that would-be butterfly gardeners abandon "any romantic idea of creating a home for these angelic creatures." The best you can do is to provide them with a good pub, with "a plentiful supply of standard drinks always on tap." Her methods accommodate the insect's entire life cycle. She notes their particularity about the host plants or food plants on which they deposit their eggs, and views with tolerance the chewed leaves the emerging caterpillars leave behind.

She celebrates the ubiquitous large white butterfly, *Pieris brassicae* (whose closest North American relative is the small cabbage white, *Pieris rapae*, long loathed and feared by gardeners as a pest that descends upon gardens and leaves naked stalks in its wake). "With a species as common as this delightful butterfly," she writes, "the garden can be a laboratory or observatory as well as an area for growing flowers and attracting birds and insects." Rothschild encourages readers to reconsider our responses to creatures we deem expendable and introduces us to marvels "beyond our imagination in creatures considered beneath our notice," pointing out that "the pest of today becomes the rarity of tomorrow." She recommends that gardeners protect what they need to eat with a fishnet and enjoy the butterflies on the rest.

For Miriam Rothschild, enjoying butterflies means penetrating the realm of appearances and proceeding, like a detective, to investigate the hidden maze of relationships implied by what she sees. The large white, she notes, acts like an exhibitionist all its life. It begins as batches of "bright yellow, torpedo-shaped eggs" that transform into "eye-catching caterpillars living gregariously on the surface of their food plant" and finally into slow, low-flying butterflies that are conspicuous in the landscape from spring until fall. "When insects adopt a self-advertising lifestyle," she writes, "it is pretty safe to assume they are well protected by the presence of toxins or intensely bitter substances in their bodily tissues." Like the monarch butterfly, the large white acquires chemical weapons from the plants it consumes in its larval stage.

Rothschild's observations of the large white butterfly demonstrate how an insect's appearance, behavior, defense against predators, and ability to reproduce result from a long-evolved relationship with a particular plant family. Mustard oils, derived from plants of the cabbage family, are critical to the entire life cycle of the large white. For fertilized females, they serve as a cue to lay eggs. Scratching and drumming green leaves with her forelegs, the butterfly releases plant chemicals and tests them with her antennae and proboscis. Once she has identified a supply of food sufficient to nourish her brood, she curls her abdomen under a leaf and begins to deposit her eggs, which Rothschild describes as objects of great beauty, "ridged and netted like a piece of modern sculpture." When the larvae emerge from their shells, the presence of mustard oils stimulates them to eat. Consumed with the food plant and sequestered in larval tissue, mustard oils also enable the butterfly to secrete a lethal protein, pierin.

In this way, Rothschild demonstrates the interconnectedness of different life-forms—a principle that underlies many current efforts in conservation. Her research and writing show that attempting to protect a given species from extinction is not enough—its habitat and interactions with other life-forms must also be preserved.

Nor are human beings exempt from such connections. "All animals—butterflies, pigs, clams, fish, fleas, whales, shrews and shrimps—all see by virtue of yellow pigments—carotenoids—which they obtain directly from plants, or indirectly from other animals which have eaten plants," Rothschild explains in *The Butterfly Gardener.* "Rhodopsin, the visual pigment, is derived (via Vitamin A) from carotenoids—and no animals can manufacture it for themselves. We depend on plants for the gift of vision; without green leaves we would all be blind."

Carotenoids have a critical role in the life of the large white butterfly. The bright-yellow color of their eggs is a result of carotenoid pigments sequestered from their food plant by the larvae. If they are fed a carotenoid-free diet, Rothschild points out, their eggs are pure white, as is the silk the caterpillar spins. Carotenoids also make it possible for the chrysalid to camouflage itself against its background. If it is attached to a cabbage leaf, for example, it will become a matching dull green. Against a stone wall, it will turn gray. A larva deprived of carotenoids will have no capacity for camouflage; regardless of its background, the chrysalid will always be blue.

The small cabbage white, the large white's cousin, was introduced to North America from Europe around 1860 and since then has become so well naturalized that it is ubiquitous and, at times, an agricultural pest. Because it is not so well defended chemically as the large white, Rothschild points out, the cabbage white's appearance and behavior are more discreet. The eggs are laid singly rather than in batches; the caterpillars are not eye-catching; and instead of feeding in groups upon cabbage leaves, they bury themselves deep within the vegetable's heart. The butterfly is also a migrant and a periodic wanderer. "Once, on the French coast," Rothschild recalls, "I saw a large flight of European cabbage whites coming in across the sea. They were accompanied by dragonflies and even a few bees. Do they orient by the sun? Can they settle on the surface of the sea to rest and rise again? We do not know. Writers have envied their 'untracked blue airway,' but it may not be as untracked as it seems to the poets."

For her, the questions continue: How does the butterfly know to avoid the few cruciferous plants that contain heart poisons? What role do plant odors play in stimulating sexual intercourse between butterflies? What are the natural enemies, diseases, and changing conditions that control the butterfly's numbers? "If, while wandering through the garden," you produce "a fair imitation of a blackbird's or thrush's whistle," she observes, you will see the large white caterpillars on the surfaces of the leaves "respond in unison by violently jerking the anterior, or front end, of their bodies from side to side." She points out that this is a "communal defensive display" intended to frighten small birds. But where are the caterpillars' ears? Not only in their heads, she concludes, for when accidentally decapitated, they still respond to a bird call by "swinging their mutilated bodies from side to side."

Today Miriam Rothschild manages a farm of several thousand acres at Ashton Wold, the family estate in Peterborough, England. One hundred and twenty native plant species, from wild garlic to bee orchids, grow in the lawns around her home, and the gravel paths are lined with "idle weeds." Tall grass covers the tennis courts and laps up to the library steps "like a green wave." Flights of blue and copper butterflies rise above this emerald sea "like bright chips of metal seen against the sun." Grass snakes hatch in the compost heap and swim four abreast across the lily pond. From trees and bushes in the center of the courtyard, the song of a nightingale breaks the silence on warm, dark evenings. To Rothschild, the Ashton garden symbolizes the new sympathy with wildlife. She believes that the conquest of nature is a thing of the past. "There is a greater interest in native flora than ever before," she writes, and asks, "Can we be more optimistic about the future of the green world?"

Catherine Caufield

The Flooded Forest

I t is pleasant to travel on the Rio Negro. There are hardly any insects (because of the paucity of nutrients), and the water is placid and silky to swim in. I traveled some seventy miles up the river with Michael Goulding, an American scientist working in Brazil, to a floating ecological-research station built by the Brazilian government in the center of a breathtaking archipelago called the Anavilhanas.

The river here is twenty miles wide from bank to bank. At one point, when we were several miles away from the east bank, I asked why the forest alongside the river was so short. The trees looked stunted. Was it, I wondered, something to do with soil conditions? Goulding looked amused and asked the boatman to take us nearer. As we approached the bank, I could see that the reason the trees looked so short was that they were largely under water; only the top halves showed above the high-water level. The boatman, to whom Goulding turned, guessed that we were floating thirty or forty feet above ground level.

Forty thousand square miles of Amazonia are regularly flooded like this—a huge area, though only 2 percent of the whole Amazon Basin. In some places the floods extend sixty miles on either side of the river. The trees and shrubs of these forests are adapted to living under water for as many as ten months of the year. Seeds can germinate in the few months of relative dryness; seedlings can live completely under water for long periods and emerge to spurt up during the short growing season. Scientists don't yet know how plants survive this degree of flooding, although some trees appear to have rootlike structures high above the flood line, where more oxygen is available.

Canoeing silently through the flooded forest is magical, like being in another, charmed world. Tropical forests are as a rule taller than temperate ones, and most of the life of the forest goes on high up in the canopy, where it is hidden from humans. We were privileged simply to drift through the canopy, silently and effortlessly. Two pairs of blue-and-yellow macaws flew close overhead, showing themselves to us like a gift. At the forest's edge, dolphins leapt out of the water. A troupe of spider monkeys scampered wildly among the branches of a fig tree; the pink and white of an orchid stood out among its shadows. Down below, a cayman, invisible in the forest shade, betrayed its presence only by the thud of its tail as it jerked against the water.

The beauty and life of this river belie a kind of poverty. Like the rich rain forest that thrives on poor soil, blackwater and clearwater rivers are so lacking in nutrients that they should not be able to support the mass of fish and animal life that they do. Goulding has discovered that, in this river and others like it, the fish depend upon the trees of the forest. Fruit that falls into the river forms the major part of the diet of at least fifty species of fish here, including a number of species of vegetarian piranha fish; another two hundred fish species eat the fruit eaters. Many fish have large molars and specialized jaws for cracking hard seeds. They eat well in the forest and build up stores of fat. In fact, many species appear not to eat at all once the floodwaters have receded and they can no longer reach the fruits of the forest. After one dry-season fishing trip on the Rio Madeira, Goulding analyzed 167 fish and found that not one had significant amounts of food in its stomach. Among the fish that depend on the flooded forest are many of the largest and most commercially important species, such as the tambaqui, which appears to depend largely upon the seeds of wild rubber trees. Goulding estimates that about 75 percent of all the fish sold in Manaus, the largest market in western Amazonia, depend ultimately upon the flooded forest.

All the rivers of Europe combined support fewer than 150 species of freshwater fish, but, exploring near Manaus, the nineteenth-century zoologist Louis Agassiz found more than two hundred species in one lake alone, Lake Hyanuary, which is only about twice the size of a tennis court. According to Goulding, there are at least seven hundred fish species in the Rio Negro alone. That is six or seven times as many species as in all of North America. No one knows how many species there are in the Amazon Basin as a whole, but five thousand (of which only three thousand have so far been described by scientists) is an often quoted estimate—making the basin the world's most diverse collection of fish. The fish market at Manaus offers more than 150 different kinds of fish, several of which, to my taste buds at least, are to plaice and cod as mangoes are to Golden Delicious apples. Fish is the major source of protein in the Amazon. Goulding cites recent studies that show that, "though poverty is at a distressing point [in Manaus], per capita daily protein intake was more than satisfactory and mostly because of a relatively cheap supply of fish from the region."

Ten years ago, no one realized that the fate of Amazonia's fish might depend so closely on the fate of the forests. Now Goulding's findings are quoted by every government official as one of the strongest arguments against clearing the riverine forests. Where these forests have been cut down, researchers, and fishermen, have measured a serious drop in the local fish population. Between 1970 and 1975, the fish catch in Amazonian rivers fell by 25 percent because of deforestation of the fishes' breeding grounds. Some Amazonian floodplain forests are dying, even though they are not being logged, according to Brazilian ecologist José Lutzenberger. Deforestation upstream is altering the pattern of flooding to which the forests are adapted, and the resulting extremes of wet and dry are damaging them.

Some scientists say that if Amazonian rivers were properly managed for fishing, their production could dwarf that of the Mediterranean and the North Atlantic. Others, such as Goulding and José Lutzenberger, argue that the idea that the Amazon could feed the world is a dangerous illusion. "There is enough for a growing local population but not for large-scale export," says Lutzenberger. Already several species, including the pirarucu and the tambaqui, are nearing depletion.

Goulding, a born-and-bred Californian, fluent in what *Doonesbury* cartoonist Garry Trudeau calls mellowspeak, is a dead ringer for the blond policeman in the television series *Starsky and Hutch*. It is somewhat surprising to discover that he is also a natural historian in the tradition of the literate, scholarly explorers of the nineteenth century like Wallace and Spruce. He is a true field scientist, in love with nature rather than with his laboratory. He has a strong sense of history and an enthusiasm bordering on reverence for his predecessors in the field—the native people of the forest, as well as earlier explorers. "We're just discovering things that the Indians have known all along. The Indians know the stories of all these fish. They know what they do. All you have to do is look at the names they've given to the fish. Lots of the fish here are named after the trees whose fruits they eat. The tabebuia tree over there, with the big pink trumpet-shaped flowers—that has the same name as the male turtle that eats its seeds."

The Uanano Indians live on a tributary of the Rio Negro. They eat mostly fish, although they also grow a few crops. Their gardens, however, are never on the riverbank; they are always deep inside the forest. The river forest is guarded as a source of food for the fish. The Uanano believe that the fish are looked after by "fish elders." The elders punish anyone who interferes with the supply of fruits to their fish, especially during the spawning period.

Spruce learned from the Indians over one hundred years ago that fish eat the fruits of the forest. He mentioned it in his journal: "The principal subsistence of fish in the Rio Negro is on the fruits of riparial trees. When the ripe drupes are dropping into the water they attract shoals of Uaracu [different species of *Leporinus*]. Then the fisherman stations his canoe at dawn in the mouth of some still flooded forest, overshaded by bushes of Uaracu-Tamacoari [the native Indian name of the tree], and with his arrows picks off the fish as they rise to snatch the floating fruits." Spruce's observation was overlooked by generations of scientists, who preferred to start their investigations from scratch.

Spruce was also much taken with the taste of fruit-eating fish. "It ought to be mentioned that the fish of the Negro, if much fewer, are some of them perhaps superior in flavour to any Amazon fish, whereof the Uaracu is an example, and the large Pirahyba is another, the latter being so luscious that it is difficult to know when one has had enough of it."

In the years Goulding has spent studying the rivers and fish of the Amazon, he has learned a great deal from the fishermen and the riverbank peasant families. "The skillful *caboclo* [Amazonian peasant]," he has written, "has several tricks for capturing the tambaqui based on knowledge of its feeding habits. One device, called a *gaponga*, consists of a ball-bearing-like weight connected to the end of line and pole; the water is beaten in such a manner to imitate falling fruit, and when the fooled tambaqui surfaces, it is harpooned."

Tambaqui are so popular that they have been overfished, not by peasants catching their own food but by commercial fishermen using gill nets. These are walls of netting that are hung vertically in the water so that fish become entangled in them. There is no effective control of gill-net fishing in the Amazon Basin, and Goulding fears that some species may be fished out if its use continues to spread.

Another fruit-eating fish is the pirarucu. It is one of the largest freshwater fish in the world—often six feet long and over 170 pounds. "Next to a jaguar and a manatee," says Goulding, "a large pirarucu is the most prestigious animal that can be claimed by a caboclo." Pirarucu breathe air and so have to surface every ten or twenty minutes, which makes them very vulnerable targets. They have been intensively hunted in the Amazon for over a century. Dried pirarucu were the main rainy-season protein food in the Amazonian interior, but because of overfishing they are now scarce and too expensive for most people. Alone of the Amazonian fishes I encountered, the name of the pirarucu was familiar to me. I could not remember why. I assumed I had heard someone raving about how delicious it is. Months later, when I was back in London, I came across a slip of paper that reminded me of my first acquaintance with pirarucu. Several years ago, staying with friends in New York, I had been unable to resist buying them something I noticed in a sort of secondhand book-*cum*-junk shop. A "Natural Nail File," with an enthusiastic message from the distributors.

What is it? Where does it come from? Your nailfile is actually one of the scales of a fish . . . yes a very large fish. The PIRARUCU fish is the second largest freshwater fish in the world, only exceeded by the sturgeon. He grows to a size of 6 to 12 feet long and may weigh hundreds of pounds. He swims in the Amazon River in South America, and has been used by the Indians there for hundreds of years. He is a basic food fish yielding succulent steaks; the tongue is dried in the sun and used as a wood rasp. The scales are used not only as nailfiles by the Indians, but also as jewelry and decorations. Nothing is wasted in Mother Nature's cycle. If engineers wanted to design a product to have the strength, longevity and functionality of NATURE'S NAIL FILE, they probably couldn't have come so close, so ENJOY!

Sylvia Earle

The Twilight Zone

At 1,000 feet . . . I tried to name the water; blackish-blue, dark gray-blue. The last hint of blue tapers into a nameless gray, and this finally into black. . . . At 1,900 feet, to my surprise, there was still the faintest hint of dead gray light, 200 feet deeper than usual, attesting to the almost complete calm of the surface and extreme brilliance of the day far overhead. At 2,000 feet the world was forever black.
　　　　　　　　　　　　　　　　—William Beebe,
　　　　　　　　　　　　　　　　Half Mile Down

n the surface of a calm, clear sea, *Jim*'s support crew wore wide-brimmed hats and slathered on sunblock for protection from the fierce midday sun.* More than a thousand feet below, I stood in near darkness, suddenly mindful of the precarious nature of my existence. It was the absence of light that prompted the reflective mood, not my dependence on the good working condition of the special dive gear I was wearing.

---

*Jim is a specially designed diving suit that enabled Earle to walk on the ocean floor.

It was one thing to know, intellectually, that the sun's energy, coupled with water and oxygen, is essential for life on earth. It was another to feel in my bones the miraculous combination of circumstances that make life possible—my life, of course, but, most incredibly, all life, through all time. I was sobered by the concept, looking upward through the dark sea, acutely tuned to the reality of sunlight sparking processes in the legions of microscopic plants that absorb carbon dioxide and water, churn out oxygen—and produce the basic simple sugar that in turn is transformed into other compounds munched upon by the countless creatures that have lived, died, and been reconfigured into other ingredients that make up the planet's current organic chemistry. Today is different from all the preceding days because of these ongoing processes, and tomorrow and all the days that follow will be slightly changed as a result of whatever happens now, and the next day, and so on. It is about the most fantastic concept I can imagine, the interacting processes that somehow work and produce, for now at least, a planet hospitable for humankind.

To understand what makes earth different from any other place, and why life can thrive here, it would be logical to focus on the part of the biosphere that supports most of the action—that is, the sea. Since I am by nature an air-breathing, sun-loving mammal, it has taken some time for the awareness to seep into the cracks of my brain that *most of the biosphere is ocean*. All of life on earth lives in the dark at least half of the time, and much of it lives in dark all of the time—in the depths of the sea.

Unfortunately, human beings do not always behave in a logical manner, either as individuals or as a species. Instead of applying 95 percent of our scientific efforts to 95 percent of the biosphere, we have focused (and still do focus) most attention on the brightly illuminated surface portion in which humankind normally functions—a dangerously cavalier bias, given the utter dependence of the 5 percent on the rest.

One of the reasons for this curious imbalance is the surprisingly widespread belief that the sea is a place apart from, not fundamental to, the basic processes that make human life possible.

Another is the continued lack of access that has until recently inhibited generations of explorers. Even in 1979, there were few diving suits or submersibles in existence to enable people to go 1,250 feet into the sea—and never before had anyone had a chance to venture solo into that nearly dark, nearly light realm with a mandate simply to explore, unencumbered with heavy work assignments or preconceived experiments that had to be accomplished during the limited time available. During my momentous dive with *Jim*, I was given license to let my curiosity take me where it would—to prowl around like a cat in a new house, whiskers twitching, alert to the slightest movement, sensitive to subtle nuances of shape, light, and sound. I was free to do what explorers elsewhere on earth take for granted they can do—to walk around, touch strange objects, look for familiar patterns, be sensitive to new arrangements, and sometimes simply to be quiet and reflect on the significance of that special environment and the nature of the creatures that live there.

Standing at the upper edge of the great sparkling cold darkness, I looked up to a full spectrum of light dancing from the waves overhead, each photon newly arrived, most having traveled from the sun through ninety-three million miles of space, a far lesser amount arriving from distant stars. When light reaches earth's blue atmospheric "cocoon," it encounters its first significant obstacles. Some is reflected back into space or is absorbed by gases, clouds, water vapor, dust, pollen, and other ingredients that make up "air." But the barriers to free passage of light through the atmosphere are slight compared with the swift changes wrought the moment light enters the sea.

First the quantity of light drops exponentially, so effectively absorbed by water that only 1 percent travels to a depth of 325 feet (a hundred meters), even in the clearest freshwater lakes or most transparent expanse of open ocean. The intensity diminishes tenfold with every 227 feet, yielding at midday a moonlightlike ambience where I stood in *Jim*. At 1,950 feet (six hundred meters), illumination is equivalent to starlight; at 2,275 feet, the intensity is approximately one ten-billionth of that at the surface, and at 2,925 feet and beyond—there is total blackness. It is not simple to determine the exact point in the sea where light fades and darkness begins, because there are numerous complicating factors: the place, the time of day, season of the year, the weather. Where the air and sea meet, light is further modified by reflection and refraction, both affected by surface roughness—waves and ripples—or the presence of ice and, in these times, perhaps floating debris or a slick of oil. Water itself appears clear when viewed in a glass, but every drop contains organic and inorganic bits, including living creatures that scatter, diffuse, reflect, and absorb light, each in its small way altering the amount and kind of light that passes downward.

Plankton, silt, and the undefinable mix of substances that flow into the sea from most urban areas cause light in many coastal waters to diminish rapidly a few feet under the surface. One sunny October afternoon, I jumped overboard in San Francisco Bay to retrieve an outboard motor that had fallen off a dock next to a boat slip. I found the motor thirteen feet down, by touch—not sight— half embedded in silty mud. Only the slightest suggestion of a dark greenish-brown glow gave me a clue as to which way was up as I turned to ascend. In harbors at San Francisco, Boston, Hong Kong, Bombay, and Tokyo—to name but a few—less than half of the light striking the surface makes it to as much as six and a half feet; by twenty-five feet, more than 90 percent is gone.

Photosynthesis is light-driven. In the sea, this process, fundamental to oxygen generation and food production, and thus to the vital functioning of the biosphere, occurs in the illuminated "photic zone," mostly in the uppermost sixty to a hundred feet, but extending downward to the gray limits of where enough light can be effectively absorbed by plants to spark photosynthesis.

There is a level of illumination in the ocean where food production precisely balances the amount of energy required for cell maintenance and growth, a pivotal place in the sea known to oceanographers as the "compensation point." In less light (at greater depths), photosynthesis may still go on, but not fast enough to keep pace with energy needed for organisms to stay alive. For many years, textbooks suggested that 1 percent of surface illumination, or, in ideally clear water, a maximum of 325 feet (a hundred meters), framed the limits where photosynthesis could not only maintain a kind of cellular status quo, but also yield a dividend in terms of growth. At greater depths—anyplace with less than 1 percent of surface illumination—the need for energy for respiration and other activities would outstrip food production and the plants would not long survive.

Alas for the authors of the texts, a number of deep-dwelling algae did not get the news. Some plants, including various remarkable bottom-dwelling algae, prosper in depths greater than 650 feet, where the quantity of light is but a fraction of 1 percent of surface illumination. In murky coastal waters, where the 1-percent level of surface illumination may be reached about thirty feet under water, and in polar seas, under several feet of ice, the photic zone is considerably more narrow. In the Arctic and Antarctic, light is also seasonal, with darkness prevailing for four months of the year and a state of twilight for another four months. Nonetheless, plants abound in polar seas, from jewellike microscopic plankton and ice-hugging diatoms to large, slippery brown kelp fronds many feet long.

How deep *do* plants grow in the sea? The deepest-growing plant species thus far discovered is a kind of crustose red alga found growing in profusion on a sea mount in waters 871 feet deep, where the light is calculated to be about .0005 percent of full surface sunlight. I am confident that plants will someday be found growing just a little bit deeper than the most recently published pronouncement of the absolute maximum depth where they can occur. Below the depth where plants can grow, plant eaters live a catch-as-catch-can existence, relying on an occasional drifting banquet followed by a long period of fasting or, if they are omnivorous, by munching on their fellow citizens while awaiting the next salad.

Though the most dramatic impact water has on light is in reducing its quantity, it also strikingly modifies light's quality: the portions of the spectrum it permits to pass. Light filtering through a dense canopy of rain-forest plants may be of low intensity at ground level, but the full range of light visible to human eyes is there in gloriously colorful hues of red, yellow, blue, and many shades between. At the moment light enters water, however, changes are swiftly wrought in the character and color transmitted downward. The long red and yellow wavelengths are quickly absorbed in the first few feet; shorter wavelengths—green and blue—penetrate the deepest. The effect is startling. In the prevailing blue atmosphere, brightly flowered swim trunks undergo a strange metamorphosis to conservative shades of Wall Street gray.

In the small area I explored using *Jim* I noted dozens of red galatheid crabs clinging to shrubs of pink coral, several bright-red shrimp, and a purplish-red jellyfish. There were no obvious plants, other than a few strands of drifting sea lettuce, a kind of bright, papery green algae that normally attaches to rocks in shallow water.

Because light in the deep sea is characteristically blue—whether from sun, moon, or starlight penetrating from the surface or from the predominantly blue light of bioluminescence—it is not such a bad idea for inhabitants of the deep to be red. In general, red pigments absorb and do not reflect blue light, and red fish thus appear dark. It probably should not be surprising that many oceanic animals living in the deep sea are scarlet to purplish red, or black, because they appear black-on-black and thus, in effect, invisible.

Some fish, sheathed in silver scales or highly reflective skin, employ a quite different sleight-of-fin disappearing technique. Their bodies, like mirrors, reflect light coming from the surface—or the searching beam of one of the ingenious light-generating devices of predators.

Other creatures escape notice by being transparent, a fine strategy for survival adopted by various jellies, squids, octopuses, certain fish, and the larval stages of many creatures. A plankton net drawn through an apparently lifeless ocean typically yields a catch resembling minute fragments of broken glass mixed with quivering iridescent lumps of jelly creatures. Some of the glistening bits are minuscule but fully grown plants and animals, but many of the near-invisible dwellers of the open sea are the offspring of lobsters, crabs, eels, urchins, and a wide range of others. All are trying to avoid being eaten while they capture and eat as much as possible to prepare for the next phase of life on a reef or craggy rock crevice hundreds or thousands of miles from where they began life as seafarers on the open ocean.

Pattiann Rogers

The Importance of the Whale
in the Field of Iris

They would be difficult to tell apart, except
That one of them sails as a single body of flowing
Gray-violet and purple-brown flashes of sun, in and out
Across the steady sky. And one of them brushes
Its ruffled flukes and wrinkled sepals constantly
Against the salt-smooth skin of the other as it swims past,
And one of them possesses a radiant indigo moment
Deep beneath its lidded crux into which the curious
Might stare.

In the early-morning sun, however, both are equally
Colored and silently sung in orange. And both gather
And promote white prairie gulls which call
And circle and soar about them, diving occasionally
To nip the microscopic snails from their brows.

And both intuitively perceive the patterns
Of webs and courseways, the identical blue-glass
Hairs of connective spiders and blood
Laced across their crystal skin.

If someone may assume that the iris at midnight sways
And bends, attempting to focus the North Star
Exactly at the blue-tinged center of its pale stem,
Then someone may also imagine how the whale rolls
And turns, straining to align inside its narrow eye
At midnight, the bright star-point of Polaris.

And doesn't the iris, by its memory of whale,
Straighten its bladed leaves like rows of baleen
Open in the sun? And doesn't the whale, rising
To the surface, breathe by the cupped space
Of the iris it remembers inside its breast?

If they hadn't been found naturally together,
Who would ever have thought to say: The lunge
Of the breaching whale is the fragile dream
Of the spring iris at dawn; the root of the iris
Is the whale's hard wish for careful hands finding
The earth on their own?

It is only by this juxtaposition we can know
That someone exceptional, in a moment of abandon,
Pressing fresh iris to his face in the dark,
Has taken the whale completely into his heart;
That someone of abandon, in an exceptional moment,
Sitting astride the whale's great sounding spine,
Has been taken down into the quiet heart
Of the iris; that someone imagining a field
Completely abandoned by iris and whale can then see
The absence of an exceptional backbone arching

In purple through dark flowers against the evening sky,
Can see how that union of certainty which only exists
By the heart within the whale within the flower rising
Within the breaching heart within the heart centered
Within the star-point of the field's only buoyant heart
Is so clearly and tragically missing there.

About the Contributors

JEANNE ACHTERBERG, Ph.D., is a professor of psychology at the Institute of Transpersonal Psychology in Menlo Park, California. She is also the author of *Imagery in Healing, Shamanism and Modern Medicine, Imagery and Disease,* and *Bridges of the Bodymind.*

Poet, essayist, and naturalist DIANE ACKERMAN lives and teaches in Ithaca, New York. Her works of nonfiction include *The Rarest of the Rare, A Slender Thread, A Natural History of Love, A Natural History of the Senses, The Moon by Whale Light,* and *I Praise My Destroyer.*

PAULA GUNN ALLEN divides her time between New Mexico and southern California. Her books include *The Sacred Hoop, Grandmothers of the Light,* and *Off the Reservation: reflections on boundary-busting border-crossing loose cannons.* She is a former professor of English at UCLA.

Born in Peru, ISABEL ALLENDE was raised in Chile. She is the author of the novels *The House of the Spirits, Of Love and Shadows, Eva Luna, The Infinite Plan,* and *Daughter of Fortune*; the short-story collection *The Stories of Eva Luna*; and the memoirs *Paula* and *Aphrodite: A Memoir of the Senses.* She lives in northern California.

RACHEL CARSON'S *Silent Spring* did more than any single publication or event to alert the world to the hazards of environmental poisoning. It was through her work as a government scientist and editor that her views about the potential danger of synthetic chemical pesticides evolved. Her other publications include *The Sea Around Us, Lost Woods: The Discovered Writing of Rachel Carson, The Edge of the Sea,* and *Under the Sea-Wind.*

CATHERINE CAUFIELD is an American journalist living in London. She is a frequent contributor to *New Scientist* and also writes for *The International Herald Tribune, The Guardian,* and *New Statesman.* She is the author of *The Emperor of the United States of America and Other Magnificent British Eccentrics, Masters of Illusion: The World Bank and the Poverty of Nations,* and *Tropical Moist Forests.*

MARY CROW DOG joined the American Indian Movement (AIM) in the sixties. Her book *Lakota Woman* is an account of a woman's struggle to survive in a hostile world. She lives in Pine Ridge, South Dakota.

MARJORY STONEMAN DOUGLAS was a journalist, writer of fiction and nonfiction, editor, publisher, and crusader for women's rights, racial justice, and conservation of nature. Her books include *Florida: The Long Frontier, Alligator Crossing, Hurricane, Freedom River, Marjory Stoneman Douglas: Voice of the River,* and *Everglades: River of Grass.*

SYLVIA EARLE is a marine biologist, author, lecturer, and scientific consultant. Her books include *The Oceans; The Living Ocean: Understanding and Protecting Marine Biodiversity; Hello, Fish!: Visiting the Coral Reef;* and *Sea Change: A Message of the Oceans.* She lives in Oakland, California.

ANITA ENDREZZE is a professional storyteller, poet, fiction writer, translator, and artist. Her books include *At the Helm of Twilight* and *Throwing Fire at the Sun, Water at the Moon,* and her poems have appeared in numerous magazines, including *National Geographic* and *Yellow Silk,* as well as in many anthologies. She lives in Spokane, Washington.

LAURA BOWERS FOREMAN lives in the foothills of the Cascade Mountains near Seattle, Washington. Her work has appeared in *Earthlight* and the anthology *My Mother's Tattoo and Other Family Memoirs.*

JANE GOODALL has been studying chimpanzees in Gombe, Tanzania, since 1960. She received a Ph.D. from Cambridge University and has become one of the world's most honored scientists and writers. Her publications include *Through a Window: My Thirty Years with the Chimpanzees of the Gombe, In the Shadow of Man, The Chimpanzees of Gombe: Patterns of Behavior*, and *Reasons for Hope: A Spiritual Journey*. She has written both *Visions of Caliban: On Chimpanzees and People* and *Africa in My Blood: An Autobiography in Letters* with DALE PETERSON, a professor at Tufts University and the author of *The Deluge and the Ark: A Journey into Primate Worlds*.

LINDA HASSELSTROM's first book, *Windbreak*, convinced her to write about what she knows, ranching and the environment. She is the author of seven books of essays and poetry, including *Going over East, Landcircle*, and *Caught by One Wing*. Now living in Cheyenne, Wyoming, she commutes to South Dakota to care for the family ranch.

ZORA NEALE HURSTON was a novelist, folklorist, and anthropologist whose fictional and factual accounts of the black heritage are unparalleled. She is the author of *Jonah's Gourd Vine, Their Eyes Were Watching God, Mules and Men*, and *Dust Tracks on a Road*.

STEPHANIE KAZA is an environmentalist, Buddhist, and feminist. The author of *The Attentive Heart: Conversations with Trees* and co-editor of *Dharma Rain: Sources of Buddhist Environmentalism*, she is a professor of environmental studies at the University of Vermont. She lives on the shore of Lake Champlain in Burlington, Vermont.

DONNA KELLEHER is a doctor of veterinary medicine, as well as a licensed chiropractor, herbalist, and acupuncturist working with small animals in her holistic clinic. Her writing has appeared in *Pets, Holistic News, New Age Journal*, and elsewhere. She lives in Seattle, Washington.

CAROLYN KIZER has been poet-in-residence at many universities, including Columbia, Stanford, and Princeton. She is the author of *Proses, Mermaids in the Basement, The Nearness of You, Carrying Over, Yin, The Ungrateful Garden*, and *Pro Femina: A Poem*. She received a Pulitzer Prize for poetry in 1985 and the Theodore Roethke Award in 1988. She lives in Sonoma, California.

CLAUDIA LEWIS wrote the title essay for the anthology *My Mother's Tattoo and Other Family Memoirs*. Her writing has also appeared in *New Age Journal, Underwire, Lilith, Tikkun, Spa,* and *The Christian Science Monitor.* She lives in Berkeley, California.

SHARON BERTSCH MCGRAYNE is a former newspaper reporter and writer-editor on physics for the *Encyclopedia Britannica*. She is the author of *Blue Genes and Polyester Plants: 365 More Surprising Scientific Facts, Breakthroughs, and Discoveries* and *Nobel Prize Women in Science: Their Lives, Struggles, and Momentous Discoveries*. She lives in Seattle, Washington.

TRISH MAHARAM lives in Seattle, Washington, with her husband, daughter, three dogs, and a ruby-throated hummingbird. Her work as a magazine editor takes her into a wide range of gardens and homes throughout the Pacific Northwest.

TERESA TSIMMU MARTINO lives on an island in the Pacific Northwest where she writes, trains horses, and oversees Wolftown!, a nonprofit organization dedicated to wolf and horse rescue and the education of young people. Her books include *Dancer on the Grass: True Stories About Horses and People, The Wolf, the Woman, the Wilderness: A True Story of Returning Home,* and *Learning from Eagle, Living with Coyote.*

RIGOBERTA MENCHÚ is a Guatemalan activist who won the Nobel Peace Prize in 1992. She is the author of *I, Rigoberta Menchú: An Indian Woman in Guatemala* and *Crossing Borders.*

KATHLEEN NORRIS is the author of *Amazing Grace: A Vocabulary of Faith, The Cloister Walk,* and *Dakota: A Spiritual Geography,* as well as the poetry books *Little Girls in Church* and *The Year of Common Things.* She lives in Lemmon, South Dakota.

NAOMI SHIHAB NYE is a poet, novelist, and anthologist. She is the author of a book of poetry, *Come With Me,* and her children's books include *Habibi, Salting the Ocean: 100 Poems by Young Poets,* and *Sitti's Secrets.* She lives in San Antonio, Texas.

SUSAN ORLEAN has been a staff writer at *The New Yorker* since 1992. Her articles have also appeared in *Outside, Rolling Stone, Vogue,* and *Esquire.*

Her books include *Saturday Night* and *The Orchid Thief.* She lives in New York City.

MOLLY PEACOCK is the president emerita of the Poetry Society of America and the author of a memoir, *Paradise, Piece by Piece,* and *How to Read a Poem,* along with four books of poetry—*And Live Apart, Raw Heaven, Take Heart,* and *Original Love.* She lives in New York City and London, Ontario.

LESA QUALE is an editorial assistant at New Sage Press, as well as a research assistant to Linda Hogan and Brenda Peterson. Her work has appeared in *The Christian Science Monitor.*

PATTIANN ROGERS is a poet whose books include *Firekeeper, New and Selected Poems, Eating Bread and Honey, A Convenant of Seasons,* and *The Dream of the Marsh Wren: Writing As Reciprocal Creation.* She lives in Fort Collins, Colorado.

SHARMAN APT RUSSELL teaches writing at Western New Mexico University and is the author of *Kill the Cowboy: A Battle of Mythology in the New West, The Fluteplayer: Seasons of Life in the Southwest,* and, most recently, *Anatomy of a Rose: Notes from the Field and Garden.* She lives in Silver City, New Mexico.

ELAINE SCARRY teaches at Harvard University, where she is Cabot Professor of Aesthetics and General Theory of Value. Her books include *On Beauty and Being Just, The Body in Pain,* and *Dreaming by the Book.* She lives in Cambridge, Massachusetts.

LINDA JEAN SHEPHERD is a biochemist, a writer, and a longtime student of Jungian psychology. She is the author of *Lifting the Veil: The Feminine Face of Science.* She lives in Issaquah, Washington.

ANNICK SMITH is the author of *Homestead,* a memoir, and *Big Bluestem: Journey into the Tallgrass.* Her essays and stories have been published in *Story* and *Audubon,* among other places, and included in *Best American Short Stories* and other anthologies. She was the executive producer of the prizewinning film *Heartland* and a co-producer of *A River Runs Through It.* She lives on a homestead ranch in western Montana.

SANDRA STEINGRABER taught biology for several years at Columbia College in Chicago and has held fellowships at the University of Illinois, Radcliffe College, and Northeastern University. She is the author of *Post-Diagnosis,* a volume of poetry, and co-author of *The Spoils of Famine,* a report on ecology and human rights in Africa. She lives in Cambridge, Massachusetts.

MARY TROYCHAK was publications director from 1985 to 1999 for the Xerces Society, an international conservation organization focused on invertebrates. She edited Miriam Rothschild's writing for the society's magazine, *Wings,* and for the book *Butterfly Gardening: Creating Summer Magic in Your Garden.* She lives in Portland, Oregon.

ALICE WALKER won the Pulitzer Prize and the American Book Award for her novel *The Color Purple.* Her other novels include *Possessing the Secret of Joy, The Temple of My Familiar,* and *By the Light of My Father's Smile.* She is also the author of two collections of short stories, three collections of essays, five volumes of poetry, and several children's books. She lives in northern California.

LOUISE M. WISECHILD is the author of *The Obsidian Mirror* and *The Mother I Carry,* and the editor of an anthology on healing through creativity, *She Who Was Lost Is Remembered.* She lives in Seattle, Washington.

LINDA YAMANE is a freelance writer, illustrator, and cultural demonstrator. She traces her ancestry to the Rumsien Ohlone, the native people of the Monterey, California, area, and has been active in retrieving the Rumsien language, songs, folklore, and basketry traditions. She is the author of *Weaving a California Tradition: A Native American Basketmaker, When the World Ended, How Hummingbird Got Fire, How People Were Made: Rumsien Ohlone Stories,* and *The Snake That Lived in the Santa Cruz Mountains and Other Ohlone Stories.*

Acknowledgments

We are grateful for all the women whose work has made of this book a bountiful garden of green life: for our astute editorial assistant, Lesa Quale, who helped us gather and unearth such an unusual variety of plantswomen; for Vanessa Adams, whose expert editorial work helped prepare this manuscript for publication; for Amy Schuring, Suzanne Edison, Laura Foreman, and Trish Maharam, for their help in final editorial and publicity work; for our farsighted agents, Elizabeth Wales and Beth Vesel, who helped envision a three-volume series on women and the natural world that began with *Intimate Nature: The Bond Between Women and Animals*. We are delighted to continue this journey at North Point Press with the generous, hardworking, and inspired editing of Rebecca Saletan and her wonderful assistant, Katrin Wilde. Finally, thanks to all the writers whose voices and visions here have taught us more than ever about our green world.

Permission Credits